BARRY LANDY is a freelance journali[...] is the editor of LouthNow.ie. His footba[...] [...] *Independent*, *Irish Daily Mirror*, *Irish Daily Star*, *The Irish Sun*, *The Irish Times*, The42.ie, and RTE.ie among others. Barry is the former editor of The Emerald Exiles, a website dedicated to following the fortunes of Irish footballers plying their trade outside of the UK and Ireland. *Emerald Exiles* is his first book.

EMERALD EXILES

EMERALD EXILES

How the Irish Made Their Mark on World Football

BARRY LANDY

NEW ISLAND

EMERALD EXILES
First published in 2021 by
New Island Books
Glenshesk House
10 Richview Office Park
Clonskeagh
Dublin D14 V8C4
Republic of Ireland
www.newisland.ie

Print ISBN: 978-1-84840-818-0
eBook ISBN: 978-1-84840-819-7

Typeset by JVR Creative India
Edited by Noel O'Regan
Cover design by Jack Smyth, jacksmyth.co
Printed by L&C Printing Group, Poland

New Island Books is a member of Publishing Ireland.

10 9 8 7 6 5 4 3 2 1

For Hannah

Contents

Introduction   1

1   The Pioneer Club   5
2   Continental Drift   20
3   The Italian Job   34
4   Once Upon a Time in America   46
5   East is East   55
6   Managing Expectations   74
7   Flying the Nest   96
8   All Roads Lead to Italy   114
9   The Euro Stars   137
10   The Second Generation   166
11   Coming to America   181

Epilogue   196
Bibliography   201
Image Credits   204
Acknowledgements   205
Index   208

INTRODUCTION

IRELAND'S WILD GEESE

Irish-born football players have earned their living in Britain's professional football leagues since the late 1880s. Ever since, the trip across the Irish Sea to England has been seen as the natural movement for footballers with aspirations of carving out a career in the professional game.

Throughout history, all but a smattering of players capped at senior level for the Republic of Ireland national team have plied their trade either at home or in England and Scotland's football leagues, and of course, more recently, in the Premier League. There is little mystery as to why – with no language barrier to overcome, a very similar culture and lifestyle to back home and close proximity to Ireland, the UK has forever been an obvious destination for our emigrants, whether they play the game or not.

Both England and Scotland have had at least three tiers in their respective football leagues since the early-to-mid-1900s, meaning opportunity has knocked for generations of Irish players. The stories and achievements of many of these players are oft told and well known to supporters of all ages. Modern-day Ireland is brimming with followers of Liverpool and Manchester United, owing to the great Irish players of the respective clubs' vintage title-winning teams under Bob Paisley, Joe Fagan, Kenny Dalglish and Alex Ferguson. The likes of Ronnie Whelan, Mark Lawrenson, Roy Keane, Denis Irwin or John O'Shea need no introduction.

In an era where the best English clubs were teeming with Irishmen, the likes of Steve Heighway, Frank Stapleton, Jim Beglin and Kevin Sheedy, as well as UK-born Irish internationals Michael Robinson, Ray Houghton and John Aldridge ended their careers with medal hauls of which Irish players in the modern era can only dream. Going further back, names such as Johnny Carey, Noel Cantwell and Tony Dunne will be recognisable to Manchester United supporters of a certain vintage, for example. Similarly, Leeds United's sizeable Irish support is owed in no small part to John Giles, a star of Don Revie's great team of the 1960s and 1970s. Those players are widely known and rightfully adored across the country and in England, where their achievements are remembered fondly.

Many of the subjects featured in these pages have also enjoyed highly successful careers in the English game, including Jack Kirwan, Liam Brady, Stapleton and Robbie Keane, who have six FA and Football League cup wins – and just shy of 2,000 appearances – between them. Here, though, we look at their experiences outside of Ireland and Britain, in places as diverse as Amsterdam, Turin, Milan and Los Angeles. We look, in other words, at those who have emigrated further afield to further their football career.

To talk about emigration, in an Irish context, is to open the wound of a great national trauma. Thoughts instantly turn to the Great Famine and, in more recent times, recessionary depths that have led to the hollowing-out of Irish society. Large swathes of the population left home behind for opportunities in foreign pastures. Football, as peculiar an industry as it is, even within the sporting world, has been as affected as any other.

For many inside the game, as is often the case with civilians who are forced to leave Ireland behind due to economic conditions, emigrating to a new club in a new country is often merely a way of surviving in the sport. Football, like few other sports, lends a nomadic status to those who play it. They move, adapt and often improve themselves as a consequence. But the move itself is often as much a necessity as it is a choice.

In the last forty years, the globalisation of the game has made the presence of foreign players in leagues the world over commonplace. Nowadays, at least some teams in most countries in the world will have cosmopolitan squads, made up of players from multiple continents. Still, Ireland has witnessed nothing like the same spread of native football talent to the other leagues outside of Britain, i.e. in Europe, and beyond. Not since Steve Finnan in 2008 has a senior men's Irish international played in the top-flight in either France, Spain, Germany or Italy. Ian Harte, playing for La Liga side Levante in 2007, was the last Irish-born player to feature in one of the continent's elite leagues, with honourable mentions to the year-long spells of Jack Byrne (SC Cambuur) in the Eredivisie and Pádraig Amond (Paços de Ferreira) in Portugal's Primeira Liga.

It remains doubtful that any of the other four major European leagues will see an influx of Irish footballers in the near future given the language and cultural differences, as well as the style of play, but also the standing in which Irish players seem to be held around the continent. (Though player movement to less prominent European clubs has become more notable in recent decades, at least.)

Still, in contrast to many smaller countries around Europe, there has never been a major temptation for Irish players to move beyond the leagues in Ireland and Britain. Perhaps it is simply due to the fact that English football continues to act, as ever, as the Promised Land for the Irish. What allure does Europe, America, Asia or elsewhere hold when fame, fortune and fulfilment can be found so much closer to home – in an English game that is piped into our homes in ever-more accessible forms? Money talks, of course, and what sets the English Premier League and Championship aside from other less-heralded leagues around the world is that these leagues offer a security that most footballers crave. It is, after all, a short career. The influence of the English game in Ireland is longstanding too, and players of all ages find it hard to shrug off the temptation of following in the footsteps of the storied greats that have gone before.

Yet with England especially becoming a more difficult place for Irish players to make it, given the influx of players from around the globe into the top two tiers, a broadening of horizons can do no harm.

These pages will profile just some of Ireland's exiles who have already looked beyond Ireland and the UK in their careers, from pre-war managers such as Kirwan – the widely unheralded Dubliner who was the first-ever manager of Ajax – and another Dub, Patrick O'Connell, a La Liga winner with Real Betis whose legacy lives on at FC Barcelona.

There will also be a focus on Italy, which once upon a time proved to be a prime location for Irish players trying their luck abroad. Liam Brady, Anne O'Brien, Ronnie O'Brien and Robbie Keane's respective spells in the country contained varying degrees of success, but none were without incident. Many other players, including Louise Quinn, Richie Ryan, Roy O'Donovan and Stephanie Roche have gone directly from domestic football in Ireland to stints in countries as diverse as Sweden, Italy, France, Canada, Brunei, Singapore and Australia.

This book is not an exhaustive history charting every Irish player and manager to spread their wings and take to the continent, or beyond. Instead, it focuses on a selection of them (those mentioned above and more besides) throughout history, from both the men's and women's game. Including sixteen interviews conducted for this book, it delves into these players' experiences and tells tales from those who chose not to follow the tired, old script and instead wrote their own chapter in the story of how the Irish made their mark on the global game.

Unless stated otherwise, all direct quotes in the book come from interviews I conducted with the players involved.

1

THE PIONEER CLUB

Ireland's footballers have a long, if not often storied, history of travelling outside of Ireland and the UK to further their footballing careers. Much of the first wave of 'exiles' headed for Europe, not so much to enhance their playing career, but to pursue a future in football coaching or management. The first notable example was a Dubliner by the name of Jack Kirwan, who would make for the continent near the beginning of the twentieth century, and go on to take a historic role with a future European powerhouse.

Born John Henry Kirwan in Dunlavin, County Wicklow in February of 1878, the young Kirwan was a natural sportsman who quickly became highly regarded in sporting circles around the capital, playing football for St James's Gate and Gaelic football for Dublin, even going on to represent Dublin in the 1894 All-Ireland final, playing in the forward line as they overcame Cork over two games. He was only seventeen.

Still, despite his passion for GAA, it was his love for football that won out, likely because – like many Irish people at the time – he sensed the prospect of a better life in England. He moved there in the late 1890s, and enjoyed a successful playing career, spending one season at Everton and then six at Tottenham Hotspur, where he helped the team, led by Scot

John Cameron, to a 1901 FA Cup final win over Sheffield United. A then world-record attendance of 110,820 had watched the first game at Crystal Palace, which ended in a draw, but Kirwan finally got his hands on the cup as Spurs won the replay 3–1 at Burnden Park.

He retired from playing in 1910. At thirty-two, Kirwan was soon looking further afield again, and would become the first exile to set sail for mainland Europe – travelling to a club with which readers will be very familiar.

Reports from the time are scarce and incomplete. What is known is that a chance meeting in London with the chairman of the recently founded Ajax football team, Chris Holst, led Kirwan in this new and unexpected direction. The club had been established a decade earlier and, still an amateur outfit, were playing second division football. Holst had come to England with a purpose: to find a British manager to help propel his team towards the top of Dutch football, as, in the early twentieth century, Britain was the country that clubs from across Europe looked to when they wanted to learn and develop their game. After that constructive – if seemingly fortuitous – meeting, Holst was convinced that he'd found his man. Soon after, Kirwan was appointed as the club's first-ever manager.

At the time, HVV Den Haag and Sparta Rotterdam were the leading lights in the country's Football League Championship, which was split into eastern and western classes. When Kirwan arrived in September 1910, HVV were the league champions, having already won nine titles since the league began in 1888. Ajax merely wanted to reach the top tier so they could test themselves against the very best.

Back then, the terms 'manager' or 'coach' were not widely used, so Kirwan was announced as the club's new trainer. In an altogether different era with an unrecognisable media landscape, managerial appointments were not considered big news in the way they are today. As a result, the Wicklow man's appointment did not make waves. Ajax's status as an amateur team outside of the top flight didn't help. Word of Kirwan's new role was reported in a small, one-sentence brief in the sport section of the *Het Nieuws van den*

Dag, a small daily newspaper in the Netherlands. It didn't even mention that Ajax was the team to which Kirwan was contracted: 'Jack Kirwan, the Irish international and former Spurs left-back, who helped this club win the cup, has gone to Holland to train as a coach. The footballer was an honest player, highly regarded in English football circles,' the story read. To indicate where news of Kirwan's arrival sat in terms of newsworthiness, it was squeezed in below the previous weekend's English football scores, including Clapton Orient's 2–1 win over Barnsley.

Kirwan arrived in Holland at the same time as Jimmy Hogan, another former player born into an Irish Catholic family, in Nelson, Lancashire, in 1882. He took up a position of trainer at FC Dordrecht on a two-year contract. Four years Kirwan's junior, Hogan would go on to establish himself as a great pioneer of the game across the continent, managing in the Netherlands, Austria, Hungary, Switzerland, Germany and France, as well as in his native England, in the lead-up to the Second World War. Kirwan and Hogan's flight to the continent was the beginning of a trend, as they sought to instil their learnings from their time in England. As Jonathan Wilson outlined in his book *Inverting the Pyramid*, Hogan – and, by extension, Kirwan – wanted to 'teach those fellows how to play properly'.

Despite Kirwan being employed largely to keep the team fit, he was determined to bring more to the role. For example, Kirwan was known to regularly play along with his team in training and in friendly matches, and he quickly became a calming presence among his players, as well as devising some shrewd tactics. This energy and enthusiasm paid immediate dividends in the 1910/11 season, when Ajax claimed the Dutch second division title and then beat Bredania 't Zesde in a promotion/relegation playoff. An Irishman – even if many in Holland failed to make the distinction between British and Irish – had just helped earn Ajax a place at the top table for the very first time in their history.

Kirwan's commitment to the club was further proven when he was joined in Amsterdam by his wife, Enith Williamson, who left London behind to be with her husband. They both registered as residents in the country in October 1911. Subsequent seasons saw Kirwan lead Ajax to a period of relative stability, as they avoided relegation from the western division of the Dutch National Championships, finishing eighth and ninth in 1912 and 1913, respectively.

However, despite the club growing in renown and fanbase, the 1913/14 campaign saw Kirwan's team finish bottom of the division, relegating them back to the second tier. A total of fifteen players left the club upon their demotion, including Ge Fortgens, a versatile midfield player who had the honour of being the first Ajax player to represent the Netherlands national team in 1911. Kirwan departed too, despite widespread assumptions in modern writing that he stayed on during their first season back in the second division. In fact, Ajax did not have a professional trainer during the 1914/15 season, and the role remained vacant until Jack Reynolds – who would go on to win eight titles across three spells at the club and is widely considered to be the founding father of Dutch football – took over in 1915.

For Kirwan, who left the Netherlands in 1915 after the outbreak of the First World War, a season in charge of Bohemian FC in Dublin followed before embarking on another continental challenge – this time at Italian side Livorno in 1923. Not much is known about his time in Italy, aside from, as was the case with Ajax, Kirwan being their first-ever manager. He stayed in Tuscany until 1924, guiding his team to a respectable third place finish in Group A of the twenty-four-team league, which then was comprised only of teams from the northern regions of the country.

Unfortunately, it is known that Kirwan endured hardship later in life. In 1924, upon his return to London following his time in Italy, the then forty-six-year-old was forced to seek a grant of £10 from the Irish Football Association to improve his circumstances. In the 1950s, as Kirwan approached the end of his life, a collection was also undertaken among Ajax club members to help him along. By that time, the club had established themselves as one of the leading sides in the Netherlands, a feat that may not have been achieved without the pioneering Kirwan. Decades on, his contribution during Ajax's formative years had not been forgotten.

Kirwan was an example other Irish players turned managers soon looked to follow. James 'Jim' Donnelly was one such figure – not that Donnelly was considered a pioneer as such when he became manager of the Turkish national team in July 1936. Having grown up in Sussex, England, he sounded British and was considered that by most he encountered. He was the third 'Brit' to take the helm of the Turkey national football side, succeeding the Scot Billy Hunter and Fred Pagnam, a former Liverpool and Arsenal forward who came from Lancashire.

In reality, however, Donnelly hailed from Ballina, County Mayo. He was born on Clare Street, on the banks of the River Moy a week before Christmas in 1893. He lived there for some years before his family emigrated to England around the turn of the century. Like Jack Kirwan, here was an Irishman who was able to convert his experience of the English game – he had played for Blackburn Rovers, Accrington Stanley, Southend and Brentford between 1919 and 1928 – into a more meaningful career on the sidelines. As with Kirwan's era, clubs on the continent were still keen to learn from those immersed in the British game, where it had all started. Likewise, the Football Association were eager to extend their influence in far-flung corners of the world.

Prior to that Turkish appointment, Donnelly had already managed in a variety of locations. Upon his retirement from playing, Donnelly took part in an FA coaching programme and was eventually shipped off first to Belgium, where he briefly held some early coaching seminars, and then to Zagreb, where he took the reins at Građanski Zagreb. In the Balkans, he replaced former Hungary striker György Molnár as coach, and while he was unable to guide the team to a trophy, he is widely considered to have helped provide the basis for near-future success under one of his successors, Márton Bukovi, who would win three titles with the club. (Bukovi is also one of the Hungarian coaches credited with pioneering the 4–2–4 formation.)

Already a long way from home, Donnelly travelled much further east for his next appointment, when he became manager of the newly formed Güneş SK, a breakaway club from the already-established Galatasaray in Istanbul. At the same time, another Jim – Jimmy Elliott – was in charge of their derby rivals Fenerbahçe, adding another element of intrigue to proceedings in the city.

Under Donnelly's management, Güneş were a coming team in Turkish football (even if Donnelly would ultimately leave before they enjoyed their greatest day, lifting the national title in 1938). While in charge of the formative club side, Donnelly was surprisingly appointed as the coach of the Turkish side set to compete at the 1936 Olympic Games in Berlin. It is understood by many football historians that Donnelly was personally tasked with heading up the Olympic team by the country's president, Mustafa Kemal Atatürk. At the very least, it is unlikely that a foreigner would have been tasked with taking charge of the national football team without the say-so of senior government figures. Unfortunately, he was unable to repay their faith, as a 4–0 loss to Norway in the first round put paid to any hopes of making a dent in the competition.

Donnelly was at the helm for a number of friendlies after the Olympics in 1936, but he soon reverted to his regular job in club management. To this day, there remains some confusion over his time in Turkey. There are claims that Donnelly managed Fenerbahçe after Güneş, but this may be an instance of the careers of both he and Elliott becoming blurred in the fog of history. Historical records from Fenerbahçe do list a James Elliott Donnelly as their manager in the mid-to-late 1930s, however no birth nor death records list Donnelly as having a middle name, so it is likely that the two men have been conflated.

Donnelly's management career in Europe spanned most of the 1930s, a time of extraordinarily hostile politics first in Eastern Europe and then across the entire continent. It is interesting to ponder what Donnelly's attitudes were towards the environments in which he was working, especially when you consider that he left Turkey in 1937 to take on a coaching role at AS Ambrosiana-Inter – known widely to modern-day supporters as Inter Milan. The country at the time was under the fascist rule of Benito Mussolini, and it is something of a surprise that he was even appointed, given that a ban had been imposed on all foreign players from playing football in the country. He was a coach, of course, but it indicates the standing that he was held in that machinations were put in place to bring him in – even if he was kept in the background. On the face of it, you see, Donnelly was not the main man. That was the recently retired midfielder Armando Castellazzi, who was the manager as far as supporters and the press were concerned. The Irishman, it seemed, was brought in to form part of a coaching team that would guide Castellazzi, who was just thirty-six.

Research formed as part of an exhibition on his career by the North Mayo Heritage Centre in 2019 found documentation that listed Donnelly as having a whole host of roles at Inter, such as a scout, technical advisor, consultant and even B team coach, which further proves this background role. However, it is fair to say that he wasn't completely in the shadows. An interview with the Italian football publication *Il Calcio Illustrato* gave him some exposure and saw him outline his own footballing philosophy – an attack-minded approach that relied on movement and the involvement of the entire team.

However, Donnelly, for all his efforts at Ambrosiana-Inter, isn't remembered for his time there; he is remembered for what came next. He left in March 1938, after Ambrosiana-Inter chairman Ferdinando Pozzani graciously agreed to release him from his contract before their title-winning season had ended. He left Inter to take up the manager's role of the Austrian national team. But this wasn't just any iteration of the Austrian side; Donnelly was replacing the great Hugo Meisl, who, along with Englishman Jimmy Hogan, had helped develop Austria into one of the great pre-war international teams of European football. Meisl had died suddenly of a heart attack, aged fifty-six, and with Hogan back in England coaching Aston Villa, it was felt someone of Donnelly's calibre was perfect for the role.

The opportunity to coach the great Austrian *Wunderteam* – featuring the celebrated centre forward Matthias Sindelar – was one he could not in good conscience pass up. The 1938 World Cup was to begin in France in little under three months' time. It was a dream job. The Austrians had finished fourth four years earlier and won Olympic silver in 1936, while Donnelly had been presiding over that chastening first-round exit with Turkey. Now leading a sophisticated side playing football deemed by many to be ahead of its time, opportunity knocked not only to make a name for himself, but to make history.

Donnelly took up the role with immediate effect. However, world events were about to interfere with Donnelly's dream move, and ultimately thwart his chance to manage the Austrian side to Olympic success. On 12 March, German troops marched into Austria to begin the 'Anschluss' (which translates as 'annexation') of the country. Donnelly would never arrive in Vienna. Their league was disbanded, Austria withdrew from the approaching World Cup, and Donnelly's elite management career looked over.

Likely distraught in losing the role, Donnelly still refused to let a little thing like a burgeoning world war get in the way of his career. Soon he was managing again, in Kirwan's old haunt, Amsterdam, where he became the coach of Amsterdamsche FC, the city's oldest but much smaller and less celebrated club. He is understood to have fully gained the confidence of his squad of players, and his time in Amsterdam also saw the club's existing team selection committee resign, as Donnelly insisted upon picking the team himself, in a move that suggested he viewed himself as much more than a traditional trainer. And his approach clearly worked, as the team enjoyed an impressive 1938/39 season, where Donnelly helped the perennial relegation battlers finish second in the Dutch league.

Unable to ignore the war any longer, however, Donnelly ultimately returned to England, living with his wife Jane in her mother's boarding house in Morecambe. The far-right's ascension in mainland Europe essentially ended a coaching career that delivered much, but had promised even more. He was only forty-five years old. But this Mayoman will always have the distinction of being the first Irishman to coach a foreign national side.

While Kirwan and Donnelly achieved some success on the continent, it was a man by the name of Patrick O'Connell who would become the first Irish manager to land major silverware on European soil. In fact, to this day he remains the only Irishman to ever win a major trophy in Spanish football. But that fact fails to do justice to O'Connell's Spanish adventure, where his legacy at one of world football's great clubs in Barcelona runs deeper than the teachings that he first brought to Spain a century ago, or the trophies he won during a twenty-seven-year spell in the country, which encompassed the Spanish Civil War and the Second World War.

His life was undoubtedly a remarkable one. It would have warranted that billing even before he left England behind at thirty-five for Spain, where he would spend the majority of his life. O'Connell was a one-time captain of Manchester United and Ireland international of some repute, despite earning just six caps across seven years spent representing his country. At the time, international fixtures were not as commonplace as in the modern day, but O'Connell nevertheless earned his place in the history books by leading his country to success in the 1914 British Home Championship, courtesy of wins over Wales and England before a 1–1 draw with Scotland in Belfast sealed a first Irish victory in the thirty-first edition of the tournament. O'Connell played the full game at centre half, despite leaving the field at one point to receive medical attention. It would later transpire that he had broken his arm.

O'Connell arrived in Spain in 1922, leaving his wife Ellen and children Patrick Junior, Nancy, Nell and Dan behind in Manchester, to take on the role of Racing Santander manager. In a letter addressed to his brother Larry in London, O'Connell went into great detail, informing his sibling of his trip to Spain and his new surroundings by the sea. His boarding house was 'a goal shot away from the beach', which he didn't appear particularly taken with. 'All told it puts me in mind of Ireland,' he wrote (all letters are drawn from the biography of his life, *The Man Who Saved FC Barcelona*). By contrast, the first correspondence sent to his wife back in Manchester was curt and to the point. He issued instructions on how to exchange the enclosed Spanish pesetas for pounds sterling, and did not begin the letter, as is customary, with his current address (as he did to his brother). He simply asked Ellen to ensure the children were behaving themselves before adding a brief line about the weather. It lacked much of the colour and descriptive qualities that the letter to Larry had possessed.

O'Connell managed Racing for seven seasons, leading the team to five regional championships. With the founding of La Liga in 1929, he left for Oviedo and then to Seville with Real Betis, who had just earned promotion to the top flight. In 1935, against all odds, he led Betis to the La Liga title. It was a victory underpinned by a watertight defence, Betis shipping just nineteen goals in the twenty-two-game season. That steadfast backline was all the more important when you consider that Betis were outscored by six of the seven teams directly below them in the table. However, the shackles did come off when ultimately required – namely, during a final-day 5–0 win over former club Santander that meant they finished one point ahead of Real Madrid, thereby confirming the league title.

Despite his previous successes with Santander, a national league success with Betis was a real moment to savour for O'Connell, especially given that the club were relatively tiny in comparison to some of the country's leading sides. (In fact, as if to underscore that point, it remains their only title win to this day.) 'What more can a manager want than to take his team to the very top? It was a great moment of triumph. A singular event. Raise your glass to us,' he wrote in a letter to his brother Larry in London.

Prior to taking over at Betis, in 1931, O'Connell had applied for the Barcelona manager's job. They declined, but once he led Betis to the title, Barca's newly elected club president, Josep Sunyol, was more accommodating to the idea of appointing this impressive Irishman as the club's new boss. O'Connell joined in the summer of 1935.

Still, O'Connell could not have picked a more tumultuous time to become manager of the Catalan club. Civil War was brewing, and an all-out war had begun within twelve months of his arrival in Catalonia. Even a high-profile figure like Sunyol, who had numerous left-wing and pro-independence militant connections, was not immune to its dangers. A little over a year after taking over as club president, he was captured by Francoist forces on 6 August 1936 and executed. It put into stark context Barcelona's defeat to Real Madrid in the Copa del Rey final six weeks earlier – the first El Clásico final in the competition's history – when two early goals put paid to any hopes of O'Connell's men claiming the cup. (The Civil War meant that match was the last Spain would see of the tournament until it returned in 1939 under its new title, Copa del Generalísimo.)

At the outbreak of the Spanish Civil War in the summer of 1936, O'Connell was actually back in Dublin on a holiday, and despite an expectation in Barcelona that their Irish coach would remain in the country of his birth, he did return – for a time, at least. La Liga, like the cup, was suspended during the Civil War, and with Catalonia within sight of Franco's forces, O'Connell and his team were soon forced to flee. Luckily, they received the opportunity to tour Mexico and the United States, where they could play exhibition matches – a potentially lucrative move for the club. Of course, extricating themselves from Barcelona for their own safety was paramount too.

O'Connell found himself at the forefront of this tour as, in May 1937, he led a delegation of twenty staff – including sixteen players – to Paris and then on to Mexico via Havana. There they played ten games in Mexico and four in New York over the course of a four-month tour, on which the Barca stars were treated like superstars. The club made $12,500 in profit, which

O'Connell was eventually able to deposit in a French bank account he had opened before the team set sail. He did not wish to risk bringing the money back to Barcelona, which was not yet under Franco rule but was a de facto stateless territory. His actions had nonetheless assured the future of the club during the most troubled time in their history.

Widely known in recent years as 'The Man Who Saved FC Barcelona' (his grandson's wife Sue wrote the book with that very title), the story of the club's tour of Mexico and New York is now the stuff of legend. And O'Connell has become a hero himself within the club, despite his failing to bring a major trophy to the club during his five years as manager (though, as you will see, that was hardly his fault).

It isn't known how exactly O'Connell avoided sanction upon his return to Franco's Spain, but he continued to live unimpeded, even continuing as Barcelona boss. However, as with Donnelly and the Austrian *Wunderteam*, an outbreak of war ended O'Connell's hopes of replicating his Betis success with Barcelona. They had won the league just once before his appointment in 1935, but with the league suspended amidst the fighting the club were forced to make do with competing in a Mediterranean League – which they at least did win once – and the regional Campionat de Catalunya, which Barcelona claimed twice. Still, these did not have the sheen of a La Liga or Copa del Rey success.

He returned to Real Betis in 1940 after five interrupted years as Barca boss, and then had a spell at their city rivals, Sevilla. He ended his managerial career in Spain with two seasons back where he began: Racing Santander.

O'Connell was considered an innovative coach during his time in Spain, one that focused on defending and quick transitions between defence and attack. For all his achievements, though, it should be stated that O'Connell was undoubtedly a flawed man. He committed bigamy when he met and married another Ellen, Ellen O'Callaghan, in Spain in 1934. (To differentiate his new wife from his first, he called her 'Ellie'.) O'Callaghan was an Irish nanny working for a British diplomat in Seville, and O'Connell hid the existence of his first family from her entirely. He only told his brother Larry about the marriage, via one of his regular letters to London. But correspondence to his wife and children in Manchester had long since ceased. In fact, when his youngest son from his first marriage, Dan, came to visit O'Connell in the early 1950s, Patrick told Ellie he was a nephew, not his son from his first marriage.

In a letter to Larry, O'Connell was matter-of-fact in his justification of his actions. He wrote: 'This is a somewhat unconventional approach however, all that is past is past. It was a different life in a different country and what is past is finished.'

Despite his early successes with Racing, Betis and then Barcelona, the last decade of O'Connell's managerial career in Spain was trophyless. By the early 1950s, O'Connell was seen as an outdated coach, and work in Spain became difficult to find. It signalled what would be a fall from grace for the Dubliner, in the game he gave so much to, and in life in general.

Soon O'Connell resigned himself to leaving Spain. He was sad to say goodbye after thirty-three years in the country. He and Ellie distributed his possessions among their friends in Andalusia and, just as he arrived with one suitcase in 1922, he left with his life packed into one in 1955.

He reassured himself with thoughts that he had, at least, made an impact on Spanish football during his time in the country. 'Though it must be said I like to consider I have made no little mark on the world of football here in Spain. It is not excessive of me to say that football in this country would not be where it is today without my contribution,' he told Larry shortly before leaving with Ellie for London, where they took up residence with his brother at the central London hotel that he operated.

He was also conscious that his return might make it difficult to keep his dual lives separate for much longer. He suspected he would not be allowed to see out his final days in peace should Manchester-based Ellen be made aware of his relocation to London, with Ellie in tow.

As it transpired, it was Ellie who learned of O'Connell's bigamy upon their arrival in London. She subsequently left him and he lived out his final years in Larry's attic and collected National Assistance, the means-tested benefit at the time, until his death. He is likely to have also sought a grant from the IFA during this time, as Jack Kirwan did when he fell on hard times prior to his own death, though there is no known record of O'Connell applying for such a grant.

Patrick O'Connell died from pneumonia at London's St Pancras Hospital at the age of seventy-one. Buried alongside his sisters Emily and Christina in Plot 216 of St Mary's Cemetery in Kensal Rise in north London, O'Connell died alone and destitute in London, ten years after ending an extraordinary career. A charming, polite man, he was an enigmatic figure who fit more than most into an extraordinary life. His abandonment of a family in Manchester and subsequent marriage to another woman is an aspect of his life that those celebrating the man in recent years have to reconcile.

Unlike predecessors such as Jack Kirwan or contemporaries like Jim Donnelly, O'Connell's story has entered the public consciousness in recent times due to efforts by campaigners and family members to remember the efforts of a man largely credited for rescuing FC Barcelona from financial ruin. Plaques have been installed in Dublin, where he grew up on Fitzroy Avenue in Drumcondra, and in Belfast, where he began his football career with Belfast Celtic as a teenager. Real Betis and Barcelona have also paid tributes with paintings and busts.

It has taken too long for O'Connell to be recognised as a true great of Irish football, given his ground-breaking successes in Spanish football at a time of unprecedented unrest in the country. Approaching the 100-year anniversary of his La Liga title win with Real Betis in 1935 and his subsequent appointment at Barca, it remains unfollowed territory for any Irish manager or player. One of only two Irish captains to lift the Home Championship, his career while in England was the stuff of legend, but it is for his achievements in Spain that 'Don Patricio' will be most fondly remembered.

He is the man who saved Barcelona, after all, and football supporters the world over should be grateful for that. If there's any justice in the world, he won't be forgotten in Dublin, Manchester, Andalusia or Catalonia any time soon. His achievements can certainly stand alongside – and perhaps above – those of Kirwan and Donnelly, in this lauded trio of pioneering Irish managers.

2

CONTINENTAL DRIFT

Irish managers weren't the only ones who would look to forge a successful career for themselves in Europe; many players – both prominent domestic and international stars and those less so – began to look to the continent in the mid-to-late twentieth century. One such pioneering figure was Noel Campbell. And his experience, in Germany in the early 1970s, was nothing if not eventful.

A skilful, goalscoring midfielder, Campbell was a fixture in an unremarkable St Patrick's Athletic team (Campbell himself refers to that Saints team as 'terrible') in the late 1960s, who had already earned international honours by the time he was approached by the German side Fortuna Köln in the summer of 1971.

Campbell had been recommended to Fortuna by Ben Hannigan, an experienced League of Ireland player who was six years his senior. With two league titles and two FAI Cup successes under his belt, Hannigan had spent much of the off-season travelling around Europe, where he earned a few trials with clubs, including at Fortuna. Although Hannigan was ultimately unsuccessful, the Germans had the foresight to ask him if he could recommend anyone else from Ireland. The forward (who passed away in February 2021) invited a man called Oskar Scheidel, one of the club's directors, back to Dublin to see Campbell for himself.

'I met them and chatted. They invited me over so I went to the club, trained for a few days and immediately they asked me to sign,' Campbell told the *Irish Examiner* in October 2014. 'For me, it was an opportunity. I was playing for Pat's, knocking around doing something work-wise but it was a chance to play professional football, so I dived at it.'

Once a trainee at Arsenal before returning to Ireland, Campbell was unafraid of the prospect of leaving home behind for pastures new, even if he feared that the language barrier would be a difficult hurdle to overcome. (As it happened, it didn't take him long to get to grips with the native tongue.) Excited, he left behind his four-shillings-a-week clerk job at the Smithfield Motor Company and Richmond Park to chase his dream in Germany.

At the time, football in the country was at its absolute peak. Within twelve months of his arrival, West Germany would claim the European Championship in Belgium, and soon after Helmut Schön's team would be crowned world champions. 'It was a massive leap,' he recalls, understating the task of swapping Richmond Park for visiting the likes of Munich's Olympiastadion and Mönchengladbach's Bökelbergstadion. Those two teams, with their respective successes in the European Cup and UEFA Cup in the 1970s, helped further cement Germany's near-domination of the elite football in the era.

Campbell, born in Terenure but brought up in Kimmage, came from a family steeped in football. His brothers Johnny, Hubert and Jim all played in Ireland's domestic league. Noel had been a precocious talent from his early days at Stella Maris, playing Under-13 level at just ten years of age. However, mixing it with World Cup winners was another level altogether. Even the unheralded, uncapped German players were usually of a standard much higher than seen on the pitches of Oriel in Dundalk or Clonturk Park.

Some young players floundered amidst the pressure of moving abroad, yet Campbell claims he took it all in his stride. 'I was an old man before I grew up,' he said. For the first two seasons of Campbell's time in Germany, he played his football in the Regionalliga West, at the time one of multiple leagues directly below the Bundesliga. Earning a good wage, he soon married his partner Anne and she joined him in the city. Her husband was under no illusions that he needed to make the most of the opportunity afforded to him. 'I felt this was my second chance, my second big chance. I was well accepted. I was quite popular with the fans.'

Not that it was all smooth sailing. By his own admission, he was fond of a drink, and during an era in the 1970s when he was new to the professional game, behaving the way expected of a high-level athlete did not often come naturally to him. Not even sharing an apartment building with the colourful chairman and millionaire benefactor of his club, Jean Löring, could dampen his partying ways, even when the close proximity to his paymaster led to no end of exchanges regarding the Irishman's readiness for games. 'It was murder. He loved the bones of me but we'd terrible arguments about my drinking and smoking and not looking after myself. I loved the gargle,' he told journalist Michael Walker for the book *Green Shoots* in 2017.

Löring's frustration with Campbell was understandable. He had, after all, ploughed millions of Deutsche Marks into the club during the years of his ownership, ultimately leading to his personal insolvency. In his later years, he even turned reclusive, owing to his personal embarrassment for his financial situation. Prior to his financial ruin, he did at least see his club reach the Bundesliga in 1973, a feat that Campbell played an integral part in. A regular starter in Martin Luppen's team during the season, Campbell hit two goals in a 6–0 drubbing of Karlsruher SC in the end-of-season playoffs to help Fortuna seal promotion. This was their moment in the sun. It was to prove brief, however, as they were relegated from the top tier on the final day of the following season, with only goal difference condemning them to demotion. They haven't been back since.

Although his lengthy time in Germany marks him out as one of Ireland's most successful exiles, his off-field antics weren't conducive to grasping that big second opportunity with both hands. Tellingly, Campbell caveats his eight-year spell at Fortuna with a regret. 'If I'd one regret in all my time in Germany, [it was that I wish] I would have been a better professional – by a million miles.'

Despite his flawed time in Germany, there can be no doubting Campbell's pioneering status in terms of Irish footballers playing outside of the UK and Ireland. In fact, Campbell proved long before most that playing football beyond these isles was possible for Irish players, even if few have tested that theory by following him directly to Germany. As Dr Conor Curran writes in *Irish Soccer Migrants*, his book on the social and cultural history of Irish footballers playing in Britain and around the world, even when the early 1990s saw Germany become the most popular destination of Irish migrants to Europe, that trend was never mirrored in terms of football migration, be it direct from Ireland or via English football. In fact, almost fifty years since Campbell last turned out for Fortuna, only one other Irishman has played in the German top flight. (Dubliner Alan Clarke spent his entire career in Germany, playing most notably for Blau-Weiß between 1984 and 1989.)

It is scarcely believable that a European country that has had over 175 players appear in the modern-day Premier League and a national team who have qualified for five major tournaments in a thirty-year period has seen just a single player appear in the Bundesliga since 1974. But as surprising as it may seem, it is true.

As is the fact that Campbell's 'second chance' placed him in the history books, when he became the first-ever player to represent the Republic of Ireland national team while playing for a team in mainland Europe. He took to the field in June 1972 against Iran in Recife, Brazil, winning the first of ten caps during his spell as a Fortuna Köln player.

First and foremost, though, Campbell was the player who helped open the floodgates – if not specifically to Germany, then to Europe in general – and more Irish players followed in his footsteps in the subsequent years and decades.

Irish interest in leagues across Europe and further afield has, throughout history, been minimal. Irish players who take their careers to shores beyond Ireland and the UK are the exceptions to the rule. So it is a quirk that five of the Republic of Ireland's top six goalscorers in international history have played the game outside of these isles.

The first of that quintet to do so was Don Givens. At the end of a twelve-year senior career in England, the Limerick native considered his options and, not seduced by the prospect of dropping further down the leagues in England, looked to the continent. A former Manchester United, Luton Town, Queens Park Rangers and Birmingham City striker, Givens was also Ireland's record goalscorer at the time, with nineteen goals to his name. His pedigree – and still-impressive goal record – meant that, even at thirty-two, Givens was still considered in demand by some within European football.

In the summer of 1981, he signed for Swiss side Neuchâtel Xamax with the help of Harry Haslam, a former Luton and Sheffield United manager who was working as the Blades' chief scout. Haslam had an eye for a player, no question. Three years earlier, while manager of the Bramall Lane club, he had come close to securing a deal for the seventeen-year-old Argentinian tyro Diego Maradona. Haslam had a contact in Switzerland, which set the ball rolling on Givens's move to the town of Neuchâtel, fifty kilometres west of Bern, not far from the French border. The team had qualified for the following season's UEFA Cup. For a player like Givens, who had only appeared in the competition once in his career while at QPR, it was an added bonus.

Still, despite their entry into European competition, life in the Swiss top-flight was a far cry from even the lower reaches of the English game where he had spent his entire career. At Xamax, which had been founded just eleven years earlier as the result of a merger between two local clubs, Givens found himself to be the only full-time player. The team trained in the early evenings, so as to allow the majority of the players to finish their day's work before arriving for practice. It took some getting used to for

Givens – not that he complained. He had joined a club with ambition, and with a new coach in Gilbert Gress and chairman in Gilbert Facchinetti who were intent on making Xamax a force within Swiss football.

Givens's time with Xamax started promisingly, with a good run in the UEFA Cup. Sparta Prague, Malmö and Sporting of Portugal were dispatched on their way to the last eight of the competition, where Hamburg – who would go on to be that season's losing finalists – ultimately ended the hopes of the (mostly) part-timers. A scoreless draw at home was not enough for the Swiss, having suffered a 2–3 reverse in Germany two weeks earlier.

The defeat came despite Givens scoring the goal of the tie in the first-leg defeat, levelling after Lars Bastrup's opener. A headed clearance by an ageing Franz Beckenbauer from their goalkeeper's punt up-field landed right at the feet of the Irishman, who attacked the then thirty-six-year-old World Cup winner. He quickly dashed into the area, sweeping the ball past Beckenbauer with his right foot before hitting a powerful shot past Uli Stein with his left. The German legend was withdrawn by Hamburg's manager, Ernst Happel, shortly after, and would make just two more appearances for the club that season before he played out his last season with a second stint at New York Cosmos in America. Givens's well-taken goal had effectively ended the sweeper's top-level career, and almost, almost carried the unheralded Swiss team to European glory. It was all so delightfully unexpected, given that the Irish striker had been languishing at the bottom of England's old Division 3 less than a year earlier. 'Funnily enough, the last thing the coach said to me when I'd got out onto the pitch at Hamburg, he said, "If you get one on one against Beckenbauer, take him on",' Givens told RTÉ in an interview almost thirty years on.

It was Givens's only goal on that year's European run, though he did hit twelve goals in an impressive debut season in the league. The European campaign took its toll on Gress's team, however, as they dropped out of the top three positions in the Swiss league that season, while a sixth-place finish twelve months later meant they had to wait two years to return to continental competition. But Givens was content to wait for his time to come again. It likely helped that he suspected that there was more to come from this team, that they were edging their way towards achieving their ultimate goal of winning the league for the first time in the club's history.

The following three seasons saw them finish fourth, third and second before, in May 1987, they finally topped the standings. By that point, Givens was approaching his thirty-eighth birthday and was playing as a sweeper at the back – his advancing years and a recurring hip complaint had meant that his days chasing and harrying at the opposite side of the pitch were over. He had been appointed captain by Gress too, a mark of the impact he had on the squad and the club as a whole.

Liam Brady remains the only male Irish player to win a top-flight title in one of the continent's major leagues – i.e. France, Italy, Spain and Germany – but Givens stands alongside a number of Irish players who have won league medals in other countries. These include his former Irish international colleague Mickey Walsh, who won Portugal's Primeira Liga with FC Porto (twice, in 1985 and 1986) – as did Phil Babb with Sporting in 2002 – and Cillian Sheridan, who more recently won Cyprus's First Division on two occasions, with APOEL Nicosia in 2014 and 2015.

Givens is considered a bona fide Xamax legend even now, which is no real surprise, as he was also part of the side that again reached the last eight of the UEFA Cup in 1986, when Real Madrid beat them 3–2 over two legs. Three goals down from the first match at the Bernabéu, Givens missed the return leg, when the home team gave their illustrious visitors an almighty fright.

To further cement his hero status, he returned to the club some years later to coach the reserves and then the first team, alongside his ex-teammate and former Real Madrid star Uli Stielike. His achievements and close relationship with chairman Facchinetti meant that the Irishman wasn't going to be forgotten in the Swiss town well known for its lakes that shimmer under the encapsulating Jura mountain range.

Givens's story is undoubtedly one of success; however, not every pioneering Irish player has had a successful time in Europe. Another figure in that quintet of top Irish goalscorers, Frank Stapleton, instantly comes to mind.

It seemed like a dream move, and that's likely what Frank Stapleton, Ireland's captain at that time, thought when he was signed by Johan Cruyff for Ajax in the summer of 1987 as a direct replacement for the legendary Marco van Basten.

Arnold Mühren had played facilitator as Stapleton swapped Manchester for Amsterdam. The two had been teammates at Old Trafford under Ron Atkinson earlier in the 1980s, so the by-then Ajax midfielder recommended Stapleton to Cruyff as the club searched for a new striker. The move made particular sense, as the Dubliner had been out of favour at United since Alex Ferguson replaced Atkinson in November 1986. Prior to the introduction of the Bosman ruling (meaning out-of-contract players could move freely to another club upon the expiration of their contract), Stapleton's contract had actually run out in 1986, but the club retained his registration as they sought a buyer.

Cruyff himself has revealed in his book *My Turn* that Stapleton had not been his first choice to replace van Basten. He had initially wanted to bring English striker Cyrille Regis, then of Coventry City, to Holland. After Regis helped the Sky Blues to the FA Cup in 1987, however, his price soared, leaving Ajax out of the running. Ironically, Stapleton, who had joined Manchester United for a then-mammoth fee of £900,000 in 1981, was now available for free. All he had to do was negotiate his release from Manchester United. Ferguson was obliging.

A veteran of fifteen years at two of England's biggest clubs – Arsenal and Manchester United – the striker had never put much consideration to a move outside of the UK, although he had followed his friend Liam Brady's recent move to Juventus closely. Now he found himself in Amsterdam – at first living in a hotel, though soon Stapleton and wife Christine, along with sons James and Scott, moved out to a rural suburb south of the city, surrounded by the city's dikes and rivers. James even went to primary school there. An unassuming family, they enjoyed the quiet life away from the city – although the couple did notice some cultural differences, and reflected that they probably appeared a little reserved to their native neighbours. 'The neighbours were very nice but they all left their curtains open. If you walked past the house at night, the lights and the television were on. They were wide open. It was very different from Britain and Ireland. We probably seemed a little out of place,' Stapleton explained.

Adapting to life in the Netherlands was a walk in the park, however, compared to adjusting to a new way of playing in the Eredivisie. 'It was difficult to adjust after playing a direct way with the teams in England and the Republic of Ireland. The stylistic difference was a big factor. It was very rare that we would get a ball from the defensive line rather than the midfield. More times than not, the ball would be delivered by wider players or the midfielders. It is only in the last few years that you realise the way many teams are set up now was the way Ajax used to play in the time before I was there and when I was there. The goalkeeper would play out from the back. They would play a flat back four because the full backs would push on and the sitting midfielder would drop in. It was a slow approach and much different to the English Football League at that time.'

Cruyff's approach also differed in other ways to Stapleton's previous managers. 'He wasn't afraid to make decisions early in games. Tactically, if you didn't do it, he would take you off,' Stapleton says of the Dutch maestro. 'Physically, he was tough. The training was really hard. He was very demanding. If he wasn't getting what he wanted, he would do something about it. He wasn't one to wait and see if it turned around. He put his neck on the line. He was looking for perfection.' Even after all that would transpire between them, Stapleton admits to being impressed by the Dutchman. 'I liked him because he was quite serious but he had a funny side as well. He was a fantastic footballer in his time, one of the best there ever was.'

Stapleton wasn't long settled in the Dutch capital before problems arose. In his 1991 book *Frankly Speaking*, he admits that he soon found himself out of the team due to his difficulty in adjusting to the style. 'It is very frustrating as a forward player because you can make half a dozen runs and never receive the ball so I found myself increasingly frustrated by the slowness of the play. I know that this sort of soccer would not be acceptable to the English supporter who likes to see plenty of goalmouth action and shots at goal,' he wrote.

Injuries also didn't help his case. A week before the Eredivisie season proper began, Stapleton was withdrawn at the break in a pre-season friendly against Italian side Torino, while he was unable to take the field against Porto in another warm-up game days later. 'Maybe it was the change in routine. I was struggling to get to a high level of fitness. I wasn't one hundred per cent. I told Johan Cruyff I couldn't go on. I was too sore.'

Stapleton did begin the Eredivisie league season in the Ajax starting line-up, playing centre-forward in a 1–0 over Roda JC at the old De Meer Stadion in Amsterdam in front of a modest 16,500 crowd in the run-down venue. However, the Irishman was withdrawn at the break with the game scoreless.

Due to these injury issues, Stapleton would spend more time watching than playing during his time in Amsterdam. And Ajax's new international striker – who was the Irish national team captain, no less – was far from blown away by the football as a spectacle. 'You would think the football was great to watch, but in essence, it wasn't. It was pretty mundane. I was injured, sitting there watching these games. One day, I walked out. I couldn't watch it. I left at half-time. I went home to get the English channel and watch *The Big Match*.'

Stapleton felt sure that Dutch football compared particularly poorly to the game in England at the time. 'When you played in England, there was no patience. The ball would come directly from the back and you were involved all the time.' In contrast, 'The hardest place to play in that [Ajax] team was centre-forward. You hardly got a touch. It always had to go back because you were double marked. It wasn't easy.'

While injury did blight his time in the Netherlands, it didn't help that he was sharing a dressing room with the likes of the experienced Mühren, as well as players of the calibre of Rijkaard and fellow Dutch internationals Rob Witschge, John van 't Schip and Danny Blind. Ajax's extended squad also contained a number of promising young players who were emerging from the club's famed De Toekomst academy. Twenty-year-old Aron Winter was a fixture in midfield while teenagers Dennis Bergkamp, Bryan Roy and Frank de Boer were already establishing themselves in the first team. Stapleton could not help but be impressed by this, describing the club's ability to produce high-calibre players at the time as 'like a conveyor belt of talent'. He added: 'They had an abundance of players. They all wanted to play for the club and make an impact. They were top players. It was a fantastic club in terms of that. I played in the reserves with Dennis when I was coming back from injury. He didn't play centre forward, he was on the right wing. He played quite a few games in the first team that season.'

In total, Stapleton would play just six times for the famous club, amounting to 356 minutes. A prolific scorer for Arsenal and Manchester United, at the time of joining the club he was chasing down Don Givens's Republic of Ireland goalscoring record. (He became Ireland's outright greatest goalscorer in 1990, and held that record until 2001, when Niall Quinn surpassed it.) For Ajax, however, he managed just one. That came early in the season, in September, when Stapleton was sprung from the bench to help his team beat some familiar opposition – Turlough O'Connor's Dundalk. The Lilywhites visited the Netherlands for the first leg of their first-round UEFA Cup Winners' Cup tie.

The match was scoreless at the break; Stapleton recalls it being another uninspiring outing against a team Ajax were expected to beat handsomely. He replaced fellow new signing Hennie Meijer at the interval. 'I think it was psychology,' he says. 'Cruyff said the Dundalk lads knew who I was, being an Irish international. He said it would help. Maybe they would show me too much respect. I went on and this psychology worked to our benefit.' Rijkaard (a very fortunate deflected effort), Blind and Winter all scored before Stapleton registered his goal, converting Rijkaard's cross at the near post beyond goalkeeper Alan O'Neill. The Irish striker raised his arms in delight before offering a word of thanks to his Dutch teammate for the assist.

His sixth and final appearance for Ajax was at Oriel Park as Ajax beat Dundalk 2–0 to secure a comfortable 6–0 aggregate win in the tie. Back on home soil, the Artane man started the game but was replaced before Ajax's two second-half goals.

A key moment in Stapleton's time at Ajax occurred shortly after this game. Ahead of a trip to Germany to face Hamburg in the second round of European competition, Cruyff took his team on a short trip west to The Hague for beach training.

During a beach rugby match – a concept that goes against the perception of Dutch coaching, especially by a purist's icon like Cruyff – the striker was turned over, hurting his back in the process. 'They would take out a rugby ball and we would play. It was just something to change the mood, to relax. Somebody turned me over and I heard a click. I knew straight away I'd done something.'

A year earlier, Blind had missed the Cup Winners' Cup final win over Lokomotive Leipzig, having broken his finger in another beach rugby ruckus. Now, Stapleton was the victim, and his injury would keep him on the sidelines for longer. Though he didn't know it at the time, it effectively ended his career at the top of the club game. He had damaged a disc in his back, and was required to go to hospital to have the disc removed. 'I went through so much pain I thought I would never play again,' he wrote in *Frankly Speaking*. He spent ten days in hospital before being discharged. Cruyff allowed him to return to Manchester to complete his rehabilitation there. Three months into a three-year deal, little did Stapleton know that was it for him and Ajax.

By the time he returned to Amsterdam in January, Cruyff had left, the culmination of ongoing issues with the club's hierarchy. Spitz Kohn, a former Luxembourg international and an assistant coach, had been installed as an interim replacement. He had Stapleton playing with the youths, but the Irishman didn't believe Kohn was making the calls. 'He didn't really have any power. I told him that he had been told to put me with the youths. He denied it. I made the point that I deserved more respect than I was getting. He didn't categorically give me an answer. But, it wasn't his doing.'

Shortly after that, Stapleton was loaned back to England's First Division with Derby County, where he played the last three months of the season in the lead-up to Euro '88. The loan move at least offered him vital minutes ahead of a first major tournament for Ireland, for which he would be captain.

The deal to take him to Derby almost didn't happen, because the club wanted County to pay £2,500 for every game he played. For a time it looked like Derby would baulk, but manager Arthur Cox was insistent that Stapleton was the man to help his team away from the relegation zone.

He was. They stayed up. And Stapleton would soon set sail for Europe once more, joining Le Havre in the French second division for the 1988/89 season, alongside another Irishman, John Byrne. It has also been erroneously reported over the years that during this period Stapleton spent a short time at Anderlecht in Belgium. He didn't.

From Artane to Arsenal to Amsterdam, Stapleton's playing career had more highs than lows. A legend at Highbury and Old Trafford, his part in Ireland's glory days as part of the Charlton era will never be forgotten. His time on the continent may have made less of an imprint on the minds of football fans but his legendary status is indisputable.

And while the likes of Stapleton, Campbell and Givens perhaps had different pedigrees – and vastly different experiences – what is clear is that they were among a charge of Irish footballers who led the way in opening new doors to mainland Europe for those who had never before looked beyond the familiar. Meanwhile, some of their contemporaries could be found in Italy, which even today remains the scene of some of the greatest triumphs of Ireland's footballing exiles.

3
THE ITALIAN JOB

At just twenty-four, Liam Brady ached to step outside of what he considered to be the safe borders of England. As a teenager, he had swapped his birthplace on the Glenshesk Road in Whitehall for north London, and after seven seasons in the Arsenal first team, he wanted to test himself in a new environment once again. 'I wanted a fresh challenge, new surroundings, tougher tests of my capabilities. If I had really wanted big money and nothing more, I could have signed for one of the top clubs in the United States, lived in a penthouse, swanned around in an open-top Cadillac, revelled in all the publicity stunts and played a very relaxed type of football on artificial pitches. But I wanted the very opposite,' he wrote in his 1980 autobiography, *So Far, So Good*, completed just as his time at Arsenal reached its end.

Brady had time on his hands and the world at his feet. After winning his first piece of silverware in professional football by helping Arsenal beat Manchester United in the FA Cup in May 1979, the Dubliner had just one year remaining on his contract. From that point on, Brady spoke openly about his intention to walk away from Arsenal in the summer of 1980. He wanted to justify his status and his reputation as one of the best players in English and European football. He described the win against Manchester

United as providing a 'marvellous sense of relief', as he felt he would now be able to leave Arsenal without regrets. Of course, he also wanted to win more trophies before departing; he had one season left with the Gunners, after all.

Arsenal, under manager Terry Neill, went on to beat Juventus over two legs in the semi-final of the European Cup Winners' Cup in April 1980, giving Brady an opportunity to win another major trophy. In a far cry from the present day, where there is virtually no Irish presence in the later stages of major European competition, Arsenal beat the Old Lady 2–1 on aggregate with five Irish players in the team. Brady, David O'Leary, John Devine and Frank Stapleton were all aged twenty-four years or younger at the time, while Northern Ireland goalkeeper Pat Jennings was among the senior pros at thirty-four.

In the final in Brussels, Arsenal succumbed in a shootout against Valencia after a scoreless 120 minutes of play, Carlos Pereira diving to deny Brady for his penalty. This meant more heartbreak for Brady as, days earlier, he had been in the Gunners team that lost the FA Cup final to West Ham, much to the shock of football spectators – partial and otherwise.

Despite Brady's hope of going out on a high, he had to accept that he would depart without more silverware in his grasp. Still, he hoped Arsenal fans would appreciate his role in helping the team to the previous year's FA Cup and a major European final, a far cry from three seasons in the doldrums in the mid-1970s, a period when a teenage Brady had been finding his way in the game.

Now it was time for a new challenge. And Brady set high expectations for himself, looking to English forward Kevin Keegan as a benchmark. Within two years of leaving Liverpool for Hamburg SV, Keegan had become only the second player after Johan Cruyff to win successive Ballon d'Or titles. 'I look at Keegan and I see a professional who improved his game all round because of his transfer from Liverpool to Hamburg.' Brady wanted to develop his game and learn new techniques. 'I believed I could achieve all these things on the continent. Tighter marking, different types of play, new training routines and a new atmosphere, devoid of the familiarity represented by Arsenal.'

In his autobiography he wrote that he knew the challenges that lay ahead for him. 'I know what to expect abroad – loneliness, perhaps initial hostility, a lack of human contact through language difficulties, frustration at what will be a very limited level of communication, days of despair when home will seem to be beckoning across the water, days of utter bewilderment as I learn how to adapt myself to a new team and a new style of football.' Still, he was determined to forge ahead with his plans to play on the continent.

Brady and his new wife, Sarah, were on the move. They just didn't know where yet. Then a man called Gigi Peronace arrived on the scene. A short, well-dressed man, Peronace was an agent who specialised in the transfers of British players to Italy. For example, he had brought John Charles to Juventus, and Denis Law and Jimmy Greaves to Torino and AC Milan respectively, among others. Based in Hampstead, his reputation for making deals was legendary.

Fresh from their honeymoon in the States, the newlyweds returned to London, where Brady actually resumed training at Arsenal. Peronace, as Brady describes it, was an Italian Mr Fix-It, acting as an intermediary who told the player that Italian clubs were interested in his signature. (What Peronace had been doing for the previous fifteen years remains a mystery, as between 1965 and 1980, there had been a ban on foreign imports into Italian football.)

Due to Peronace's machinations, it soon became clear that Brady was to be the first foreigner to sign for a Serie A club since the ban was lifted. It transpired that the run to the Cup Winners' Cup final had offered Brady – a player in possession of a cultured left foot and a keen eye for picking a pass – the showcase to secure his move. In orchestrating Arsenal's win over Juventus in the last four, he had impressed the hierarchy at the Stadio Comunale sufficiently to buy.

His welcome in Turin was likely more than he expected, too, as he was carried on the shoulders of fans the very day he arrived, lifted from tarmac to terminal as Juventus supporters celebrated a first foreign import in a footballing lifetime. But he knew even then that the hard work was still to come.

With his arrival, he became the first Irishman in over thirty years to play in Italy – the first since Paddy Sloan, a journeyman who appeared as a guest player for numerous clubs throughout the Second World War, before the Lurgan-born Sloan played one season at AC Milan in 1948, and went on to have further short spells at Torino and Brescia.

The Juventus manager at the time of Brady's arrival was Giovanni Trapattoni, then a sprightly forty-one-year-old. He was hopeful that the Irishman could make an immediate impact on his team; however, things did not start off according to plan. After the Coppa Italia group stages dominated the fixture calendar for the early weeks of the season, what Brady considered to be his debut 'proper' came against Cagliari, at the Stadio Comunale Sant'Elia in Sardinia. As he remembers it, the day itself was 'fucking boiling', a far cry from the British and Irish climate to which he was accustomed. The game finished 1–1, the Irishman suffering in the suffocating early-autumn Sardinian heat.

The newspaper reports were not favourable towards Juve's new import. Nor was the instant reaction of one of the club's directors, after a game in which the eighteen-times champions were expected to win. Even off the pitch, Brady continued to feel the heat. He explained to writer Michael Walker for his 2017 book *Green Shoots*, 'We were on the bus, ready to leave. I was sat on my own. One of the directors, a dirigente, asked somebody how Inter had got on, because they were the champions.' The reply came: 'They won 4–0.' The director asked, 'And Prohaska?', referring to Inter's new foreign signing, the Austrian playmaker Herbert Prohaska. 'Yeah, he played well' came the reply. Then Brady, with his developing grasp of Italian, heard something that stuck with him. '*Forse abbiamo lo straniero sbagliato*,' the director snapped. From what he had picked up in his seven weeks at the club to date, he knew two words: *straniero sbagliato* – the wrong foreigner.

The director saw no reason to hide his disdain for the debut league showing of the club's new man, even with the player in earshot. Perhaps he underestimated the Irishman's grasp of the native tongue. The incident never left Brady. Football, he knew, was fickle. 'Directors are like that. I remembered it when he was kissing me at the end of the season,' Brady added to Walker.

His season with the Bianconeri soon turned a corner, however, when Brady was the star man as Trapattoni's side beat Inter Milan in November, in what was just the club's second win in eight attempts that term. Fresh from a penalty and an assist for Gaetano Scirea, he was carried off the field that day on the shoulders of his teammates, such was his impact on a game of the magnitude of the so-called 'Derby d'Italia'. The *'straniero sbagliato'* had come a long way in nine short weeks.

And things only improved from there. At the season's end, Juve had won the league title by two points. A 1–0 win over Fiorentina clinched it at the Turin Comunale. A first career league title brought a profound sense of vindication for Brady's decision to make Turin his temporary home. 'When we won the title, I felt really, really proud. A lot of people had said, "What's he doing going to Italy? It's defensive, horrible." I remember Keegan saying he didn't want to go to Italy because his wife was frightened his children might be kidnapped. It was shite. There were a lot of people who said I was going to fail, that I'd made a mistake going abroad, maybe they saw me as being a bit of a bighead leaving English football.'

Today, were an Irish international to represent one of the continent's best, it would be the biggest story in town. In 1980, Brady's Italian adventure received little press attention, although this was prior to the era of readily available TV coverage. Bar a weekly diary in the *Irish Independent*, ghost-written by Sean Ryan, Brady was out of sight, out of mind. There was a detachment to home – and global – life from his perspective too. 'There was no internet then, no mobile phones. I used to go to get the Sunday papers on a Monday at Turin station. That's how I kept up with what was going on. But I was detached. One of the things I do remember from 1980 was being told John Lennon was shot. I was in a car with three teammates. I think we were going to get Christmas presents and I heard them talking in the car. "*John Lennon e morto*," they said. I was in shock.'

He would go on to help bring Juve to the brink of another title in 1982, before owner Gianni Agnelli decided he wanted French star Michel Platini in his team, leaving Brady facing the exit. At the time the ban was lifted, clubs were limited to one foreign player and then two. With Polish midfielder Zbigniew Boniek also in the mix at Juve, three into two didn't go – even though he had a year remaining on his deal.

He recalls asking Giovanni Trapattoni about it one day after a training session only to be assured that there was nothing to worry about. Brady could see that the manager was lying to him, but concedes that he was in a situation not of his making. Giampiero Boniperti, the then director, would tell Brady that afternoon that he was to be made available for transfer. His response?

'Stick it up your ass!'

The Irishman was devastated by the news that he would be forced out of the club to make way for Platini's arrival. He had been made aware of the situation weeks prior to the league's final day, in which he would have a seventy-fifth-minute penalty kick to secure Juventus a 1–0 win over Catanzaro – and a second league title during his spell at the club. Juve supporters in the crowd that day reasoned that Brady, bitter over his treatment by the club, would miss on purpose. They were grateful when he didn't.

He admits at the time that he was shocked by the club's treatment of him but, approaching forty years on, Brady has long since come to terms with how his time at the club ended. He didn't sulk off to England, as appealing as the prospect of home might have been. Instead he remained in Italy for five more years. Money talked too. 'I've no problem saying I didn't go there just for the challenge,' he said.

Two good years at newly promoted Sampdoria – who had hot prospect Roberto Mancini in their ranks – prompted a star-studded Inter Milan to move for him. In a dressing room consisting of Karl-Heinz Rummenigge,

Walter Zenga and Giuseppe Baresi, Inter fell short in both the league and UEFA Cup in Brady's two seasons there; coach Ilario Castagner couldn't get them over the line. The lack of silverware during his time at Inter is Brady's main regret from his time in Italy.

Another was his decision to leave Inter for Ascoli in 1986, a club where Brady's largely happy Italian time was soured. 'I rushed myself into it,' Brady would tell the journalist Hunter Davies in an interview with the *Independent*. 'I should have waited for a better club. It was the money that did it, which was stupid of me. The town was small and provincial, and we didn't like living there. I was soon at loggerheads with the president. I had a bust-up and refused to play. It was a very unpleasant time.'

Ultimately, with Ascoli struggling badly towards the foot of the division, Brady's former manager at Inter, Ilario Castagner, was brought in to try and salvage their season. Appearances by Brady at that point were rare, with a dispute over unpaid wages creating a division between player and club. By March of that year, Brady had finally decided to return to London, to play with West Ham United.

A source of frustration for Brady is that, in the decades that followed, his time at Juventus – and his seven years in Italy as a whole – became remembered almost exclusively for that title-winning penalty, and not for his wider achievements. No Irish player since has enjoyed such longevity at a top continental European league. Brady remains the only Irishman ever to win a league title in any of Europe's elite top-flight leagues, outside of Britain. 'They made it out to be this wonderfully professional effort on my part not to miss it purposely. I'm remembered at Juventus as the guy who was so professional and all that but I'd like to be remembered for more than that.'

Penalty aside, Brady's move to Italy remains one of the most successful transfers ever completed by an Irish player. However, there was one other Irish player who had an even more successful time in Italy, and that was Anne O'Brien.

⊕

No Irish player in history comes close to Anne O'Brien's achievements, with her haul of nine league titles with Stade de Reims in France and Lazio in Italy surpassing all in the professional game.

O'Brien is an inspiration to Ireland's modern-day stars and the young girls hoping to follow in those footsteps by reaching the pinnacle of the club and international game. It is with no small dose of irony that, while her Republic of Ireland career spanned just a smattering of caps – for reasons we will soon get into – no player in the near fifty-year history of the national team has since come close to achieving the global recognition that O'Brien continues to hold among those who saw or worked alongside her.

Born in 1956, O'Brien was a cousin of Irish football greats Johnny Giles and Jimmy Conway (third and first, respectively). She grew up in an age in Ireland during which there were very unyielding perceptions over how young women should live their lives. A football-mad girl, she would while away hours of her childhood kicking a ball around on the streets of Inchicore. The only girl among hordes of young boys, she was an outlier then and would remain so across an illustrious career.

O'Brien came to the attention of Stade de Reims when the French side embarked on a tour of Ireland in August 1973. Part of a Dublin selection playing a friendly in Dundalk, she caught the eye of manager Pierre Geoffroy, and was subsequently asked whether she would consider joining the visitors on the next leg of their Irish tour, in Limerick, as the team were short players due to injury.

At the time, Geoffroy coupled his duties as Stade de Reims boss with that as manager of the French national team. Two months after first spotting O'Brien, Geoffroy's French team would beat a brand-new Republic of Ireland national team 4–0 at the Parc des Princes in Paris. O'Brien starred for her country that day. Her performance, despite the scoreline, only served to reinforce Geoffroy's desire to bring her to Reims.

For a teenager like O'Brien, who had previously turned out for the Julian Vards women's club and the All-Stars in Ballyfermot in Dublin, to get an offer like this was no small feat. After all, she had only owned a pair of football boots for three years.

O'Brien ultimately accepted the offer, with her parents' say-so, to travel over to France for a trial of sorts with the club. In December, the seventeen-year-old played in three friendly games for Reims, where she impressed once again. Still weeks away from turning eighteen, a deal was agreed for her to join the club in advance of the 1974 campaign.

An RTÉ news report, conducted by reporter Tom McCaughren and broadcast on bulletins on Monday, 24 January 1974, showed the teenage O'Brien playing on the street outside her home on Oblate Drive in Inchicore. There was plenty of space to play on the streets back then, when neither side of the road was obstructed with parked cars – though the player's renowned close control suggests she would have been just as at home honing her skills on more confined modern-day streets too. When asked by the reporter whether she expected a long career in the game, she replied, 'I hope so.'

While the full extent of O'Brien's achievements have only been given widespread exposure in Ireland in the last decade, her move into the professional game did make headlines at the time, though more for the novelty of it than anything else. News of her move to Reims also made headlines in France, via ITN in London. She had become the first female player, Irish or British, to play the professional game.

Leaving behind her family and boyfriend in Dublin, the youngster took her new-found fame and the responsibility of spearheading an expectant Stade de Reims to success in her stride. Known for her balance, vision and cultured left foot, O'Brien quickly became central to Reims's play, and acted as the team's main source of goals. She helped them to three successive league titles from 1974 to 1976, as well as a cup win in which she hit a hat-trick in the final.

A star had been born, and at a time in France when the women's game was booming in the aftermath of the 1970 decision to lift the ban on women playing professionally, O'Brien developed into a superstar of the game.

However, just as Stade de Reims had acquired O'Brien on a tour, they lost her to a bigger team when they embarked on an end-of-season tour to Italy in 1976. Lazio's offer of superior terms and the chance to play in Italy proved too good to turn down.

In Italy, she helped Lazio win the Coppa Italia in her debut season before they claimed a first league title in 1979. They repeated the trick a year later, with O'Brien the key player in the coveted number 10 shirt, often playing behind the strikers in the trequartista role. Colleagues at Lazio included the prolific Danish star Susanne Augustesen and Swedish great Pia Sundhage, though she played with the latter in her second spell at the club. Her time at Lazio was split up by a season with Trani, a small club on the Adriatic coast, which she helped lead to their first league title in 1984. All this meant that in her ten years since leaving Dublin, and still only twenty-eight, O'Brien was toasting her sixth league title in the professional game.

Back in Dublin, news of her achievements were largely lost amidst the travails of the men's senior international football team, the League of Ireland and the popularity of English football from across the channel.

Her involvement with the national team would undoubtedly have provided a boon on the pitch and off for a team in its infancy. The Women's Football Association of Ireland was at the time a separate entity from the organisation that governed the men's game, and there was little in the way of resources to fly O'Brien in and out for international camps. She won only four caps for the national team, and just one of those came after her move to the continent in 1973. That was in 1990, when, back in Ireland anyway, she linked up with Fran Rooney's team for a European Championship qualifier against the Netherlands at Dalymount Park. She lined out against a Dutch team that included the future Irish manager, Vera Pauw. O'Brien stated later in life that the Irish association never approached her with a view to coming home for games. While it was supposed that it was unfeasible to bring back Ireland's best player for international competition, her family

– including her mother Rose and her seven siblings – regularly made the trip to Rome and elsewhere to see her.

Back in Italy, the diminutive playmaker's star never waned. Despite trophyless campaigns at Modena, Napoli and Prato, she helped Reggiana to back-to-back league titles before moving to Milan and winning her sixth and final Serie A title in 1992, aged thirty-six. O'Brien's standing in the women's game at the time did not suffer from her lack of recognition at international level.

Looking back, it was felt that O'Brien's learnings from childhood, where she developed her skills playing against boys on the roads around her home, provided her with the street-smarts to not merely survive but thrive in Italian football – a place where the defenders were seen to be as cynical and physically imposing as their famed male counterparts.

She remains closely associated with the Italian striker Carolina Morace, whom she played with at Lazio, Reggiana and Milan. The Italian legend first encountered O'Brien when the Irishwoman was twenty-two and Morace was just fourteen and a member of Belluno's squad. Speaking to The42.ie after O'Brien's death in 2016, Morace recalled their first meeting in 1978. 'She was an amazing player. She was smart, she had class but she was dynamic too and she'd never stop running because it came so easily to her. That night in Rome, she came up to me during the match. I was just fourteen but in a Roman accent she said to me, "*A regazzi sei proprio brava!* – Young girl, you are very good!" She was absolutely one of the best players in the world. But, at that time, there was no TV or social media to celebrate her.' The two would go on to become friends and remained so for decades.

O'Brien's commitment to the game was absolute. For example, while still playing at the highest level, Anne gave birth to a son, Andrea, but according to her brother Tony, the pregnancy only kept her out of the game for a minimal amount of time. 'She was back playing straight away,' he told The42.ie in 2019. 'I'm sure it was four weeks later that she was back playing for the team again. And she used to breastfeed Andrea in the dressing room.' O'Brien asked Morace to be Andrea's godmother, an offer that was duly accepted.

Over a decade after her retirement, O'Brien coached with Lazio and the Italian Football Federation. Rome had been her base since first moving there in 1976, and after forty years in the Italian capital, it was home. O'Brien remained in Italy until her death in August 2016, after a short illness. She was just sixty years of age.

It is perhaps the most remarkable aberration in Irish football history that a player widely considered to be one of the finest players of her generation amassed just four international caps across a twenty-year professional career. For years, she had been Ireland's only female professional player.

To this day, she remains one of only two Irish players to ever win a top-flight league title in France or Italy, the other being Brady, who followed in her footsteps by moving to the continent in 1980. He won two Scudetti with Juventus, but this pales in comparison to O'Brien's six, plus her three league wins in France with Stade de Reims. Nowadays, O'Brien holds the unenviable title of the 'Greatest Ever Irish Sportsperson You've Never Heard Of'. A lack of match footage – even of the grainy, 1980s retro variety, sometimes seen on YouTube – is clearly partly at fault for this.

Nonetheless, it's never too late to admire her achievements, nor to push to cement her legacy in Irish sporting history. After all, O'Brien's career was the perfect example of taking an implausible dream and using it to create an incredible reality.

4
ONCE UPON A TIME IN AMERICA

By the middle of the twentieth century, Europe was considered the epicentre of club – and perhaps international – football. Meanwhile, the sport had little foothold in the US, and the standard of the football played in the States was far below that seen in Europe. However, attempts were being made to try and rectify that by the nascent United Soccer Association (USA) – and an Irish team, with plenty of Irish players, would participate in this experiment of sorts that hoped to capture the hearts and minds of an untapped market in Boston and around the country.

The USA organisation was a new concept that sought to create the first professional nationwide soccer league in the US. Initially slated to launch in 1968, its maiden season was brought forward by one year after a deal was brokered with the network CBS to broadcast games, with almost immediate effect. What stood in the way was the lack of any teams at that point. Faced with a dilemma, an invitation was made to teams in the established football centres of Europe and South America to enter franchise teams that summer.

The imported teams – there were twelve in total – were given new names and assigned to cities and existing stadia around the country, with some locations chosen on the basis of the club's ethnic background. Among the teams to enter were Sunderland, Stoke City, Wolverhampton Wanderers, Aberdeen, Dundee United, Glentoran, Cagliari and ADO Den Haag, from the Netherlands, as well as Brazil's Bangu AC and CA Cerro of Uruguay.

And then there was Boston Rovers – an offshoot of Shamrock Rovers, and Ireland's sole entrant in the competition. They were set up in Boston, where a teeming Irish population was considered a ready-made audience for the team. Liam Tuohy, the club's player-manager, brought over a panel of fourteen players from his League of Ireland squad, while two guest players – Brazilian brothers Carlos and Gilson Metidieri – were added to their ranks.

While Ireland's squad had virtually no global cachet, there were some big names in the league, notably at Cleveland Stokers, where Stoke City's World Cup-winning goalkeeper Gordon Banks played just a year after his career-defining success. The Cleveland squad was stacked with players who had years of experience in England's Football League, as were the squads of the Los Angeles Wolves and Vancouver Royals, Sunderland's USA franchise.

One of Rovers' Irish players, Paddy Mulligan, a right back, was yet to become a full Republic of Ireland international, and was two years away from earning a move to Chelsea, where he would go on to win a UEFA Cup Winners' Cup. He looks back fondly on his time in the States, even though his participation in the 1967 competition was cut short by a career-threatening knee injury. That was after he'd already lost his job to travel to the States.

Working in the accountancy department of the Irish National Insurance Company, he had previously been refused leave to represent the Republic of Ireland on a week-long trip to Austria and Belgium. They saw no reason why they should make allowances for a twenty-one-year-old, earning a meagre £3 a week, to represent his country, especially in *that* sport. Mulligan left anyway, and received a stern telling-off upon his arrival home. As a result, he knew what would come from leaving his office behind for an unsanctioned seven-week tour of America in the summer of 1967. Again the request was made, and again it was denied by the company's directors. Mulligan, again, departed anyway, and he wasn't welcomed back upon his return. He didn't mind too much, even after his injury.

In truth, that entire season was a bit of a disaster, not just for Mulligan, but for the entire Boston franchise. The team was getting a scant 4,000 people per game at the Manning Bowl. It was meagre even compared to the poor average league attendance of 7,500. Rovers' total of seven points from twelve games likely didn't help draw crowds, a tally that saw them finish bottom of the six-team Eastern Division with the worst record of all twelve competing teams.

However, that poor performance did not spell the end of soccer in Boston, as the club would return in the next season – the inaugural North American Soccer League (NASL) campaign, after the USA had merged with a rival league – as Boston Beacons. So too did Mulligan. Doctors back in Dublin had already warned him that he, aged twenty-two, may have no longer than two years left playing football. Undeterred, he played one game in Ireland, against Shelbourne at Milltown for Rovers, before he headed back Stateside. 'I'd discussed it with my Dad – we'd lost my mother to cancer in '65 – and he backed me on it,' he told the *Irish Examiner* in March 2015. 'I was committed to football by then and my thinking was that I'd give it at least a year. At that stage I wanted to taste professional football and there was nothing happening across in England.'

It turned out that twelve months was all he could commit to the project anyway, with the Beacons folding within a year of their formation. He had been joined there by another Rovers man, Tommy Kelly, and Sligo man Davy Pugh, who had joined the previous year as a guest of the club. Mulligan had at least racked up twenty-one appearances and notched four goals.

Still, despite Mulligan and Rovers' failure in the US – and the general failure of that newly established league to capture hearts and minds in America – it gave a first opportunity for Irish players to experience playing in America.

It would be another decade before John Giles became the most prominent Irish player to join the burgeoning, star-studded ranks of the NASL, then frequented by World Cup winners such as Carlos Alberto and Franz Beckenbauer. (Pelé had been and gone by then too.) Those players were approaching the end of their careers by the time they took their detour into the glamour and riches of the celebrity-infused and endorsement-filled NASL – a league that ultimately fizzled out.

The next big American opportunity would come decades later, with the founding of Major League Soccer (MLS) – a league in which a young graduate from Walkinstown would be the first Irish footballer to play.

A football fanatic growing up, Paul Keegan had held Frank Stapleton in great reverence for as long as he could remember. An ex-Arsenal, Manchester United and Ajax star who captained the Republic of Ireland national team under Jack Charlton, he was a fixture on the television in the Keegan household on Walkinstown Avenue on the southside of Dublin. Now, here he was, in the summer of 1996, having just joined the New England Revolution for the inaugural MLS season. And Stapleton was his manager.

As Keegan remembers, Stapleton – then thirty-nine – was the best player in training, with no player pushing him particularly close. Keegan believes he should have played in the MLS that season. That, as written about in a later chapter, was mooted at one point, but Stapleton declined. Now was the time for him to focus on managing. Keegan, meanwhile, was determined to improve as a player in the familiar surrounds of Boston. Even if part of him was still surprised that he'd made it this far.

Keegan admits he had little in the way of expectation when it came to the first MLS College Draft in 1996, where franchises from all over the country took their pick of the cream of the collegiate soccer scene. This was despite his achievements at Boston College, where, twenty-five years on from graduation, he still holds team records for goals, assists and points amassed. A four-time NSCAA Regional All-American, Keegan was a three-time NSCAA All-American and three-time Big East first team honouree. In 1992, Keegan received the Big East Rookie of the Year. He led BC to two NCAA Tournament appearances and helped the Eagles win the 1994 Big East Championship.

The inaugural MLS College Draft was held on Monday, 4 March 1996 in Fort Lauderdale, Florida. Keegan was in New Hampshire, skiing with friends. His coach Ed Kelly managed to get through to a friend on the landline. 'Paul, you've been drafted by the Revolution and you're sixth pick,' he relayed. Keegan could hardly believe his luck. Not simply because he was deemed the sixth most desirable college player in the country, but because he could also stay in Boston. It was home away from home, by then. Tampa Bay Mutiny had shown an interest in drafting the Irishman, but the Revs were his number one choice. And he, theirs.

Towards the end of March, the players had to report to Foxboro Stadium, their home ground, which they were to share with American football franchise the New England Patriots. Keegan had been there as a spectator before, taking in the Patriots as part of a 60,000-capacity crowd. Growing up, he used to watch the coverage of American football broadcast on RTÉ and Channel 4 during the 1980s. He recalls arriving on day one and first bumping into Alexi Lalas, the flame-haired and flame-bearded national team star. 'To be part of something that big was amazing. I was in awe of all these footballers. Then, I was one of them.'

Due to his four years at Boston College and the large Irish community in Massachusetts, Keegan didn't feel like an outsider at the new franchise. After all, Stapleton's squad contained players from Yugoslavia, Czechoslovakia, Brazil, Cape Verde, Nigeria and Argentina. In contrast, he considered himself something of a native, a local boy done good.

That local connection, especially among the Irish-American community, meant Keegan became one of the more recognisable faces among the roster at the Revs. He would regularly attend football camps or children's birthday parties. It went some way to cementing his popularity among fans, and contributed to the strength of positive feeling towards the club, battling for attention in New England Patriots territory. Keegan was happy to undertake such duties that the likes of Lalas, a full US international, did not. 'I didn't mind that because I felt I was a local and you did gain popularity from it. The kids would come to games and want my autograph. I related to that.'

Keegan certainly began his career at the Revs well. He holds the honour of being the first Irish player to play and score in Major League Soccer, two accolades he pipped Corkman Ian Hennessy to in 1996. Hennessy was on the roster at MetroStars, coached by the future Portuguese manager Carlos Queiroz. A former Arsenal youth, Hennessy had played under Ed Kelly at Seton Hall before spells lower down the food chain in the Boston and New York areas. At thirty years of age, and in the middle of studying for a PhD in Molecular Biology at New York's Columbia University, Hennessy was handed an opportunity to play alongside and against some leading names in this new league. It was difficult to pass up.

Keegan arrived with a bang in the MLS. He can acknowledge, though, that it helped that he had applied for a Green Card during his time at Boston College, having been prompted to do so by Kelly. Therefore, when drafted to play in MLS, he did so as an American college player – not as a foreigner. At the time, clubs were limited to two national team players and two additional foreign imports. The Dubliner admits there was no way he would ever have warranted one of those places.

Despite the Green Card, he was very much tethered to home, to his family. In May 1996, Keegan welcomed his father, Peter, and brothers to Boston for a busy week of activity. They were at Foxboro Stadium to see him in action against the MetroStars. Within eighteen minutes, Keegan had scored to double the Revs' advantage. The game finished 2–0. He was walking on the moon.

The Keegans stayed for another week to attend the graduation ceremony of the class of 1996 at Boston College, where Paul donned mortarboard and gown. It was another proud moment for Peter, whose heart had been swelled by the achievements of his eldest son. It worked both ways.

In 1992, after Brian Kerr had offered Keegan a contract at St Patrick's Athletic, it was Peter who pressed his son to see the world and get an education. 'You can always come back and play,' he said. Peter hadn't been inclined to education but wanted something different for his children. 'Get away from here, get your education,' was the message.

The academic side of life had its challenges for Keegan, who would on occasion be assigned a tutor for help with his studies. Calculus was a particular challenge. Eager to maintain a grade point average to facilitate his availability to play for Boston College, the athletic department would arrange classes for athletes from all codes. Keegan remembers he would predominantly be joined by American footballers. Linebackers as far as the eye could see.

He recalls expensive phone calls as he, at first, struggled to settle into Boston life – £1.50 a minute in old Irish currency. He would record his voice on blank cassette tapes and send them back to Ireland. It was tough on his mother, Mary, adapting to life with not one but two of her two eldest sons across the Atlantic. It was certainly difficult for the self-confessed mammy's boy. He was a real home bird. 'There were a few times the phone was cut off at home because of the cost of calls going over. It was hard.'

The distance was made all the worse when a family tragedy struck. In March 1994, Paul and his brother Wayne, who were both in the middle of their sophomore year of studies at Boston College and Southern Connecticut State University College respectively, received individual phone calls that would change their lives forever. 'You need to come home straight away, your mum's been in an accident,' said the voice down the line.

It was a dark, wet night. Mary and their sister Kim had been returning home from the nearby community centre when Kim dropped a lollipop, forcing both mother and daughter onto the road to pick it up. They were knocked down. Mary was in a critical condition in hospital. The boys – Paul was aged just twenty-one,

Wayne only nineteen – immediately booked flights home. Unfortunately, they didn't arrive in time to say goodbye to their beloved mother.

Paul and Wayne remained by their father's side for months afterwards. His adaptation to life without his wife of twenty-three years was underpinned by their support. They even offered to withdraw from study and stay in Dublin permanently, an offer that filled Peter with pride. However, he wanted his sons to return to the States to resume their academic and sporting endeavours. Eventually, in the summer, they did go back to Boston. 'It was an awful time,' Paul recalls. 'He was so proud. He knew what was better for us and as hard as it was getting on that plane, I'm glad we did it. It was a tough time. Such is life.'

And when Keegan returned, he brought with him a desire to give his father something to treasure. His graduation and on-pitch success with the New England Revolution would do just that.

Keegan remained at the Revs for five seasons, playing under five different managers – starting with Stapleton and including his teammate-turned-coach Walter Zenga and Steve Nicol. A Liverpool supporter from a young age, the latter's appointment had excited Keegan as much as the prospect of playing under Stapleton. While managers and players came and went, the Dubliner's longevity at the club contributed to his acceptance among the fanbase and the wider Boston community. 'I was there for five seasons under five different managers so I like to think I did something right. I always think of that as a badge of honour.'

Keegan ultimately returned to Ireland in 2000, despite having options to remain in MLS, with other offers on the table from clubs in Sweden and England's third tier. But family matters back in Walkinstown made the twenty-eight-year-old's mind up for him. His father Peter, having lost his wife seven years earlier, had been diagnosed with cancer. Paul came home to be near his father in the final year of his life. 'I will always say my dad was my best mate. We were always close but we got really close. It was special to go home and spend the last year with him. I'd love to think I would've gone somewhere else but family has always been a big part of my life. Should I have stayed in America? Should I have gone to Sweden? Should I have gone to Bristol Rovers? I'm glad I didn't. I'm glad I spent that time with him.'

He went on to represent four League of Ireland teams across six seasons, his time in the league seeing Keegan win every major honour available to him, starting with a Premier Division win with Bohemians in 2003. A year later, Keegan helped an unfashionable Longford Town to a domestic cup double in 2004, including scoring an eighty-eighth-minute winning goal against Waterford United to cap a dramatic late comeback in the FAI Cup final.

Nowadays, Keegan looks back fondly on his time in the US, proud that he was there at the beginning of the MLS, a league that has gone from strength to strength since that inaugural season in which he featured. 'Was it ever going to fail? No, because of the attendance figures. I remember playing in front of 60,000 people at the Rose Bowl. How was this going to fail? You can't keep football down, if it's the number one sport in the world – even in America.'

And while Keegan would be the first Irishman to live the American dream in MLS, he would be far from the last.

5

EAST IS EAST

The history of Irish footballers playing in Asia is not abundant, but it is perhaps more plentiful than people assume. In recent years, Irish-born players like Roy O'Donovan, Joe Gamble, Andy Keogh, Shane McFaul, Éamon Zayed and Anthony Stokes have played in countries as far-flung as Brunei, Indonesia, India, Thailand, Iran and Azerbaijan. English-born Ireland-qualified players such as Caleb Folan and the striker Billy Mehmet are well travelled too, with stamps for Malaysia, Myanmar, India and Singapore on their respective passports.

The launch of the Indian Super League also opened doors for Irish in the region. Darren O'Dea became the first Irish player to play in the league in 2015, joining a league that had launched to considerable fanfare a year earlier. Robbie Keane joined Teddy Sheringham's ATK in 2016, before going on to replace his former Spurs' strike partner in a player-coach capacity for a period. Their international teammates Andy Keogh and Anthony Pilkington went on to join franchises in Assam and East Bengal, while former Arsenal goalkeeper Graham Stack and Donegal's Carl McHugh have also appeared in the league. One-cap Ireland striker Owen Coyle became head coach of Jamshedpur in 2020, while Terry Phelan and Gerry Peyton have coached Kerala Blasters and Odisha FC respectively. Peyton had also previously coached at two clubs in Japan's J-League in the 1990s.

Hong Kong has also seen plenty of less heralded Irish players. Eligible for the Republic of Ireland through his maternal grandparents, Salford-born Sean Tse was once called into the Republic of Ireland Under-17 squad, in April 2009, under then boss Sean McCaffrey, but he did not participate in either friendly as part of a double header against Poland. After leaving Manchester City in 2012, Tse has played for a number of clubs in the Hong Kong Premier League, including Kitchee and South China, where he was part of the title-winning side in 2013. However, he is not the first Irishman or player with Irish heritage to play in Hong Kong. Peter Foley, a Republic of Ireland Under-21 cap while an Oxford United player in the 1970s, spent a season there, while another ex-Under-21 player, English-born Tim O'Shea, also played in the league during the 1990s, as did Colin Baker, who would be familiar to some League of Ireland fans as a winger who played for his local side, Limerick, in 2008. He spent eighteen months in the country prior to his spell in his native Ireland, representing Hong Kong FC and Hong Kong Rangers.

However, one footballer's journey to Asia predates all of these players. Dating back to the early 1970s, Terry Conroy was an early trailblazer in this regard.

A Dubliner who grew up in Cabra, Conroy spent twelve successful seasons at Stoke City during what was undoubtedly the Staffordshire club's heyday. Conroy helped the club win the 1972 League Cup – to date their only major trophy – and was a regular as the Potters competed in European competition for the very first time. A tricky winger with an easily identifiable mop of ginger hair, Conroy was also a regular fixture for the Republic of Ireland during the 1970s, eventually going on to become assistant manager of the national team under Eoin Hand.

After leaving Stoke in 1979, aged thirty-two and having played almost 350 games for the club, Conroy declined offers to drop down to English football's Fourth Division with Tranmere Rovers and even further down the pyramid with non-league Worcester City, then of the Southern League Premier Division. Instead, he, his wife Sue and five-year-old daughter Tara set off for pastures new a world away from Stoke. Conroy joined Hong Kong (then a British colony, as it remained until 1997) side Bulova, a team only established two years earlier and sponsored by the American watch company of the same name.

The club had entered league football in 1977 when they competed in Hong Kong's Third Division. Two consecutive promotions underlined their ambition and the investment that had catapulted them quickly towards the summit of football in the country. Conroy, with ten years of top-flight football in England under his belt, and a full international to boot, was seen as a marquee signing. One who represented hopes of further success.

In his 2015 autobiography, *You Don't Remember Me, Do You?*, Conroy recalls how he was excited by the prospect of being a big fish in the small pond of Hong Kong's domestic football scene. 'I was intrigued. Hong Kong sounded so glamorous and I fancied it. I wanted to see how the other half lived. The two-year adventure appealed to me.'

Within weeks of his arrival, however, Conroy could see that the move had been a mistake. Five months in Hong Kong, he wrote in his book, felt like five years. The family didn't settle, nor was Conroy enamoured with the standard of football. He described the level as 'pretty appalling, which was roughly equivalent to lower non-league in England'. Similarly, the training at Bulova was 'exclusively woeful', the team competing with joggers and tai-chi enthusiasts for space in the local park. Still, as he had signed a two-year deal, he expected that he would have to see it through until the end.

Conroy had signed on as a player-coach at Bulova, who were the pretenders to the throne held by rivals Seiko, who had dominated the domestic game in the country for years, and were also sponsored by a major watch manufacturer. Straight away, there were culture clashes in the dressing room, as Conroy sought to improve standards so that they could compete with Seiko. 'The Chinese culture was such that you couldn't even hand out a rollicking, as they took offence. It got very heated very quickly.

I had arrived to quite big headlines as I had transferred from a team that had been one of the best in the English First Division,' he said.

Performances, and results, did not go as expected. 'Now here I was being part of a distinct failure. There was such expectation on me to lead the team into being a better team but they didn't want to be led. I ended up having to bite my tongue.' Conroy had other gripes, too, such as how too much emphasis was being placed on the professional European players in the squad to win the games.

His association with Bulova was a ticking time-bomb, one that came to a head shortly before Christmas, when the club chairman ordered Conroy to play, despite him suffering a hamstring injury. The Irishman lost his cool and shoved the chairman, a reaction he still today describes as the one major act in his life that he feels ashamed of. 'He was the owner. I was supposed to show him deference and respect, especially as a foreign national. Everything which had been building up during my five months in Hong Kong boiled to the surface. I pushed the chairman. He staggered back, but didn't fall,' he recalled.

The players were stunned to witness such an act of disrespect. After recovering, the chairman stormed out of the dressing room and left Conroy to consider the consequences. He was summoned to a meeting the next day. The player-coach described the scene as one from a James Bond film, evoking images of a small but powerful man sitting in a large chair, behind a wide desk, flanked by trusty henchmen in tow.

An agreement was reached regarding the remainder of his contract and the club paid for the family's flight back to London, where they arrived at Heathrow Airport just two days prior to Christmas Day 1979. Rather than two years, Conroy had lasted mere months in the role. Given his dislike of his time in Asia, however, it was likely as welcome a gift as he could have hoped for.

Conroy's autobiography alludes to fears for his safety in Hong Kong after his altercation with the club chairman, Mr Chim, who was alleged to have contacts within the Triad. He believed Mr Chim was the sort of person who could have made him disappear. In the end, the Dubliner was perfectly happy to perform the disappearing act himself. He needed no invitation to cut short his stay in the Fragrant Harbour.

His Asian adventure did not go as planned, nor was he able to help upstarts Bulova reel in the mighty Seiko. At least he had forged a path into Asia that some Irish players would follow.

If Conroy was a pioneer for male players, Claire Scanlan would perform a similar role for Ireland's women footballers.

'If you can see it, you can be it – but back then, there was nothing to see.'

Claire Scanlan readily admits that, while she harboured serious ambitions of becoming a professional footballer from a very young age, she didn't know much about the paths available to her, or how she would actually go about fulfilling her dream. Hailing from Rush in North County Dublin, Scanlan was a Manchester United obsessive as a child, following the era in which her Irish heroes Kevin Moran and Frank Stapleton played for the club in the 1980s. Her dream was to play for the Red Devils, who at the time did not have an official women's team.

At fourteen, she wrote to her beloved club's fiercest rivals, Manchester City, enquiring about their girls' and women's teams. It was indicative of just how desperate the teenager was for any opportunity to play the game at a high level.

Growing up, Scanlan was admittedly naive about the opportunities available to her to play the game she loved, either at home or abroad. Becoming involved with Rush Athletic and later with Swords Celtic eventually led to a call-up to the Republic of Ireland's Under-18 team. It was here that she had her eyes opened to the international game and the high-calibre players with whom she longed to compete.

A diminutive, attack-minded playmaker, Scanlan was a highly technical player who started as a striker and worked backwards until she settled into the coveted number ten role for club and country. At twenty, she chose to leave home and take up a soccer scholarship at Erie, Pennsylvania's Mercyhurst College, where she undertook a degree in Business. Having won her first senior cap three years earlier, leaving for the States meant that she was forced to give up regular involvement with the national team for the duration of her time in the States. Unlike today, where international players are dotted all around the world, there was no budget to fly players back and forth across the Atlantic Ocean and elsewhere (as Anne O'Brien had also discovered during her time in Italy) for international camps. Scanlan's hiatus from the Irish team would ultimately extend to six years.

After graduating from Mercyhurst in May 1996, it took the twenty-four-year-old an entire year to sign a professional contract, via a try-out in San Jose, California. The opportunity to take part came at the end of a letter-writing campaign by Scanlan, who reached out to as many American coaches as possible in the hope that some connections could point her in the right direction.

Little did she know that this endeavour would take her all the way to Japan, with coach Mark Krikorian ultimately providing a link, through those trials, between Scanlan and a team called OKI FC Winds, a team playing in Division 1 of Japan's Nadeshiko League, the top flight at the time. Sponsored by OKI Electric, a company familiar to some for manufacturing printers, the Winds had previously been known as OKI Lady Thunders before a name change in 1995, two years before Scanlan's arrival. Based in Honjō city in Saitama, the team were in just their second season in the top flight when the Irish international joined.

Still, it was a long way from home, even further away than the States. Like most footballers spoken to for this book, she describes herself as a 'homebird'. Travel was more of a necessity for most. 'Because I wanted to play, I had to travel. I would never let travel get in the way of me playing. Wherever the game took me, I had to go.'

Scanlan was the lone representative from Ireland or Britain playing in Japan when she arrived, though the league was among the few fully professional female leagues at the time and was home to some notable talent. This included Norway's World Cup-winning midfielder Hege Riise, who played for Nikko Securities Dream Ladies, and several US internationals such as Saskia Webber and Tammy Pearman, who were both teammates of Scanlan's at OKI Winds.

Investment was forthcoming for the women's game in Japan and, as it offered Scanlan the chance to play the game full-time, she considered it a no-brainer to make the move. Leagues in Germany, Sweden and Iceland – countries with strong and full-time domestic set-ups nowadays – were only semi-professional in the mid-nineties, and could not scratch her itch. The improving Damallsvenskan in Sweden was another option, but she believed Japan suited her football and her personality the best. Culturally, it appealed to her too. 'The Japanese were a very dignified people. Emotions never got too high, not too low. It was all very balanced. I loved Saitama too. I didn't think I was going to beat anyone on strength and power but I'm a more technical player so it totally suited me.'

Though professional, not everything was up to the standards expected. 'We trained on dirt pitches. The fields weren't grass, they were hardened dirt pitches and the sessions would go on for four hours. I thought that was quite interesting although I felt they were quite underdeveloped in their coaching at the time.' Furthermore, attendances were scarce in Japan at that point, with the league failing to capture the attention of the wider public outside of a small, hardcore fanbase – unlike today. 'They went on to win the 2011 World Cup, but at the time in the late 1990s, I felt the coaching was below par and the pitches weren't as advanced. The match pitches were these beautiful 40,000 to 50,000 seater stadiums. They were fantastic but the training facilities weren't great. You train all week on this dirt field and then you play on this gorgeous, immaculate pitch.'

Scanlan arrived on a one-year deal and had there been scope to extend her stay in Saitama, she would have done so. However, a stock market crash and subsequent banking crisis led many of the companies sponsoring the women's teams, including OKI, to withdraw funding. The foreign players left, and for Scanlan that meant a return to Ireland, with Shelbourne, and the international fold. 'It was a bit of a low point for me,' she says. 'I was probably feeling a bit unfulfilled in Ireland. I seemed to be achieving things when I was out of the country. In Ireland we were training just two, three times a week. There were no coaching jobs. No future really.'

One positive of her return to Ireland was that she got to play with the international team again. Within a year of her return she had won the FAI International Player of the Year award, which pointed to her importance to the team under boss Mick Cooke and her immediate impact on the national side after six years out of the fold.

While her time in Japan did not last as long as she would have liked, at least she'd forged a fresh path for the next generation of Irish women footballers, showing them what was possible, an example for others to follow. She had become the type of inspiration she didn't have growing up. 'There was no player in any other country or any other team that I was aware of. And within the Irish set-up, the only person I was aware of who had gone away was Anne [O'Brien],' she says. 'There weren't loads of options like now when girls have lots of choice, which is great.'

She remains the only Irish-born player – male or female – to play professionally in Japan, or indeed in neighbouring China or South Korea. But Scanlan remains one of the few female Irish players of the era to look beyond Ireland, the UK or the collegiate system in the United States for her football fix.

The road less travelled naturally leads to more unique experiences. It is something a number of players have found out for themselves in the decades since.

Caleb Folan didn't have any answers to give, nor (unlike Terry Conroy) did he deem it smart to engage in any form of backchat with his new paymaster. However, the exchange between players and Ahmad Samsuri Mokhtar did serve to illustrate the environment that the former Republic of Ireland striker had walked into.

Samsuri Mokhtar was the chairman of Malaysian Super League side T-Team, based in Terengganu, Malaysia's royal capital. It was early 2013 and he had recently bankrolled the signings of Folan and the former Dutch international midfielder George Boateng, a duo who had been Premier League teammates at Hull City just three years earlier. For a team established a mere seven years previously and with little trophy-winning pedigree to speak of, the outlay on Folan and Boateng was substantial.

The ambitious team were managed by Peter Butler, an English football manager who, by the time he arrived at T-Team, had spent over a decade managing a host of sides in south-east Asia. Best known for being part of the West Ham United squad promoted to the Premier League in 1993, Butler was the first foreign coach appointed at the club. It was Folan and Boateng however, not Butler, who bore the brunt of Samsuri Mokhtar's agitated line of questioning after a 2–2 draw in a pre-season friendly with local rivals Terengganu FC.

After full time, the chairman – who was also a high-profile politician in Terengganu – entered the dressing room at the Sultan Ismail Nasiruddin Shah Stadium and took aim at the high-profile signings. 'Why didn't we win?' he asked, eyes fixed on good friends Folan and Boateng. It was at this point that Folan realised that his time in Malaysia – however long he might spend there – would take on a unique dynamic, with added expectation placed on him by those who had brought him to the club. 'Their mentality was the onus is on us,' he recalls. 'If we didn't win, it was on us. The mentality was, "You played in the Premier League, you're going to score 100 goals for us." Genuinely. Their expectation was very high.'

Folan, who had played in the top flight of English football with Wigan Athletic and Hull City and earned seven senior caps for the Republic of Ireland under Giovanni Trapattoni five years earlier (the striker represented Ireland because of his paternal Irish grandfather, John Michael Folan, who hailed from the west coast), had only just returned from a long-term and damaging nerve injury in his right leg that had seen him play no football throughout the entirety of 2012. He had left MLS side Colorado Rapids at the end of the 2011 campaign, expecting to return before a change in manager left him surplus to requirements. A mooted move to Wolves, then a Premier League outfit under Mick McCarthy, failed to materialise, and so he signed for Birmingham City, where another Irishman, Chris Hughton, was in charge. However, the aforementioned nerve injury put paid to his time at St Andrew's, where he failed to make an appearance. Between the not-so-conscious uncoupling from the Rapids, months on the treatment table at Birmingham's Wast Hills training facility and a subsequent six months with no gainful employment prior to his move to Malaysia, 2012 had been an annus horribilis for Folan.

At the end of the year, however, it seemed like things were improving. Folan first learned of the possibility of moving to Malaysia during a phone call with an agent friend in December 2012. After that, it all happened very quickly. Ten minutes after putting down the phone, his friend was back on the line. Butler wanted him at T-Team. A short time later, details of a long-awaited contract were in Folan's email inbox.

The prospect initially excited Folan. 'I'd always wanted to play in Asia. I told my friend about my fitness. I told him I was fine, which I wasn't. I was far from 100 per cent but I was just so eager to play. I would have taken anything half decent just to get back playing again. After so much looking and waiting for that opportunity, it came at the wrong time. I had been six months out and had not been able to train properly. I tried my best to wing it out there. I definitely didn't succeed.'

He didn't score in ten league outings. Hence the chairman's outbursts.

This failure to score ultimately led to a parting of the ways. It was no surprise to the Leeds-born centre forward, given the level of expectation on the shoulders of T-Team's marquee imports. Unlike his shock departure from Colorado a little over a year earlier, he was mentally prepared for this. 'I knew where I was within myself. I was mentally prepared for it. I knew I wasn't 100 per cent. When you know that, you have a more understanding approach to things. I knew it was going to be a challenge on the pitch,' he says.

Pre-season had gone well for Folan, but once the season began in earnest, he had little left. 'I was finished. I had almost given so much in the pre-season. I just couldn't take that next step. My body just wouldn't allow it.'

Folan left the club at the end of March 2013 and was followed by Butler before the season reached its climax in July. T-Team finished third bottom of the twelve-team division, avoiding relegation only by goal difference.

So much for winging it. But, it wasn't all bad for a player who had longed to spend time in Asia. An innately spiritual person, Malaysia had been the perfect next destination or step in Folan's life. 'Change for me was a new experience. It wasn't just finding a new team or a new club. It was finding a new country. Aside from the football, it was the most amazing time. It was incredible, just as I'd imagined. I couldn't have asked to be in a better place, in terms of being in connection with yourself on a deeper level. Spiritually and mentally, it was educational. Malaysia felt like my spiritual home.' He adds, 'I found out a lot more about myself than I ever had before in places I had been previously. I don't know whether that was where I was in life or whether the location triggered something within me. I definitely found comfort in that part of the world.'

A short spell back in England – in Yorkshire, specifically – at League One side Bradford City followed, but upon leaving the club in December 2013 Folan endured a year-long spell without a club.

It soon dawned on the striker that other opportunities would be hard to come by in England. He would have to look further afield again for his next chance. His time in the Ireland set-up, under a manager in Giovanni

Trapattoni who Folan enjoyed a strong bond with, counted for little after three seasons outside of British football's sight and mind. Injuries had played their part but so too, Folan believes, did a reluctance by English clubs to take a risk on a player who had spent much of that time in Malaysia and America. Major League Soccer is maligned by many as a league for players looking to wind down their careers in cities more salubrious than Stoke or Sunderland. 'There was definitely that mindset that when you're playing in these countries, they're not too sure about you. I couldn't even get in the doors of a club. I had no interest from anyone. No calls, nothing.'

Folan found himself emailing clubs and using LinkedIn in the hope of being given a chance to show, at thirty-one, that he still had plenty to offer. Based from his home in Leeds and training individually at nearby Roundhay Park, the striker was frustrated but motivated. He felt he had more to give and was not prepared to stop playing without giving more of himself. He would continue on, he decided. With that, his attention turned again to Asia.

Folan soon found himself in Thailand, where he trialled for Army United, among other teams. However, his reputation after Malaysia – the Premier League striker who failed to find the net – damaged his prospects of finding a club there.

Next he turned onto the not-well-worn path of Myanmar, namely Kanbawza FC, who were based in Taunggyi, the capital of Shan State. Kanbawza (which shortly after Folan departed changed their name to Shan United) saw the best of him during his season-long spell at the club in the 2014/15 season, as here the targetman enjoyed his most prolific goalscoring season. Perhaps that is no real surprise, given that it was most certainly the weakest league he played in. Factor in that 6'2" Folan was playing in a country where the average height of men is 5'4", it is little wonder that he flourished during his ten-month stay.

One of just four European players in the league where clubs are limited to four foreigners per squad, Folan hit thirteen goals in seventeen games, striking up a fruitful partnership with Georgian attacker Giorgi Tsimakuridze. However, as in Malaysia, expectations were, in Folan's own words, 'ginormous'. He recalls, 'I still think they expected more. They expected to win the league, the cup, everything.' The duo performed well but both missed games, Folan being absent for five, and the team could ultimately manage only a fifth-place finish, eighteen points off the summit and one agonising point adrift of qualification for the group stage of the AFC, Asia's UEFA Europa League equivalent.

As with his time in Malaysia, even if the football didn't quite go to plan, Folan still found solace in the culture. Always alternative, artistic and increasingly attuned to spirituality as he got older, his time in Myanmar was where he connected to more holistic affairs, to life and healing. 'I found out certain things there that helped me stabilise myself,' he says, referring to the anxiety that he had lived with in some form for years by that point. 'During my time in Malaysia and then Myanmar, I was tapping into that and learning. It gave me direction, something I wanted to pursue. I was awakened.'

What stood out to Folan – once a £1 million footballer when he became Hull City's record signing in 2008 – during his time in Myanmar was how content the people there were with what little they had. He was drawn to their internal happiness, how they were not reliant on, nor were they in pursuit of, material things in order to determine their mood or spirit. 'People have little in comparison to those in the Western world, but they are happy. It's quite a powerful thing. I found that incredibly humbling.'

Since he was a teenager in the Leeds United academy, he had harboured ambitions of playing around the world. Not in Spain, Germany or Italy, the leagues readily available to British and Irish audiences on television, but Asia and elsewhere. While football offered the platform to do so, it was his receptiveness to these other cultures that opened doors most players would not dare approach. (His experiences certainly fed into his life post-retirement. Now living back in Leeds, Folan works as a holistic wellness and massage therapist.)

Folan left Myanmar after a ten-month stint in the country. To this day, he remains the only player to play in the Premier League and Myanmar's

National League. Still, he was not quite finished exploring. Folan finished his career in 2018 after a short spell in Trinidad and Tobago with Central FC, a team based in Couva on Trinidad's west coast. Issues with non-payment meant Folan's stay there was a brief one. By the end of his first season he was offered the chance to continue, but he'd finally had enough. Even he, with his wanderlust, called it quits at thirty-five.

Still, he has no regrets, and is glad he chose this route rather than dropping down the leagues back in England. 'I was more driven by the travel aspect of it – the opportunity of playing in Asia and the Caribbean. I was driven to explore these locations. It was the travel side of things. You think about people who want to go travelling and they go thousands of miles around the world. I always liked the idea of travelling and I was able to incorporate playing football into that. That was the happiest I've ever been. I loved that. That for me was my ultimate happiness.'

As a young boy, Folan had set his sights on travelling the world, with Asia a location high on his list of destinations. Roy O'Donovan had never looked so far afield, but at twenty-eight and in need of a career reboot, all of a sudden it was calling.

Two days. That was all it took for Roy O'Donovan to realise that his latest career move would not go down as a success. It was February 2015 and the former Cork City striker, who had previously turned out for eight teams in a seven-year spell in the United Kingdom, was sitting alone in his hotel room in central Tenggarong, a small town in the East Kalimantan province of Indonesia. Speaking to his wife Ellen via FaceTime, the striker couldn't disguise his frustration. He didn't want to. He needed to get it off his chest.

Following a career-best season with Singapore club Brunei DPMM, in which he had hit twenty-six goals in all competitions and helped the club to the Singapore League Cup, O'Donovan had found himself as one of a number of new recruits for Indonesian side Mitra Kukar, managed by well-travelled Englishman Scott Cooper. As well as O'Donovan, who had garnered a lot of interest from clubs across Asia and Australia after his season leading the line for Brunei, Cooper signed a Spanish duo, creative midfielder Cristian Portilla and defender Jorge Gotor. Big things were expected for the club, O'Donovan had been promised. And he was to be a central part of that.

But he had been sold a dream. Now, in his own words expressed to his wife, the then twenty-nine-year-old felt trapped.

Having flown into Balikpapan airport two days earlier, it took a three-and-a-half-hour car journey via dirt country roads to reach Tenggarong, a town with a population in excess of 100,000. He recalls having to board a ferry to cross the Mahakam River, which runs alongside the town, and then embarking on a ninety-minute drive to reach the city of Samarinda, where O'Donovan says the nearest supermarket was located. 'Tenggarong was in the back arse of Borneo. People didn't speak English, not even in the hotel. There was no supermarket in the town. It was very hard. I felt isolated, a bit lost straight away.'

The Corkman was disheartened to learn that after arriving in the dead of night at his hotel in the town after his treacherous journey from the airport, they didn't even serve breakfast. This was a culture clash he wasn't expecting.

Before jetting off, O'Donovan had conducted rudimentary research on what was to be his new home. In photos online, the sun was shining. That was a start. However, the truth was that Tenggarong had a tropical rainforest climate, meaning while it was hot all year round, heavy rainfall was also par for the course. What else caught his eye while checking out the city online was the impressive Kutai Kartanegara Bridge, a suspension bridge which connected Tenggarong and Samarinda. What the jet-setting footballer discovered upon his arrival, however, was that the bridge had in fact collapsed over three years previously. Twenty people had been killed and scores more injured in what was a devastating event for the region. Hence the ferry crossing.

All of this information was relayed to Ellen.

What irked him more was how all this was a world away from his time in Brunei. It also helped that Ellen had spent much of the previous year in Brunei with him, along with fellow Corkonian Joe Gamble and his family. While there, they enjoyed the modern and comfortable surroundings Brunei offered. Mistakenly, that modernity and comfort had led O'Donovan to the belief that elsewhere in the continent – even across the vast expanse of Borneo – would be similar.

Both on and off the pitch, however, it was to prove a far less fruitful experience. For one thing, the standards were much lower. 'It was the polar opposite of what I was used to in Brunei. The stadium [the 35,000 seater Aji Imbut Stadium] was left to rack and ruin. The grass was knee high. The players would turn up in all different sets of training kits. It wasn't professional, it wasn't ready. It wasn't what I was used to,' he says. 'The football wasn't ready and the lifestyle didn't fit what we were used to.'

As it turned out, there would soon be no Indonesian Super League to compete in anyway. Indonesian Youth and Sports Minister Imam Nahrawi first postponed and ultimately cancelled the season, owing to what the government claimed were legal verification reasons. Indonesian President Joko Widodo claimed the government's stance against the Football Association of Indonesia was part of a broader attempt to reform the sport in the country. That did not fly with FIFA, who responded by suspending Indonesia from international competition. That meant that by the time the league was cancelled, in mid-April, Mitra Kukar had played just two league games, both defeats.

The Irishman featured in one, a 2–3 away defeat to Gresik United. (He had at least some fruitful outings during pre-season, hitting braces in wins over local amateur sides Harbi Putra and PS Mitra Teras.) The contract he had signed was for one year, with an option to extend for a further twelve months. However, with no football to play, his stay lasted just two months. 'I couldn't get my head around how I got suckered into it really. At the back of my mind I thought everywhere would be like

Brunei, that it'd be straightforward. It was the longest two months of my life. I think had I gone to Indonesia first and not Brunei, I would've been burned and I probably would have gotten out of there as quickly as I could. Every day I was frustrated; when I went back to the hotel, I was frustrated.'

That year-long spell in Brunei, where he'd played for the former Blackburn Rovers boss Steve Kean and alongside his friend Gamble, himself a former Cork City player with experience in England, really had been a polar opposite experience both on and off the pitch. As already mentioned, O'Donovan was part of the DPMM team that won the Singapore League Cup in 2014, as well as coming within a whisker of winning the league – losing 1–2 to Tampines Rovers on the final day of the season to concede their place at the top of the table to eventual winners Warriors, who beat Albirex Niigata 1–0 to complete the dramatic final-day title grab. DPMM would exact revenge on Tampines Rovers at least, beating them in the League Cup final five days later.

However, perhaps it was O'Donovan's life off the pitch that differed the most from his time in Indonesia. Brunei was palatial and was the antithesis of what O'Donovan came to dislike about Tenggarong. A wealthy country, all the mod-cons were very available to an Irish couple already out of their comfort zone. At twenty-eight, the move was a leap for a player who hadn't given up on another call-up to the senior international fold, where a full cap had eluded him to that point.

The fact that Steve Kean, a Scottish manager who O'Donovan was familiar with from his time in charge of Blackburn Rovers, was the coach was a major selling point, as too was the presence of a fellow Corkman in Gamble. It softened what would have been a harsh change in terms of football and culture.

Primarily, though, Kean added credibility to the project. 'He'd got criticised at the end of his time at Blackburn. He needed a bit of a recharge and a reset, and so did I. It was the right opportunity at the right time. I never looked back. It was the best possible thing for me.' O'Donovan and Gamble were joined by three other foreign imports at DPMM in 2014: Croatian midfielder Robert Alviž, Bosnian Boris Raspudić and Brazilian Rodrigo Tosi – who would later spend a year in the League of Ireland with Limerick.

While a rapid start to the league campaign ultimately came painfully short of success – O'Donovan believed the team 'froze on the home stretch' – the team were treated well by the club's owner, the Crown Prince of Brunei, Prince Al-Muhtadee Billah. While players could never get too close or familiar with the Crown Prince, they did attend the Sultan's residence on occasion for birthday celebrations. Post-game audiences with the Crown Prince were also not uncommon. He did, however, make occasional demands of his team. For example, every training session tended to follow a familiar pattern. The players would be partaking in drills when they would hear a cavalcade of cars and sirens approaching. That was Kean's signal to abandon the drills and begin a five-a-side game, as this was what the Crown Prince was coming to watch. 'Everybody was happy,' O'Donovan says. 'We got our game of a ball and he got to watch his team score a few goals with a few combinations. He wasn't coming to watch the warm-up.'

As much as O'Donovan enjoyed his time in Brunei – certainly compared to Indonesia – his departure was an acrimonious one.

His friend and advisor, George O'Callaghan – himself an ex-Cork City player – had become general manager of Sabah FC, a team in the nearby Malaysian Super League. Located a short twenty-minute flight from Brunei, the two clubs are historic rivals, as Brunei used to compete in the Malaysian leagues before joining the Singapore S League in 2009. O'Callaghan had already asked O'Donovan whether he would be interested in joining the club, where he had secured the services of League of Ireland stalwart Éamon Zayed and controversial former Liverpool forward El Hadji Diouf. Preferring to stay at Brunei for another season, O'Donovan declined the offer but still decided to visit his friend in Kota Kinabalu, before he travelled back to Cork for Christmas. That was to prove an irreversible error.

An overzealous club official at Sabah FC mistook O'Donovan's visit as confirmation of a new signing and proceeded to publish news of his arrival on the club's official website, a story which included a photograph of the player arriving at the airport.

That marked the end of any relationship O'Donovan was to have with Brunei DPMM. The Crown Prince was suitably embarrassed by the incident, meaning the contract the club had offered to extend his stay for another year was withdrawn. Despite Kean fighting his striker's corner, nothing could be done. Kean's protestations fell on deaf ears. O'Donovan's attempts to prove his loyalty to the royal family were deemed too little, too late. 'They had to save face,' O'Donovan remembers. 'I showed a disloyalty to them. They cut me before I decided to cut them. It came down to pride for them. You can't be seen to be doing the dirty on the royal family. It wasn't the done thing. I was upset. I was happy to stay there for another year.'

O'Callaghan, himself a former DPMM player after a brief spell with the club in 2011, was made persona non grata by the club, with accusations that he had engineered a situation where O'Donovan would ultimately leave for Sabah.

In the end, of course, he played for neither in 2015, instead choosing to join Mitra Kukar, which was an altogether different experience, one that ended his Asian experiment on a sour note after such an eye-catching start. Australia was calling next for him – along with a return to prolific form in front of goal – but at least O'Donovan could say that he had seen two very different Asias, where most Irish footballers don't even see one.

6

MANAGING EXPECTATIONS

While Jack Kirwan, Jim Donnelly and Patrick O'Connell set sail for mainland Europe in the early part of the twentieth century, more recent Irish coaches have trained their sights much further afield for opportunities than in previous eras. One such coach, Conor Nestor, who was made head coach of Cambodian C-League side Preah Khan Reach Svay Rieng in 2018, is an eye-catching example of the new generation.

He is an unlikely man to find in charge of such an improbable team in a remote outpost. At thirty-four, Nestor was a baby in football management terms upon his appointment. Most future managers haven't yet retired from playing themselves at that age, while many are only then embarking on the tentative initial steps required to leave the pitch and move into the dugout. Within weeks of his start, however, he had already been to hell and back – thanks to a riot that threatened to end a football management career still in its infancy.

It occurred eight games into his tenure at the club, in June 2018, and was just one element of what he describes as the 'season from hell'. For all his qualifications and learnings – Nestor had worked as an FAI Development Officer in Limerick for nine years and is a UEFA A License holder – nothing had prepared him for something like this, or the consequences that would follow.

His side trailed 1–2 against the Cambodian army's National Defense team when a scuffle broke out among the players after Svay Rieng midfielder Nob Tola reacted badly to being on the receiving end of a late, hefty challenge from Korean Song Chi-Hun. From there, things escalated quickly. As the players grappled on the field, punches by this point flying indiscriminately, the club's kitman decided to enter the fray. As he approached a National Defense player, fist clenched and primed, the opposing player struck a pre-emptive blow. Cue chaos. The benches emptied onto the field, as did many of the fans occupying the small stand behind the dugouts. The offending player dashed off at speed, as a number of Svay Rieng players chased him with revenge on their mind. On a continent where age is an important determinant on social behaviours, raising a hand to an elder – as the player did to the kitman – could not be overlooked. This was regardless of the latter's likely violent intentions when he illegally entered the pitch.

Nestor, meanwhile, was standing completely still in the technical area, watching the chaos unfold. He wondered, given just how surreal this moment was, whether Mike Murphy would appear and tell him he was on candid camera, a nod to the popular *The Live Mike* variety show broadcast on RTÉ in the late 1970s and early 1980s (Nestor vividly remembers watching repeats of the programme broadcast on RTÉ as a child). Alas, the retired seventy-five-year-old Irish TV personality was not in Cambodia, and had no hand in what Nestor was witnessing. It would have been funny, had it not been so serious. 'A collection of people lost their minds. They lost control of their emotions. Their emotions controlled them, effectively,' Nestor recalls. 'I was rooted to the floor. I was in complete shock. I was eight games in and my professional career as head coach was over. That was the logical thought process.'

Nestor assumed, wrongly so, that he was doomed. His first season in Cambodian football was a busted flush, however. While the referee only sent off two players for their part in the melee, the Football Federation of Cambodia conducted their own post-mortems. Seven players from Svay

Rieng ultimately received bans, including five who were banned for eleven games each. National Defense sacked Korean Chi-Hun, who was involved in the initial scuffle, while Japanese player Yudai Ogawa, who landed the punch on the kitman, was heavily fined. The kitman also received an eleven-match ban for his part in the melodrama, but with seven fewer players to provide shirts, shorts and socks for, perhaps that loss wasn't as keenly felt as the others.

Their season, with fourteen games left to play, was effectively over. Fines accompanied the bans. The club's next fixture was to be played behind closed doors, and the club were warned that if they failed to control their players and fans in the future, more substantial financial penalties would be incurred.

Back in the dressing room on that fateful day, 3 June 2018, Nestor told his players that football was a game of emotion. That was why they were there, how they had come to this point. But he reminded his players that they were not animals, but humans, and humans were expected to control their emotions. The Limerick-born coach eventually reached the conclusion that institutional issues were at play at Svay Rieng. He later found out that this sort of incident had happened, to a somewhat lesser extent, in previous seasons.

The club were roundly criticised for not sacking some of those involved in the incident. But Nestor and his team, including Scottish general manager Christopher Grant, stood firm. 'In a family or in a home, you don't throw your child out in the street. You're part of the solution process, educating them and disciplining them. You don't wash your hands of the problem and say, "It's them".'

Without a doubt, at that stage of his fledgling managerial career, Nestor was missing the familiar terrain of Limerick. Hailing from Foynes, a small town sitting on the southern bank of the Shannon Estuary, a young Nestor had been captivated by Irish football's emergence on the world stage under the direction of Jack Charlton. Born in 1984, he remembered with particular fondness the World Cup campaigns in 1990 and 1994, played out on the fields of Cagliari, Palermo and Genoa, New York and Orlando.

Having represented Limerick's district league as a teenager, leading to Ireland trials, Nestor's interest was piqued even at that age by coaching. By seventeen, he was balancing his Leaving Cert studies with coaching an Under-14 boys team at Foynes AFC. He thought he could do a better job than some of the local parents. He duly did. A student of English and History at NUI Maynooth, by this stage, he had succumbed to the coaching bug. A spell as caretaker coach of the third level college's soccer team led to a time spent coaching at inter-league level before Nestor was employed by a US-based coaching company called UK Elite.

It was during a spell back in Limerick while in-between work visas that the role of FAI development officer in Limerick came to his attention. Aged just twenty-three, he didn't think he would get it. But he did. From 2007 to 2016, Nestor ran coaching courses and looked after player development in his home county. He worked with schools county-wide and helped grassroots clubs implement structures. At the same time, he worked alongside Tommy Barrett with Limerick FC's Under-19 team, helping them to a league title.

Still, this wasn't enough for him. Nestor had begun his coaching journey at seventeen years old and he wanted to get back in the saddle. More pitches, less PowerPoint. What was next? A return to the States was an option, but through friend Keith Garvey, he opted for Australia. There he would work at a newly established Football Star Academy.

While awaiting a new visa, Nestor was advised to spend time in Cambodia, where he could live cheaply for however many months it took for his application to be approved. Via his extensive online network, he knew someone in Phnom Penh: Christopher Grant, who was then academy director at Svay Rieng.

The Irishman initially passed the time spent waiting for the visa in Cambodia by coaching a semi-professional team in the evenings. He also picked up some background on Svay Rieng, like how the club was founded in 1997 and played in Cambodian football's top-flight. Champions for the first time in 2013, the club had enjoyed some success in recent years, winning the Hun Sen Cup – the country's knock-out cup competition – four times between 2011 and 2017.

As it happened, within weeks of arriving, Svay Rieng were suddenly looking to change their coach. The planets were aligning. In conversations with chairman Dy Vichea, Grant put forward Nestor's name. All of this meant that by January 2018, eighteen months after leaving the FAI, Nestor had a coveted senior role. It was not the exact role he would have craved, but it was a head coach position at a club that were going places.

He wasn't naive to the pitfalls of senior club management. It was a rat race. He could be out of a job after six games. His gut told him not to do it. But in preparation for a presentation – one, final dastardly PowerPoint – to the club's chairman and technical director, Nestor's due diligence convinced him that Cambodian football was on an upward trajectory. 'I got this sense from very early on. I had a real belief that football in Cambodia had the potential to go boom.' He compared the potential to pre-Celtic Tiger era Ireland, when, during the halcyon days of Jack Charlton's reign, football instilled a feel-good factor that changed a nation. He believed something similar could happen in Cambodia. 'The technical quality of the players here is much higher than I expected for a country so low on the FIFA rankings. There was a clear love for football visible on every street too, with jerseys from around the world on every street corner and kids playing on every available space they could find. It's a country that can only rise economically after a troubled past. A country with a required hunger to go and make the climb.'

As if to confirm his suspicion, in August 2018, months after Nestor's appointment at Svay Rieng, the Japanese superstar Keisuke Honda became manager of the Cambodian national team. A former AC Milan player and veteran of three World Cups with the Samurai Blue, Honda's arrival prompted an all-in investment from supporters and pundits alike.

That is not to say that Nestor and his team haven't played their part in this investment. In the aftermath of the now-infamous riot, and despite his belief that that season was a write-off, Svay Rieng bounced back reasonably well, winning seven of the remaining games to secure a respectable mid-table league finish. The new manager had been up against it that first season in any case, as his appointment in late January 2018 had given him just five weeks to scout and secure the maximum four foreign signings for the beginning of the season, as well as embed them into a team – and region – with which he was just growing familiar. After all, Nestor had never been to south-east Asia before arriving in 2017 for his supposedly short stay. The town of Svay Rieng is small, with a population of a little over 40,000, but the province itself is home to half a million. In size and lifestyle, it was a world away from Foynes.

Still, while in Nestor's own words, that first campaign was 'the season from hell', he was determined that the next season would be a different story.

In some ways, the riot turned out to be a sort of blessing. What happened after was that Nestor was afforded the time to coach the team without the pressure of expectation. Saying that, he knows that had they decided to change the coach, he wouldn't have had much grounds for complaint. 'In south-east Asia, it's not unknown for coaches to be gone after five games, especially foreign coaches,' he explains. 'It's not then unknown for that foreign coach to wait a long time, or until they die, to get paid after being fired.'

But ultimately there were no such concerns for the Irishman. By the time the banned players returned, there were three league games remaining in the season. Svay Rieng won them all, including hitting five in two separate wins over Soltilo Angkor and Visakha. Those came either side of a 1–0 away win to National Defense. It was cathartic to defeat the team with whom they had rioted, but of more importance was the visible improvement in the team.

That manifested itself in a 2019 season that ended in Svay Rieng as C-League champions, for just the second time in their twenty-two-year history. Nestor's side won twenty and drew five of their first twenty-five games of the campaign. The title was wrapped up by the time they fell to their one-and-only defeat on the final day, losing 1–2 to NagaWorld.

Coupled with the three wins at the end of the previous season and five victories in the Hun Sen Cup, the Irishman had led the club through thirty-three unbeaten games.

It was a success that he surprisingly got to share with his mother. As the team celebrated their 2019 league win, Nestor's seventy-six-year-old mother Teresa decided she would like to travel the 10,000km and be part of the festivities. Flying into Phnom Penh with her daughter Bríd and son-in-law John, she then embarked on the treacherous two-and-a-half-hour drive to Svay Rieng for that final game against NagaWorld, the 2–1 defeat. 'Mam came to jinx us and break our unbeaten run. That's how superstitious I am. She'll never be invited to a game again.' But he counters how, 'It was a great moment to be able to give the winner's medal to my Mam.'

When Teresa Nestor from Foynes isn't jet-setting around the world to watch Cambodian league football, the topic is never far from her lips. It's often discussed during trips to the local butcher, while pubs in Foynes are known to stream games for locals to watch as they enjoy a pint on a weekend afternoon. Her son and his title-winning team.

It says something about the competitive nature of the league that, despite their extraordinary run of form, they won the league by – only – seven points from second-placed Visakha. Four teams had won fifteen or more of their twenty-six outings, while three teams scored eighty or more goals. At the other end of the table, Kampong Cham were relegated, having ended the season with a goal difference of negative 170. Remarkably, even they won two of their matches.

A clean sweep of league awards would soon follow, including Coach of the Season for Nestor. His Cameroonian striker Befolo Mbarga finished the season with thirty-six goals, earning him the Player of the Year gong. Goalkeeper Aim Sovannarath, with eight clean sheets to his name, was named Goalkeeper of the Year. But it was another accolade that Nestor took the most pride in. His team, still full of the riotous reprobates of Svay Rieng, ended the season with the best disciplinary record of the division. The coach employed a number of tactics, including delivering empowerment coaching to his squad, in a bid to help them control their emotions better on the field of play. It had worked.

In 2020, a year interrupted by Covid-19 but less so in Cambodia, where the virus was virtually non-existent until a major outbreak in the spring of 2021, Svay Rieng were unable to retain their title, losing out on the final day via their head-to-head record against Boeung Ket. Both teams had finished tied on forty-one points at the end of a truncated, seventeen-game season.

Starting the day two points behind, Svay Rieng had to win and Boeung Ket had to lose. Nestor's side did their bit – beating NagaWorld 4–0 – but a ninety-seventh-minute leveller for the league leaders away to Phnom Penh Crown meant the league title was lost. That was a bitter pill to swallow at the end of a year that offered little respite from despair and despondency. As well as the pandemic denying him a route home to see family, Nestor also saw a career-highlight AFC Cup campaign cut short.

Playing on the continent was an entirely new experience for his largely home-based squad. Ahead of a pre-season trip to Malaysia, work began on obtaining passports for players who had never left the country before. Many had never even been on a plane before, nor had they sampled food other than the local cuisine. To some, an Irishman from rural county Limerick was as exotic a fruit as they'd ever been exposed to.

Still, despite the players' lack of travel, Nestor still led the club to a 7–1 aggregate playoff win over Master 7 of Laos, meaning Svay Rieng qualified for the tournament proper for the first time, the AFC Cup being the Asian equivalent of the UEFA Europa League. Hopes were high for a run deep into the competition – until the pandemic meant the tournament was cancelled halfway through the group stage. In an attempt to bolster his squad during the pandemic year, Nestor found himself looking back to Ireland. Shortly before Christmas 2020, Nestor pulled off a coup by securing the signing of former Dundalk centre-back Paddy Barrett. The Waterford man decided to swap the US for Cambodia, and as a trophy-laden member of Dundalk's

Europa League squad in 2016, his signing made headlines. Barrett's eastern adventure did not last, however. The defender opted to leave after less than two months in the country. He re-joined St Patrick's Athletic, citing a failure to adapt to life in Cambodia. His decision disappointed Nestor, who was left to scramble for a replacement. However, that's football, and he knows it. Perversely, he wouldn't have it any other way. It is just another challenge he relishes meeting. And he can understand the pull of home.

Being away from Ireland often gives Nestor a bigger sense of Irishness than when he's back in Limerick. That is true for many of Ireland's great diaspora. He can feel the warmth of home even from afar. He comes from a special part of the world. And there are special people who are still with him. His father Larry passed away in 2005. Conor believes that there are moments when his dad is definitely helping him along. 'None of those moments were in 2018. He must have been playing golf in 2018, that's what I tell my mother. In 2019, he decided to talk to a few saints and angels for me.'

When he visited the stadium for the first time soon after his arrival at the club, Nestor saw a groundsman walk along the pitch with a push lawnmower that was ten years old. It took the ground team one day to cut the field. Almost four years later, Nestor is a championship-winning manager and progress is the buzzword at the club. They are improving their small stadium, building a training ground, and have assembled a professional backroom staff, with some bringing experience of English football. The push lawnmower is long gone, too. 'I chose the obsession and I don't regret it. It's an unhealthy profession. I'm completely married to it. I love it all, but you have to be winning.'

Another long-time FAI employee with a remit for development, just like Nestor, Brian Kerr is also married to the game. After a spell as Republic of Ireland senior coach, he found himself in an unexpected location for his next management role.

⊕

The Faroe Islands is considered one of the safest places in the world, and with good reason. The country is an archipelago, an island cluster, consisting of eighteen small islands, while the country's population is a mere 49,000. It is home to one prison in the capital Tórshavn, located on the island of Streymoy. It can hold twelve prisoners at a time, but largely operates as a detention centre for non-violent offenders. Criminals convicted of violent or capital offences, as rare as they are, are sent to serve longer sentences in Denmark. In 2012, a Croatian national was convicted of killing a Faroese local – twenty-four years on from the last recorded murder on the country's Sandor Island. So when Brian Kerr decided to up sticks and leave Dublin behind to take on the role as Faroe Islands manager in 2009, three-and-a-half years after leaving the Republic of Ireland job, his personal safety could be assured. Job security in football is something that can hardly ever be taken for granted. But this was something, at least.

In fact, so small was the island, and so limited the resources, the prisoners from the nearby jail would be routinely bussed in to act as groundsmen at the Tórsvøllur, the 5,000-capacity national stadium in Tórshavn. The capital city has only one set of traffic lights, and even they are unnecessary, for the most part. Its approximate 20,000 population isn't much more than modern-day Drimnagh, where Kerr was born and grew up.

While 600 miles from home, Kerr never felt like an outsider. In fact, he revelled in the chance to represent a country he had developed an affection for during a previous trip, when he was the Ireland manager. Ian Harte and Kevin Kilbane scored Ireland's goals in a 2–0 away win on that June evening in 2005. The three points would ultimately prove fruitless in the wider context of Ireland's World Cup 2006 qualifying campaign. But Tórshavn's tranquil, contemplative air had made an impact on Kerr.

So in April 2009, he took the opportunity to become the country's new coach, signing a two-and-a-half-year deal, bringing him to the end of the Euro 2012 qualification campaign. Halfway through the South Africa World Cup qualification series when he signed on, the Islanders languished as ever at the bottom of a group that contained France and Serbia. Actually turning the Faroese no-hopers, who had not won a competitive game in eight years, into a team that could stake a claim for a major tournament place was surely beyond him. But improving them wasn't, in his eyes.

'It's a big challenge to say the least,' he told Mary Hannigan of *The Irish Times* prior to his first game, a visit of Serbia. 'When you take on a team that's 166th in the FIFA rankings that last won a competitive game in 2004, you have a fair idea of what you're coming into. The ability of the players is obviously not as high as what I've seen or worked with in the past, and looking at the four group games so far, they had less than ten per cent of possession.' Kerr wanted to change their style of play. 'My own instinct is to have a go. I don't like watching my teams playing in their own half and hanging on and hoping they don't concede by defending deep. I'm not used to that. They seem to be quite calm about it, but I don't know if I can be.'

Kerr often joked that the largest population of the Faroes was probably the sheep, who grazed on much of the luscious and vast green land beautifully compressed within the 540 square miles of the islands. But the people were passionate about their football. And it was by far the most popular sport on the islands. In a country of fewer than 50,000 inhabitants, there are sixteen amateur teams playing in the top three divisions of the domestic pyramid, with the other fourteen teams made of reserve sides of those clubs. Everyone in the Faroes knows someone who plays football, be it internationally or at club level.

The one-time St Patrick's Athletic boss and Irish youth supremo, Kerr wasn't the first foreigner to take charge of the Faroes. Danish duo Allan Simonsen and Henrik Larsen both had spells as manager between 1994 and 2005, where they managed a combined tally of thirteen wins. The Dubliner spoke often about the honour of taking on the role of Faroes coach, despite their standing in the world prompting questions as to why someone of his stature had taken the job. 'I considered it a huge honour,' Kerr said in a 2020 interview with Virgin Media's Tommy Martin. 'I was humbled by the idea that they would let somebody else take their country, be responsible for their matches and listen to their national anthem. I thought it was a big deal.'

Isolated from mainland Europe, and the British Isles to boot, when Kerr visited, he could concentrate on the job at hand in Streymoy and the surrounding islands. Distractions were at a minimum, which suited a football man like Kerr down to the ground. He was consumed by the game, and being in a country he knew little about allowed him to immerse himself freshly into learning about the players at his disposal and the culture of the game there. Driving from island to island, via underground tunnels, through mountain valleys, past fjords and along coastal roads, he felt a serenity there that had been hard to come by in a bustling Dublin city, especially in his years as an FAI employee.

And naturally, he engrossed himself in the football. 'The best thing has been the enthusiasm. There's huge interest in football,' he told Mary Hannigan. 'One day, I went to three league matches. I reckon there were about 4,500, combined, at the games – that's almost ten per cent of the population. In many ways it's like the tradition of the GAA in the country. It's one of the smallest places in Europe, yet they have these rivalries between the different towns, much as we'd have in intercounty football and hurling – places like Runavik, Toftir, Klaksvik and Tórshavn, it's nearly like Cork and Dublin and Galway and Tyrone, it's a fierce rivalry.'

As with the GAA, his team consisted of fish factory workers, carpenters, teachers, a politician, students, a builder, two policemen, an accountant, a sports shop worker and a man who worked in a bowling alley. A small number of his charges did play full-time in Denmark and Iceland, but his pool was, obviously, quite limited.

Kerr's assistant manager was initially Jens Martin Knudsen, a Faroese legend and former international goalkeeper who won sixty-five caps for the country between 1988 and 2006. When starring for his national team – in 1992, he was a hero in the country's seismic 1–0 over Austria in September 1990 – Knudsen also worked as a part-time forklift driver at a fish factory in Runavik. Twenty years on, he owned one of the biggest fish factories on the island. Due to his work commitments, Knudsen could not always attend away games. That proved an issue for Kerr, who would ultimately bring in his former St Pat's defender Johnny McDonnell as his assistant.

Kerr was realistic about what could be achieved with the Faroes, but remarked in a 2009 RTÉ documentary *Away with the Faroes* that he 'wouldn't have come here if I didn't think I could make a difference'.

The challenge of being the underdog certainly appealed to Kerr. He had no playing career, yet had risen to become the manager of the Republic of Ireland senior team, following Mick McCarthy, World Cup-winner Jack Charlton, Eoin Hand and Johnny Giles, one of Ireland's finest ever players. Steering Ireland's youth to Under-16 and Under-18 European Championship success and a third place World Cup finish in Malaysia had been just the start. Now, after a mixed spell managing the Irish senior side, he was ready to lead the Faroes.

'I remember my first couple of matches were Serbia and France, and I could see them going out before the match and there was almost smoke coming out of their ears. They were really up for it. We lost 0–2 to Serbia and 0–1 to France and the disappointment was massive.' Still, there were undoubted positives to be taken from the results, particularly given the resources at his disposal; after all, he'd gotten the same result against France for Ireland, with a team full of top-tier professionals. 'I'd lost 0–1 to France with Ireland. I knew Fróði [Benjaminsen] would be back doing the roof tomorrow. Símun Samuelsen would be back working in the bank tomorrow. He'd been trying to take on Patrice Evra. Atli Danielsen, he'd be selling ads for the newspaper.'

The French game, just Kerr's second in charge, reunited him with the team that had crushed his hopes of World Cup qualification with Ireland four years earlier. Much of the same team travelled to Tórshavn in August 2009, but mercifully Thierry Henry, whose goal at Lansdowne Road had all but denied Ireland qualification, did not travel. So small was the capital that both the home team and Raymond Domenech's France shared a hotel in the build-up to the game. Kerr believed that David and Goliath was an insufficient analogy to describe the task at hand for his team. He likened it to comparing a hill in Dublin's Phoenix Park to Mount Kilimanjaro.

Gignac's winning goal for France was all that stood between the minnows and a famous result. Greek fourth official Anastasios Kakos bore the look of a man who hadn't met an opposing manager in the ilk of Kerr during his time officiating in Athens, Thessaloniki or Piraeus. Kerr had given him an earful throughout the course of a match in which he felt the illustrious visitors were benefactors of the majority of decisions.

Still, despite signs of progress – and their minnow nature – there were demands from the Faroe fans. 'I was realistic, but that is part of the nature of international football. Every country thinks they should be doing better, and every player who plays for that country understands the responsibility. There was pressure, there was an expectancy to win matches. They [the supporters] used to think we should win all the matches, all the home matches anyway. They did think we should do better, but it was unrealistic. They didn't understand what it was like to be out there.'

A month after the French defeat, Kerr delivered a riposte when the Faroes beat Lithuania 2–1. It was their first competitive victory in 2,930 days.

Kerr still recalls the joy that permeated the islands in the days and weeks after the Lithuania win. 'I can remember going to the airport to come home, a small airport. It wasn't Heathrow, but it was a very vibrant Knock-type airport. Everybody was smiling. The check-in people, baggage handlers, pilots – these results affected the morale of these people.'

He would later guide his side to a draw against an improving Northern Ireland, before seeing his team beat Estonia 2–0 in a European Championship qualifier in June 2011. What was remarkable about the victory over Estonia was that the former Soviet nation would go on to pip Serbia, Slovenia and a distant Northern Ireland to second place and a playoff spot. It would be folly to suggest the Faroese victory condemned them to a runners-up position – Italy would win the group by ten points

– but the Estonians had produced an all-time-best qualifying campaign and still succumbed to a loss to the 'lowly' Faroe Islands. (Estonia would go on to lose 5–1 on aggregate to Giovanni Trapattoni's Republic of Ireland in the playoffs for the European Championships, to be held in Poland and Ukraine. Kerr, given his fractious parting of the ways in 2005, wasn't contacted to offer a scouting report.)

In fact, they had almost done the double on Estonia. His team had thrown away a 1–0 lead in injury time against Estonia in Tallinn to lose 1–2 earlier in the campaign. 'That was one of the most disappointing days in my career, because I schemed hard for that one and prepared well.' Still, beating them 2–0 in the return fixture had been sweet revenge. The Faroes had done what Serbia or Northern Ireland had failed to do in the group, neither side picking up a point against them. 'It was wonderful. I enjoyed it more because of how small the place was and how brilliant the players were and how much they hurt [after] every match we lost,' he told Tommy Martin on Virgin Media's *Sport Stories* series in 2020.

Kerr is both a football man and a people person. He is in his element when bringing the two aspects of his personality together, holding court and regaling an always-captive audience with stories of this player and that player. More often than not, the player is one few can remember. But Brian can. Looking back on his time with the Faroe Islands, he holds the people and place in high esteem. 'They were very welcoming to me. They were very respectful to me. They embraced my ideas and my personal style, my commitment, and they gave me that opportunity and we got a few results. They were great lads with great commitment, playing in a league that was one of the lowest standards in Europe.'

Of course, Kerr was not the first Irishman who had roots in youth football that went on to have a spell in charge of a national team other than their nation of birth. In 1996, Joe McGrath left his role as FAI director of coaching to take on a similar role with New Zealand, which would ultimately lead to a role in charge of the senior team.

The Dubliner had spent time playing in Australia in the late 1960s, in-between two stints at Limerick FC. A striker, he had previously turned out for Dundalk and Drumcondra. He succeeded Liam Tuohy as coach of Ireland's youth teams in the 1980s, and worked for the FAI until early 1996, when he left for Auckland.

McGrath believed that the standard of the league in New Zealand wasn't too dissimilar to the League of Ireland, but there were travel issues for clubs due to the elongated country. 'Picking the national squad was difficult, because you had players here, there and everywhere.'

He had not intended on stepping into the breach with the senior side, but when Scot Keith Pritchett left the role in 1997, McGrath was asked to take over. 'I hadn't really wanted to take on the senior team. I would have preferred to have waited for a few years when some of the younger players had come through, but it's hard to say "no" when you're asked.'

He took charge of the All Whites for nine games in his two years in charge, winning three, drawing one and losing five. His team scored thirteen and shipped thirteen, leaving him close to par for the course during his time in Oceania.

Hopes to qualify for France '98 were dashed when Australia enjoyed 3–0 and 2–0 wins in their two-legged tie in June and July 1997. Speaking to *The Irish Sun*'s Neil O'Riordan in 2019, McGrath recalled the dramatic scenes in Melbourne, when Australia were subsequently pipped to qualification in a playoff by Iran. 'Terry Venables was managing Australia, and he invited myself and my wife over. Some yahoo ran onto the pitch and cut up the net and Iran ended up scoring two late goals. Everyone was in tears, Terry was on a $1 million bonus to qualify, and the federation needed the money too.'

Although he failed to lead them to qualification for the World Cup in 1998, he was offered a new contract by the country's football association.

He would ultimately decline, instead deciding to return to Ireland to take over at Bohemians.

Outside of the international football arena, new opportunities were springing up for Irish coaches and managers in emerging club markets too – like with Nestor in Cambodia. The most eye-catching of these in recent decades has been in the United States with the advent of Major League Soccer, the country's latest attempt at establishing a sustainable, truly nationwide soccer competition. Among the esteemed managers and players hired to be part of its launch was one of Irish football's favourite sons.

In 1996, along with two aforementioned players, Paul Keegan and Ian Hennessy, the Irish spotlight on the newly founded Major League Soccer was trained on Frank Stapleton. Still Ireland's record goalscorer at the time with twenty goals, he was a renowned figure in Ireland, as well as in the red parts of north London and Manchester.

The Dubliner arrived in America as a newly retired thirty-nine-year-old, taking his first steps in management with New England Revolution, based in Boston. And it wasn't long before he found out what being based in Boston entailed. Stapleton first arrived in the north-east in mid-winter, greeted by snowstorms that are the norm in that part of the country. Having flown out to interview with the club's owners, Robert and Jonathan Kraft, the billionaire family who also own the NFL's New England Patriots, it seemed unlikely that he would get back home in time for Christmas, which he had planned to spend in Manchester with Christine and his sons James and Scott. With further snowstorms forecast for Tuesday, 19 December 1995, there were fears no flights would depart Boston Logan International Airport. There were certainly no flights to Manchester, with British Airways staff informing him that all flights had been cancelled. Fortunately, Ireland's own Aer Lingus had adopted a more laissez-faire attitude towards the severe weather conditions. Their flights to Dublin were still running, meaning Stapleton would at least get to Dublin. Reaching Manchester from there was a journey he had taken countless times while representing Manchester United and the Republic of Ireland.

Informed he had got the job of taking New England Revolution into their maiden MLS season over the Christmas period, Stapleton returned to Boston in January with his wife and boys. They were met with even more snow. An Irishman who had spent most of his adult life in England, the conditions were beyond anything he was used to.

Stapleton had signed a two-year deal to take the Revs into the unknown of MLS. There were clearly high hopes for Stapleton's tenure. At a press conference announcing Stapleton's arrival, Jonathan Kraft said: 'We interviewed a wide range of coaches, including some very high-profile people who were very interested in coaching the Revolution. We were most impressed with Frank Stapleton, and feel he understands the challenges ahead for this new league, while sharing our family's commitment to putting a championship team on the field in Foxboro.'

In the second week of January, at the campus of UC Irvine in Orange County, California, Stapleton attended try-outs, where he would build much of his squad. It was clearly a relief for Stapleton to get away from the north-east cold. 'The weather was unbelievable, even in January. It was like a cracking summer's day.' Reality would soon bite, when he went back to Boston. And this included his attempts to sign players, the Revs struggling to bring in marquee players from Europe, while teams like New York/New Jersey MetroStars, Tampa Bay Mutiny and LA Galaxy had no such issues. Then thirty-six-year-old Paul McGrath was one mooted marquee foreign signing, but he didn't arrive.

At the outset of the league, each team in the ten-team division was assigned two national team players and two foreign recruits. Outside of this, the squads were built from the Inaugural Player Drafts, College Drafts and Supplemental Drafts. A man who had spent the majority of his career at Arsenal and Manchester United wasn't particularly impressed with what was on display. Asked by a reporter from *The Boston Globe* how he assessed the successful trialists, he said they weren't good enough.

That would come back to bite him.

The paper came out the next day and Brian O'Donovan, the club's Clonakilty-born general manager, said he couldn't say that. Stapleton responded: 'What do you want me to do? Do you want me to lie? Even if it was to a journalist, I can't lie.'

Years later, Stapleton can admit, 'I probably shouldn't have said that', even if he still stands by his comments. 'If this was to be a major league, the standards had to be higher.' It did prove problematic. 'It was naivety in understanding how they did things. In America, they promote things. They are positive. In hindsight, I could have said something else, but at the time the guy asked me a straightforward question and I gave him a straight answer.'

Another trial in Florida, where there was a sizeable Cuban community, helped him bring in two South American players to the roster. Still, Stapleton believed he was playing with a handicap, having arrived in the US less than three months before the season's opening day. He had less preparation time, and less familiarity with the playing pool. 'As we travelled around to different places, I noticed players who weren't in the trials were playing [for opposing teams]. We never got to see them. They were hidden away. That was cheeky. It was a privilege if you lived there, had been a coach in those leagues and knew the players. It was difficult to deal with that. It wasn't fair. Nowadays, you wouldn't get away with that.'

The Revs endured a poor season. They finished bottom of the five-team Eastern Conference, winning just nine of their thirty-two regular-season games. Of the ten teams in MLS, only two missed out on the end-of-the-season playoffs, the Revs and Colorado Rapids the unfortunate couple. New England were the lowest scorers in the entire league, with Italian striker Giuseppe Galderisi struggling to provide goals for the team. At one point, thirty-nine-year-old Stapleton briefly considered taking on the responsibility himself. Now, he says the notion was dismissed immediately. But not so quickly that it wasn't discussed with O'Donovan. 'You feel like you can help the players if they copy some of the things you do. In the end, I decided no. I just couldn't do it. The job was too much in itself. Brian said I could do it. But it wasn't realistic with the workload.' Still, it may well have helped turn their fortunes. Paul Keegan, his fellow Dubliner who was in his squad in 1996, believed the former Irish international should have played for the team that year, saying the manager was the best player in training by some distance.

Midway through the season, Galderisi was traded to Tampa Bay, having failed to hit the target at all in Boston. A one-time teammate of Liam Brady at Juventus, he later claimed that he wasn't enamoured with the training methods. Stapleton mused that the Italian perhaps just preferred to be where the sunshine was. (Though, saying that, after the manager's departure at the end of the season, Galderisi actually returned to the Revs in 1997.)

While Stapleton had no particular run-ins with the striker, the same could not be said for Alexi Lalas, who would become a major adversary for the manager in the dressing room. One of the two US internationals on the roster – the other being Mike Burns – Lalas was a regular in the US men's national team, and had just shy of two seasons' experience of playing in Serie A, following Padova's promotion in 1994. Instantly recognisable with his distinctive long red beard and shaggy mop of curly hair, Lalas was one of the stars of US Soccer at the time, especially given that he had experience playing in what was, at the time, the strongest league in the world.

Despite Lalas's strong CV, Stapleton had issues with the player. 'His attitude wasn't good. I had run-ins with him,' Stapleton recalls. 'He didn't adhere to the training schedule. He didn't turn up some days. I confronted him about it. I think he had this idea that he was going to be running the show in Boston when he came. I spoke to Brian about it. What was I supposed to do? Just accept it?'

Stapleton also didn't care for Lalas's off-field interests. In 1996, perhaps to capitalise on his burgeoning status as one of the marquee players in the new MLS, Lalas released a debut solo record, called *Far From Close*. He was also in a band, The Gypsies. 'He was more interested in that,' Stapleton opines. 'If that was his priority, why was he playing football? He wanted to do things his way. He wasn't running the team, I was. I had to leave him out of the team. If you don't have discipline, you have nothing.'

The pair's relationship, or lack thereof, came to a head in August when Stapleton left Lalas out of the team for an away game to the MetroStars at Giants Stadium. Lalas watched from the bench as the Revs went down 0–4. Afterwards, he described the situation as a 'joke'. He told *The Boston Globe*, 'Today has been a difficult day to say the least. The audacity of someone to question my commitment to New England Revolution boggles my mind.'

While the straight-talking but mild-mannered Stapleton had little interest in currying favour with the Boston press, Lalas was a friend to the media in the city, and the Irishman believes his power struggle with his star player ultimately led to his exit. 'As soon as players start making managerial decisions, you're in trouble. I don't think he could back it up with ability,' Stapleton reflects. 'He was a poster boy for MLS, in the northeast certainly. The league had a problem. The club were trying to move him around but the money he was earning was crazy. I had tried to shift him earlier in the season but we couldn't do it. The salary was too big. There weren't too many takers.'

Soon it was Stapleton who was forced to depart.

It was a disappointing end to ten months spent in a bustling Irish-American community, one that the owners had been hopeful Stapleton could tap into. That he did achieve, at least. The Revs, for all their on-field struggles, averaged the third-highest attendance in the season, largely thanks to the large Italian and Irish immigrant communities in the city.

But then the truth is that the season wasn't as bad as it first appeared. While they finished bottom of the Eastern Conference, in reality, they were only four points short of a playoff place, and six shy of third-placed MetroStars. Two more wins would have secured them mid-table respectability. They enjoyed some significant wins too, beating LA Galaxy 1–0 at the Rose Bowl on 4 July and enjoying a 4–2 home win over Eastern Conference winners Tampa Bay Mutiny. Lalas scored his one and only goal under Stapleton that day. Galderisi, by then lining out for the opposition, notched one of the Mutiny's consolation strikes. 'In real terms, we weren't too far away. That's what time gives you. You don't always get time to develop. Clubs that stick with their man get better returns on it. When I was there, they were looking for automatic success. That just isn't going to happen.'

The fact he'd managed some success likely explains why the Krafts did ask Stapleton to stay on in a different capacity. However, at forty, he wasn't prepared to move to 'Front Office', as they call the upper administrative staff in the US.

Stapleton remains contemplative about the end of his time in Boston, believing that forces conspired to have him out of the way. Funnily enough, Lalas would eventually depart New England at the end of the 1997 season, having outlasted Stapleton by a mere twelve months. By that time, the former Irish international and his family were in Manchester, having settled back into life in the north-west, where they still live today.

Sometimes the American dream isn't an everlasting one. Managers especially tend not to last too long, never mind forever, regardless of where they go. That reality hasn't dampened the desire of Irish coaches to travel the world in pursuit of managerial opportunities.

7

FLYING THE NEST

Over the years, both the League of Ireland and the Women's National League have proved, if not fertile ground, then certainly an occasional hunting ground for a bargain for clubs further afield than the British and Irish isles.

In the women's game in particular, where leagues in Scandinavia, mainland Europe and the US have been ahead of the curve in terms of offering professional opportunities to players, it has been almost commonplace in recent years to see stars plucked from domestic obscurity to ply their trade at a higher level on foreign fields.

One such figure was Stephanie Roche. And it was all thanks to an exquisite goal, scored during Peamount United's 6–1 win over Wexford Youths at Ferrycarrig Park in the Women's National League in October 2013. From a cross, Roche, with her back to goal, controlled the ball with a touch to her left, then returned it back over her own head and that of her marker before swivelling and sending a dipping volley into the corner of the net, beyond a stranded Youths goalkeeper. The idea was audacious, the connection was true; it was the perfect mix of ingenuity and precision.

The goal became a worldwide sensation, viewed all around the globe millions of times, and ultimately leading to a FIFA Puskás nomination for the 'most beautiful' goal in the world. It catapulted Roche to stardom, something normally far beyond players in the part-time Irish domestic league. Even stars of the national team, of which Roche was a part, were starved of anything close to the attention that came from the goal. It also made outsiders sit up and take notice. It was the start of something for Roche, a journey that would take her to Europe and the US.

The following summer Roche left Ireland behind to test herself in the environs of the professional game for the first time. She joined newly promoted French Division 1 Feminine side ASPTT Albi ahead of the 2014/15 campaign. However, her time there was to last just six months, and can be summed up by one incident.

It was New Year's Day 2015, two weeks out from the FIFA Ballon d'Or awards ceremony in Zurich, where Roche would find out whether she had won the public vote to claim the Puskás award. Roche had just returned to France, having spent Christmas at home with her family. The league had broken off for two weeks over the holidays, so a friendly match had been organised ahead of the club's return to action against lower league opponents US Saint-Romanaise in the Coupe de France on the following Sunday. Roche, who didn't drive at the time, always left her apartment in the middle of town on match days and made the short walk to a nearby car park, where she would be picked up, usually by a teammate. She repeated the routine that day, and stood in the car park in her club tracksuit with her gear holdall in tow. No one came. She waited for forty-five minutes. 'What the fuck is going on here?' she wondered. When she finally gave up hope that someone was coming to pick her up, she returned to her apartment, booked a flight back to Ireland and left the next day.

The player had already given serious consideration to leaving France while at home over the Christmas period. Being close to family and friends had brought into stark focus the isolation she felt on a daily basis. This was all the more disappointing, as only months earlier, she had jumped at the chance to play professionally. Reflecting on it now, she admits she was naive in certain aspects when leaving Ireland behind for the continent. 'I jumped in with two feet a little bit,' she says. 'It became a bit of a nightmare in the end. It ended up being too much for me.'

The image of the twenty-five-year-old standing on the kerb of the car park in this small French town, isolated from her family, friends and, more worryingly, her own team stands in stark contrast to the Stephanie Roche that the Irish public saw on a regular basis during that period. At the time of her Puskás Award nomination and the award ceremony itself, she was the most in-demand Irish sportsperson around. Everyone wanted a piece of her.

She attended the glitzy award ceremony on 12 January, just weeks after being forgotten about by her own team back in France. Previous winners of the Puskás Award included Cristiano Ronaldo, Neymar and Zlatan Ibrahimović. A woman had never won the prize before, and standing in Roche's way were global superstars Robin van Persie and James Rodríguez, with the latter ultimately beating her to the award, despite her receiving a very creditable thirty-three per cent of the public vote.

The most memorable image of the night from an Irish perspective is of Roche walking past seated Ballon d'Or nominees Ronaldo and Lionel Messi in her pink, Helen Cody-designed dress, with the two greats of the modern-day game looking on, suitably impressed. Days later, Roche would appear with Ryan Tubridy on RTÉ's *The Late Late Show*.

However, it was all a world away from the reality that Roche was living with on a day-to-day basis. Now without a club, she was taking time to reassess her options before deciding what was next. 'In France, I felt like I was abandoned. I was by myself. It was a strange kind of feeling. A lot of the players there in France didn't speak English and didn't try to. They wouldn't ask me out to do anything. It was difficult for me because I was only starting to learn the language. Those first few months are really crucial in terms of getting to know your teammates.'

The forward player had started French lessons upon her arrival in the south of France, but after her teacher left for Montpellier, it took the club over a month to arrange new lessons. That was a major setback, especially as things had begun well on the pitch.

Roche had started impressively under manager David Welferinger, playing in ten of the club's opening fifteen games of the season. She scored twice, both goals in a 2–0 away win to another newly promoted side, Issy. By early November, she felt close to peak form. But the loss of French lessons deepened the void between her and her teammates. The situation was made worse when dressing-room friends Chloé Bornes and Solène Barbance – whom Roche had known from Peamount United – left the club.

Meanwhile, she was struggling without the close support of her family, including footballer boyfriend Dean Zambra, while the Puskás Award hype was reaching fever pitch. 'It was a huge thing for me and my family. Being away from everybody was so tough. I just wanted to celebrate with them and prepare for things.'

After training sessions, which Roche cycled to and from, she would arrive at her apartment and go straight to bed. Sleeping shortened the day and the misery. 'I was in a bad place mentally. I was suffering from a little bit of depression. I didn't want to be there. I tried to shut it all out.'

Being left behind for the mid-season friendly match proved the final straw for her. Welferinger put the incident down to a simple miscommunication, but Roche had made up her mind. 'I felt I had given it everything I could. That part of my career was a saga. Without meaning to, they treated me quite badly. I was naive, thinking it was the best move for me when it probably wasn't. There was no organisation.'

Her manager believed the success that came from her Puskás nomination had turned her head and she was looking beyond Albi. 'She doesn't want to return to France. She has benefited so much from her success, inevitably, she has had other offers from richer clubs. We're not going to hold her back,' he told *AFP*.

The reality was different, says Roche. 'I was feeling so low. I felt I had to look after myself. When I was in France, I always tried to maintain professionalism and tried to give my best. It wasn't a case of I'm getting out of here because I had better options. It was a case of this isn't the right fit. At the time I had made the decision to leave, it was spur of the moment. I just couldn't do it anymore.'

Hurt but not scarred by her French ordeal, Roche was adamant that she wanted to stay in the professional game. That meant leaving Ireland again. In mid-February, she signed with Houston Dash of America's National Women's Soccer League, making her the first Irish player to compete in the league since its inaugural season just two years earlier. 'I always planned to stay professional. I didn't want to be put off by what happened in France,' Roche explains.

That could have been in England, but having turned down options there, Roche felt choosing America was wise. A two-year deal offered her the kind of security she craved, and in the US, where all of the US national team players plied their trade at the time, the professionalism and seriousness in which women's football was treated was unmatched. It was something she couldn't turn down. As far as America was concerned, Roche believed, it was all business. That would be a far cry from the issues she had experienced in France, where she had been paid just €700 a month, plus lodgings, and had been left unhappy at what she perceived to be a lack of support from the club. (In a later interview, Roche conceded she signed her deal with ASPTT unaware of what professional female players were paid on average.)

Joined by her partner, Dean, Roche flew to Texas with months of intense media interest and spotlight behind her. 'I am so excited about the signing of Stephanie,' Dash coach Randy Waldrum told official club media at the time. 'We are getting a player that has great technical ability, a superb left foot, and possibly the best goalscorer to come out of Ireland since Olivia O'Toole.'

Waldrum was certainly accurate in his description of Roche. A prolific scorer in the Women's National League, Roche had twice claimed the league's Golden Boot in three seasons with Peamount United, prior to her move to the continent. Additionally, her six goals for the national team included strikes against leading sides France and Germany.

There was considerable excitement on both sides of the Atlantic that Roche was to be paired up front with US soccer icon Carli Lloyd, who had been traded to Dash the previous October. At the time that Roche teamed up with her, Lloyd had already plundered sixty-one national team goals and was a 2012 FIFA World Player of the Year nominee.

It would transpire, unfortunately, that their time together on the pitch would amount to just twenty-five minutes, as Roche – who had been given the number nine shirt – went on to only make substitute appearances in two of Houston's opening three games of the National Women's Soccer League campaign.

Roche had uprooted her life to move to America, believing she would have a two-year stint in the country. Circumstance dictated otherwise.

Defender Stephanie Ochs suffered an anterior cruciate ligament tear in the club's third league game of the season against Boston Breakers, in what would turn out to be Roche's final appearance for the club. Ochs joined a number of other defenders on a lengthening injury list, forcing Dash to look elsewhere for reinforcements. Due to restrictions on the size of rosters and the number of non-US players a club could register (only five of the twenty-player panel could be foreign), Roche was deemed dispensable. In order to make way for two new defensive reinforcements – Australian Ellie Brush and Brazilian youth international Camila Martins Pereira – Roche was waived, meaning she was essentially freed from her contract. It was a merciless decision.

Roche had received an email the previous night, 19 May 2015, summoning her to a meeting with Waldrum and managing director Brian Ching, a former USMNT international. 'I thought it was a bit strange,' she recalls. Roche met the two men the following morning and emerged a short time later with an envelope in hand. It was a formal letter informing her that the club had waived the right to keep her on the roster. Waldrum had barely made eye contact during the short meeting. Roche knew it wasn't what he wanted, but that did nothing to soften the almighty blow. Almost three months to the day after joining – and with a mere twenty-five minutes of league football to her name – the American dream was over.

It was a bolt from the blue. The goal she scored against Wexford in the unassuming surrounds of Ferrycarrig Park nineteen months earlier was evidence of football's capacity to change lives in a single moment. Now she saw that it worked both ways.

'I came back out with the envelope and said "they're after cutting me".' 'You're joking,' Dean replied. 'No,' was the solemn and matter-of-fact reply.

That was it. Roche's acquisition by the Dash had made headlines at home and abroad, and had been subject to sizeable fanfare. In contrast, her departure was publicly announced via a brief six-word sentence on the club's website.

This really was *all business*. 'In America, it was very cutthroat,' she says. 'That was it. They decided out of nowhere and it was out of my hands. It uprooted my whole life. It was a shock to the system.' Before that, all the noises from coach Waldrum had been positive and the Irishwoman had been keen to build on her start in Houston.

In a tweet acknowledging the news, Roche responded with dignity and a gratitude that belied her evident shock and disappointment. She wrote, 'Impossible to appreciate the highs without experiencing the lows.'

In March of that year, Roche had played a major role in the Irish delegation's St Patrick's Day celebrations in the United States. She met Taoiseach Enda Kenny while he was attending the opening of the brand-new Irish consulate in Austin, Texas, and she visited the Obamas at the White House. 'He seems to have a bit of charisma about him,' she had told the *Irish Independent* in rather understated fashion about the then US President. For a spell in the US that had begun with such glitz and promise, it was now ending in the most deflating fashion possible. Not that this was the end of her story.

⊕

Players in the League of Ireland were also increasingly looking beyond Britain and Ireland to further their careers. Richie Ryan was one such footballer. In his own words, Ryan took a long time to grow up. Hailing from Templetuohy, a tiny village in Tipperary, the entirety of his football career has occurred a long way from home – taking him from Sunderland to Sligo via Antwerp and, since 2014, Ryan has embarked on a whistle-stop tour of North America.

Ryan's football awakening arrived in the week after the 2009 FAI Cup Final, during his time at Sligo Rovers. Sligo had lost the cup final to Sporting Fingal, with two goals in the final five minutes putting paid to the Bit O'Red's hopes of claiming their first major trophy in eleven years. A technically gifted midfielder, Ryan was a key component of the Sligo midfield in a team that would become cup specialists under manager Paul Cook. Twenty-four years old and with considerable experience in the UK and Belgium already behind him, he was a mainstay in the team's engine room alongside Liverpudlian Danny Ventre.

Impressive as he was, there was more to give. Ryan credits the conversation with then Sligo chairman Dermot Kelly as a turning point. The two men were in talks regarding a new contract. 'Last week, you were the best player on the park for sixty minutes, but then you were nowhere to be seen for the last thirty minutes and injury time,' Kelly told his young charge.

In football, everyone has an opinion, but when your chairman is casting doubt on your ability to last the course in meaningful games, it would make any professional sit up and take notice. Having been on a professional contract at Sligo for two years, Ryan was offered reduced terms on an extension. It was, in essence, an amateur contract. Even worse, the offer was not borne of a need to tighten purse strings. It was based purely on performance and attitude.

It was an affront to the player, but one that ultimately prompted a change in mindset. Over a decade later, Ryan credits that conversation with Kelly as a watershed moment for him. 'It was the best thing that happened in my career. It was the wake-up call I needed. I needed to dedicate myself to my profession a lot more than I had done in the previous years.'

Ultimately, after discussions with Cook, a compromise was reached with better terms. The newly focused Ryan would go on to reap the rewards of this wake-up call in the years that followed, helping Sligo to FAI Cup wins in 2010 and 2011, while he also picked up two EA Sports Cup winners medals at Sligo and then Shamrock Rovers. He was named the PFAI Players' Player of the Year in 2010, at the end of a season in which Sligo finished third, just four points off the top spot.

After those achievements, Ryan decided to take this more dedicated version of himself away from the League of Ireland. A move to Dundee United in the winter of 2011 followed, but not before the possibility of a move Stateside was mooted. Days before Sligo's FAI Cup semi-final with Bohemians, Ryan had been approached by an agent working on behalf of FC Dallas of Major League Soccer. Ironically, helping Sligo reach the showpiece final meant Ryan could not link up with the Texans; the dates just didn't line up.

An opportunity to play in MLS wasn't something Ryan sniffed at, nor should it have been. Irish eyes were fixed and, as ever, smiling on the league after Robbie Keane's high-profile move to LA Galaxy five months earlier. 'From then, it was always something I thought wouldn't be a bad move to go and challenge myself somewhere else,' Ryan recalls. 'I believed and trusted in myself that I was capable of playing at MLS level. The goal of moving to North America was to play at the highest level and that was MLS.'

He achieved his goal of playing in North America in early 2014, when Ryan and his partner Nik began their new life in Ottawa, Canada. He joined Ottawa Fury, a brand-new North American Soccer League franchise, the NASL being a second-tier division under MLS. (It had no connection to the original league of the same name that helped popularise soccer in America in the 1970s.)

As far as spanners in the works go, Ottawa Fury's most high-profile new signing was dealt the biggest one shortly before he flew out to start his new adventure. The city's two new arrivals would soon be three. Nik's pregnancy brought fresh questions to the fore, such as were the soon-to-be new parents right to raise their child thousands of miles away from grandparents and family? Ultimately they decided to stick with their decision and stay. 'We're easy-going people. We said we'll go and give it a shot.'

His choice was soon vindicated. After all, the nascent Ottawa Fury provided Ryan with opportunities that would have otherwise been elusive during a career in Ireland, Scotland or lower down the food chain in England. Here he was in Ottawa, no less, lining out for a club playing in a stadium that was part of a wider $500 million redevelopment. The 24,000-capacity TD Place Arena was home to the city's soccer, rugby, Canadian football and ice hockey teams, with a 10,000-capacity rink built underneath one of its stands. It was shiny, state-of-the-art and a world away from the League of Ireland.

What the Fury also afforded Ryan was the chance to test himself against some pre-eminent opposition. American soccer's most glamorous team in the 1970s, the original New York Cosmos, brought players such as Pelé, Carlos Alberto and Franz Beckenbauer to the US. Now back after twenty-five years away, the Cosmos franchise had joined the NASL in 2013. As with their predecessor, star names were part of the attraction. Their squad included Spain legend Raúl and Euro 2008 winner Marcos Senna. 'For players like me to come up against players like that, it makes it all worthwhile. Just to have the chance to play against players of that calibre in a regular league game. It's not a pre-season friendly.' There was a whole other world out there, and Ryan was living in it. 'Playing in the Premier Division in Ireland or in League 1 or 2 in England or the Scottish Premiership, you're not going to come up against that calibre of players. Granted, Raúl and Marcos Senna were coming to the end of their playing days, they were still by far the best players on the field when I was playing them.'

By his second and final season in Ottawa, the Tipperary man had been made captain, and had been joined by another well-travelled Irishman,

Cork's Colin Falvey. Fury went toe to toe with their illustrious big-city opponents, winning the Fall Championship and finishing tied on points at the top of the combined season standings. The sides met for the third and final time in the season finale Soccer Bowl, which the Cosmos edged 3–2. The game was refereed by Ireland's Alan Kelly.

Ryan transferred to Florida's Jacksonville Armada, also of the NASL, shortly before Christmas 2015. His time at the club would last just five months. At the time of his signing, Jacksonville had planned on building their team around Ryan. However, the club were then made an offer they couldn't refuse – $750,000, to be exact. Few on this side of the Atlantic would bat an eyelid at the three-quarters-of-a-million purchase, but it was record breaking for the NASL, where trades and drafts are the norm.

It was notable too for who was doing the buying. Miami FC were a new NASL franchise, debuting in 2016. Their coach was Italy's World Cup-winning defender Alessandro Nesta. The record-breaking fee was an outlier, but it marked out Ryan, who still harboured ambition of reaching the MLS as a standout performer. 'For me, it wasn't a big deal. It was normal. At home, that's how the game works – if you want a player, you go and pay for them,' he says. Ryan recalls that many in the game were making a lot of the transfer fee, saying that it was 'a bigger thing than it needed to be'. He had become, on occasion, an easy target for opposition fans if not for opposing players. They were often more envious.

His new club was co-owned by Italian businessman Riccardo Silva and Italian legend Paolo Maldini, and with Nesta in the dugout, it is little surprise that the Italians went about their business in the way that served them so successfully in decades past. Just as he had revelled pitting himself against Spanish superstars a year earlier, Ryan found himself in the desirous position of becoming one of Nesta's most trusted lieutenants. Some days were easier than others, but the experience was unmatched. 'I learned so much from him on the game tactically, but even more so as a person – just how humble he was.'

A cordial man away from the pitch, the tendencies of a serial winner were never far from the surface, Ryan noticed. Nesta could be intense and demanded the highest of standards from his players. 'His standards were far too high for the level of players and the level of the league we were at, so he had to rein it in a bit. If you weren't reaching the level he believed you should be at or you could be at, he wouldn't think twice about telling you. He was probably over the top some days with how he spoke to some players.' He does admit, however, that, 'As a player, you need to put demands on yourself and you need to reach a certain level. If you're not doing that consistently, the manager probably has a right to have a go at you.' Those demands were felt on the training ground, as Ryan says that the pre-season he underwent with Nesta at Miami in 2017 was as hard as he's experienced in his career. He described being 'worked like dogs to the point you were nearly physically sick'.

Still, at least Nesta had no need to worry about relegation, which wasn't a feature of the NASL. Recent events had brought the idea of relegation – and competitiveness – back to his mind when he spoke to me for this book. In April 2021, a cabal of Europe's biggest teams attempted to push through a new closed-shop competition – the European Super League – where no qualification was necessary and relegation was not a factor. The idea was quickly shut down amidst supporter protest, most notably in England. What was football without competition? It is a question Ryan has posed to himself on many occasions. A benefactor of the stability available to him in America, he has mixed feelings on playing out his career in franchise leagues with no promotion or relegation. 'You don't really need to be successful in America and you can stay in a job. The way I've been brought up in the game is that it's hugely important to be successful. I don't think you should be rewarded for being poor, but it offers you that stability. It's a mixed bag. You have to win. I love playing football. It's the best job in the world. I love playing it because I love winning.'

Overall, for Ryan, it is just another way in which Stateside football is different than back in Ireland or the UK. Not better, not worse. Just different.

He spent a little over eighteen months at Miami before a year with FC Cincinnati. He signed with El Paso Locomotive in January 2019, and he has now spent longer there than at any of his previous four teams Stateside.

Unlike many of the Irish footballers and managers who have taken to the skies and seas in search of new opportunities, Ryan has made the United States home, having started a young family there. His daughter Polly has started primary school in El Paso, with two younger siblings at home. He has begun work on obtaining a US Soccer License too. He acknowledges that opportunities to coach will be easier to come by over there whenever the time comes to stop playing.

An easy-going type who admits he was a latecomer in acquiring the maturity needed for a long career, Ryan is focused on marrying his reignited love of the game with the commitments that come with a growing family. Life in El Paso is grand; he sees no need to move again. 'It's not fair on the family to keep pulling them from pillar to post every year. It's definitely something that's become more difficult, and I have to give more attention to it. I always say with footballers – it's easy to build a network of friends because you have a ready-made network, twenty-four or twenty-five fellas, so you're going to kick off a friendship with a few of them. The hard part is the family, trying to make sure your wife and kids settle in. The happier they are, the happier I am.'

Of the ex-League of Ireland players to have swapped domestic affairs for foreign pastures new, Ryan is certainly among the most successful in a lot that includes Noel Campbell, Roy O'Donovan and Dominic Foley, the former Bohemians and Limerick striker who played professionally in Greece, Portugal and, most notably, Belgium.

For others, however, the route to play the game professionally outside of Ireland is unexpected and often unheralded.

Conor Powell stands alone. Across six seasons in which the Professional Footballers' Association of Ireland sent a squad of out-of-contract players to the FIFPro winter tournament in Oslo, the left back from Portmarnock was the sole Irish player from those panels to secure a contract, professional or otherwise, outside of the island of Ireland.

FIFPro was the worldwide players' union, composed of sixty-five national member player associations. Held every January (until the final edition in 2016) at the Vallhall Arena in Oslo, the tournament involved teams from Ireland, Sweden, Finland and hosts Norway. Each team was made up of out-of-contract players from each league, with the aim of the players securing a contract for the upcoming season. Coaches from all four leagues were present, as were scouts and agents representing Scandinavian and Irish interests, as well as those from elsewhere in Europe.

In 2011, the first year of the tournament, the PFAI squad contained Brian Gartland, Mark Rossiter and Darren Meenan, all three of whom would play key roles in the first of Dundalk's four league titles under Stephen Kenny two years later. Liam Burns had won a domestic double with Bohemians in 2008, Brian Shelley was a one-time PFAI Players' Player of the Year and a winner of eight major trophies, while Glen Fitzpatrick, Bobby Ryan and Stuart Byrne were multiple Premier Division title winners.

Each year, the squad would train together for a month in annual close-season training camps in preparation for the trip to Norway. Potentially, players could have been sought after in Scandinavia or elsewhere. At the very least, the camps allowed out-of-contract players to maintain their fitness in the hopes of securing a contract back in Ireland as the season edged closer.

Powell signed for Norwegian third-tier side Vard Haugesund in early 2014, having impressed scouts at the winter tournament that year. Then twenty-six, Powell had left Shamrock Rovers months earlier after two years at the club. A former Republic of Ireland Under-21 international, he had won a clean sweep of domestic trophies during his time at Bohemians, where he had made his debut at sixteen.

He is the only player to move from Ireland to one of the participating nations, at least directly via the FIFPro tournament, but players have gone the other way too. Galway United manager Tommy Dunne, who now coaches in Iceland, signed Swedish defender Armin Aganovic in 2016. He would later have a brief spell at Derry City before returning to his native country.

Which begs the question: how open were Irish players to the idea of leaving Ireland behind to play in Norway, Sweden or Finland? 'I think the majority would be open to the idea,' PFAI player executive Ollie Cahill says. 'We've seen the likes of Éamon Zayed playing in Iran and in America who'd been at the tournament; James Chambers was at the tournament as well, he's over in America now; there are guys in Australia. The world opens up, you would have looked further afield at any opportunity to play and experience something new. The majority of them would have jumped at it.'

The squads assembled for the training camps and the tournament in Norway were always a mix of players at different ages and subsequently at varying stages in their career. Cahill believes that, while some players would attend with an open mind to where it might lead, many merely wanted to keep ticking over in the winter months. Making such an effort would also be viewed positively by coaches in Ireland. 'A lot of them then would have been going for the chance to go to Norway to play in the tournament, it being possibly where they could go further afield as well. There is a lot of pressure on certain players. Some players revel in that, but then [for] other players it's a big ask for one game, to really stand out, and for a manager to maybe take a chance on someone.'

As for Powell, he had reached a stage – having also taken in English football with Colchester United – where he was ready for something new. 'I had been having thoughts of whether I wanted to stay playing in the league here again, and I decided that at this point in my career a new challenge would be best for me,' he said. 'At my age I might not get many other opportunities to play abroad again. I didn't really expect to end up in Norway, as it happened, but that is football I suppose. I was ready for a change so I was prepared to move.

Obviously when myself and my girlfriend Kirsty talked about moving it was Australia or America, so it was a bit of a shock to her and my family as well. But this move came up and I wanted to give it a shot. If I stayed playing in the League of Ireland until I retired I would have had regrets about not trying something different, like living in a foreign country and experiencing a different style of football. I felt the move was the right thing to do.'

Powell believed that Irish domestic football had stagnated. 'The good times have passed by,' he told the *Irish Independent* at the time. Vard was Powell's only definite offer on the table. He believed, having lost his love for the game over a number of years, that Norway could revitalise him.

The security of a two-year deal in 2014, admittedly much more commonplace now among clubs like Shamrock Rovers and Dundalk, was a draw too. 'The season is April to November, so I'll come home over Christmas and not have to worry about being unemployed like I used to be.'

After signing the two-year deal with Vard Haugesund (the smaller of two clubs that occupied the hearts of the 37,000 inhabitants of the town that sat on the North Sea coast; the bigger club, FK Haugesund, have played in the top flight since 2010), the left back helped Vard to a credible third-place finish in the league, even if they finished fourteen points off promoted champions Åsane. Vard lost nine games in their twenty-six-game campaign, but Powell had a personal highlight when he scored the winning goal in extra time against Byrne in the second round of the Norwegian Cup. Another dramatic match for Powell was the final game of the league season, in which the Irishman scored and was then sent off as Vard went down 2–3 to Ålgård. It would prove to be his last action for the club, as he returned to Ireland in the close season. This was despite his having one year left to run on his contract.

But at least he'd given Scandinavia a go – and he still has the distinction of being the only Irish footballer to get a deal through the FIFPro tournament.

If the Irish players were open to moving, though, why was Powell, in six years of the FIFPro tournament, the only Irish player to earn a contract in one of the Scandinavian countries? After all, as outlined above, the calibre of players that made up the PFAI delegation included some serial winners, among them the league's leading lights. Cahill says it was hard to gauge why there weren't more Irish players approached with contracts or offers of trials. During the annual tournaments, Cahill and PFAI general secretary Stephen McGuinness would often ask themselves what the Scandinavian clubs and scouts were looking for – and perhaps more pertinently, why the Irish weren't it. 'Are these players not suited to what they're looking for?' they would wonder. He theorises, 'Maybe they think it's a safer bet taking a Swedish player into Finland than taking an Irish player. Maybe it would cost them more to get an Irish player over than a more local-based player.'

Over the years, players who have left the League of Ireland behind to try their hand outside of Ireland and the UK are in relatively short supply. Like Powell, Shane McFaul has spent time in Scandinavia in recent years. An FAI Cup winner with Sporting Fingal in 2009, McFaul joined FC Haka for a season in 2012 either side of a stint with St Patrick's Athletic, where he won a league title in 2013. He later returned to Finland to join Kotkan Työväen Palloilijat in the Veikkausliiga, where he enjoyed promotion in his first season and endured relegation in his second. Since then, he has spent a season in India's I-League with DSK Shivajians and in the US with FC Arizona – both of which where he played under League of Ireland stalwart Dave Rogers – while, most recently, McFaul has turned out for clubs in Finland's third-tier Kakkonen.

Shane Robinson, a league and cup winner with Drogheda United in the mid-2000s, spent two seasons with FC Haka, having joined in 2011, after a year in Australia's National Premier Leagues Western division with Stirling Lions. Australia and New Zealand have been popular locations for Irish players seeking new personal and playing challenges away from home. Jason Gavin also turned out for Stirling Lions, while Steven Gray played in Australia – making one appearance for A-League side Melbourne Heart – before linking up with Brian Shelley at Auckland's Waitakere United.

Pádraig Amond's move from Sligo Rovers to Portugal's Paços de Ferreira made headlines in 2010, while stories of Joe Kendrick's time in Azerbaijan with Neftchi Baku and the aforementioned Éamon Zayed's time in Iran with Persepolis and Aluminium Hormozgan are well known. Zayed's spell in particular is considered the stuff of legend, at least in Tehran, where he is fondly remembered to this day. (Zayed was Dublin-born but represented Libya at full international level, and went on to play under George O'Callaghan at Sabah in Malaysia before a fruitful spell in America's NASL and USL.)

Prolific striker Declan O'Brien spent six months with Maltese side Valletta in 2010, while lesser-known Christopher Harrington – brother of Olympic gold medallist Kellie – who began his career with Dublin City and Shelbourne, played in the Icelandic lower leagues with UMF Tindastóll. There he played with Steven Beattie, who would return to Ireland to considerable success before jetting off to the United States. Beattie himself was a one-time draft pick by Major League Soccer's Toronto FC, then managed by former Netherlands and Ajax star Aron Winter.

The number of League of Ireland players playing in the tiers below MLS in America have grown in recent years. Paddy Barrett, Colin Falvey, Derek Foran, Dan Casey and Iarfhlaith Davoren are among the recent players who have also left the domestic league behind for America.

Liam Buckley turned out for teams in Canada, Belgium, Spain and Switzerland in-between spells at five different League of Ireland clubs. Shamrock Rovers' double-winning defender Jacko McDonagh joined French Ligue 2 side Nîmes in 1985, where he spent two seasons before joining KSV Waregem in Belgium. Another hotshot striker, Mick Byrne, spent six months in the Dutch Eredivisie in 1988, playing for ADO Den Haag.

A league and cup winner with Dundalk in the late 1980s, Dessie Gorman moved to France, where he represented FC Bourges, while, years earlier, Noel King played for second-tier side Valenciennes. Fran Hitchcock also had an injury-interrupted season at SC Cambuur in the Netherlands.

The question was posed whether enough League of Ireland players would opt to take the route into foreign countries, mostly in Europe, should the opportunity arise. As outlined above, many aren't opposed to the idea at all.

8
ALL ROADS LEAD TO ITALY

Italy has been the scene, arguably, of Irish exiles' greatest successes, with Liam Brady and Anne O'Brien winning multiple titles between them. Given their success, it was perhaps inevitable that members of the next generation of Irish footballers would travel there, looking to mirror their achievements. For all their success, though, neither Brady nor O'Brien had an association with the iconic *Time* magazine. Few soccer players do.

Hunched around a desk in one of the many editorial meeting rooms in the Time-Life building in Manhattan's Rockefeller Center on a sweaty, summer's day, the team responsible for running *Time* magazine's Person of the Century online poll contemplated their next move.

The online poll, in 1999 a novelty of the emerging technology, was open to the public to determine who would be selected as the most worthy newsmaker of the twentieth century. Spanning a period where societal and technological change transformed life like no other in time, there were many to choose from: Martin Luther King Jr, Winston Churchill, Bill Gates, John Paul II, John F. Kennedy, Mahatma Gandhi and Yitzhak Rabin, the former Israeli prime minister who worked tirelessly towards Middle Eastern peace, were all popular names put forward for consideration. It was a crowded field, and that therein was the problem. The vote was split, ripe for a usurper to steal in and take the glory.

No one, bar some mischievous sorts in Ireland seeking to inject some divilment into their lives, thought a suitable contender would be a young Irish football player who, earlier that year, had been released by Middlesbrough without ever making a first-team appearance for the club.

The name Ronnie O'Brien had likely never been uttered in the offices and along the corridors of *Time*. Even if there had been a Middlesbrough or Republic of Ireland supporter on the payroll in some capacity, they wouldn't have wasted much breath discussing the merits of O'Brien, who was deemed surplus to requirements at Boro – one of the Premiership's more modest outfits at the time, notwithstanding their penchant for merging South American flair with Teesside steel.

Yet here the staff at *Time* found themselves with a dilemma. A small – and ever growing – army of internet early adapters in Ireland had decided to press forward O'Brien's claims for the prestigious title. They had done something similar months earlier when they hijacked a poll on the official Juventus website to support O'Brien as the club's most promising newcomer.

Of course, the Bray native was not the century's most noteworthy newsmaker. Nor was he that decade's, or year's. Or Ireland's. The magazine had made an error in allowing an open vote. They hadn't countenanced how the internet could be harnessed for such mischief. It was 1999, after all. The word 'viral', in an online sense, wouldn't become part of the everyday vocabulary for years to come.

The folks at *Time* hadn't yet figured out a way to restrict multiple votes either, or maybe they merely hadn't thought of it. O'Brien, who by that time had signed for Serie A giants Juventus in an admittedly seismic move for a player of his standing, received more than 57,000 votes to provisionally make him the Person of the Century. He held the title for all of twelve hours before the magazine's editors removed him from contention. 'Whimsical candidates will not be counted,' they argued.

The click of a mouse ended O'Brien's candidacy, but his bizarre legacy in Irish football history remains the stuff of cult legend decades later.

The midfielder had been part of Brian Kerr's Under-18 European Championship-winning team in 1998, alongside Robbie Keane and Richard Dunne, among others. A youth prospect at Middlesbrough, he had been released towards the end of the 1998/99 season. Days later he was snapped up on a multi-year deal by Juventus.

O'Brien was about to go from playing second, or even third, fiddle to the likes of Robbie Mustoe and Phil Stamp to sharing a dressing room with legends of the game, such as Zinedine Zidane, Filippo Inzaghi and Alessandro Del Piero. It was a dramatic reversal of fortunes for a previously unheralded player whom Boro boss Bryan Robson publicly declared as not being good enough to get into his team: 'Ronnie O'Brien is not good enough. People jump to the ceiling because he has gone to Juventus but he hasn't done anything yet,' Robson told newspaper reporters. 'People have said this about kids coming through, but they have to be good enough. I want kids who can get in the team, stay there and become seasoned professionals. If kids are good enough, I like them, if not, I have no time for them.'

The then twenty-year-old returned to Bray, where he kept himself in good shape ahead of his summer arrival in Turin. A media frenzy ensued, naturally enough for Ireland's first representative in Serie A since Liam Brady. Soccer correspondents flocked to the seaside town to speak to O'Brien, where he also posed with a Juventus shirt, a club-branded kit bag and an issue of the Italian football magazine *Guerin Sportivo*.

His Ireland youth manager, Brian Kerr, with whom O'Brien had run-ins on occasion, thought the move would be beneficial for the player. He didn't betray too much surprise about the signing either. 'Ronnie may just have the game for the continent, he'd have the skill and the pace that would really impress the Italians,' he told *The Irish Times*. 'He has good control and that bit of dash, and when the flicking session starts on the training ground, Ronnie will be well able for them. His performances will improve if his confidence grows. When he's buzzing, he's a cheeky little winger who can cause real danger.'

The deal had been brokered by agent Steve Kutner, who acted on behalf of Juventus in the UK, as well as representing high-profile players such as the then Middlesbrough star Paul Merson. 'Paul Merson recommended that I should have a look at Ronnie. I passed the recommendation onto Juve and the result is a five-year deal for Ronnie,' Kutner explained to Paul Hyland of *The Herald*. 'I told them to go and look at Ronnie in Cyprus [during the Under-18 European Championships] and they did. They've also seen him playing for Boro reserves. I see no reason why more Irish players who can boast talent like Ronnie O'Brien shouldn't head for Juventus. Why not?'

Despite the excitement surrounding his move, O'Brien never got ahead of himself, though he was hoping to prove his doubters wrong. 'If I'd been promised a chance I would have stayed at Middlesbrough,' the player said, speaking to Michael Walker for *The Guardian*. 'But I've signed for a club Bryan Robson never signed for and hopefully I can prove him wrong. Even if I don't, I'll take the picture from the team photo call, get it signed and frame it. That'll do me. Not many have that. My time will come.'

Upon arrival in Turin, O'Brien was immediately thrust in to training with his midfield contemporaries Zidane, Antonio Conte and Edgar Davids. Too old for their youth team and with no reserve system to play in, the right-sided midfielder fully expected to be loaned out soon after his arrival. He duly was – but prior to that he did make his debut for the Italian giants. His first appearance in the famous colours of the I Bianconeri came in the Intertoto Cup. With Juve 5–1 up on the night (and leading 9–1 on aggregate) against Russian side Rostov, O'Brien was introduced with thirteen minutes remaining by coach Carlo Ancelotti. It wasn't much, but it was something.

Soon afterwards, as expected, he found himself in Switzerland on loan, representing Lugano in the country's top flight. A loan move was common for young players striving to get into the teams of Serie A's elite. While he had been taken under the wing of club stalwarts such as Davids and captain Conte, during his brief time in Turin, he knew the lay of the land. This was a long-term project. Earning in excess of £3,000 per week and already having made a first team appearance, O'Brien was in a happy place.

In reality, the following few years saw O'Brien's career take a nomadic turn. He followed his time in Switzerland with a spell with Serie B's Crotone and then in Serie A with Lecce before moving on loan to Dundee United in Scotland. The Wicklow native pulled up no trees at any club, and with each failed attempt to make his mark in senior football, the hope of a breakthrough at Juventus became less likely.

He would call time on his Juventus spell in 2002, those thirteen minutes against Rostov the only time he'd worn the famed Juve colours. Leaving Europe behind, he joined Major League Soccer franchise Dallas Burn. O'Brien would enjoy the best spell of his career in America, representing Dallas, Toronto and the San Jose Earthquakes over a seven-year period before his retirement from the game at twenty-nine. He was named to the MLS All-Star team for four straight seasons, and made the league's Best XI in both 2004 and 2005, while he starred for Dallas.

Texas is home now for O'Brien, who has moved from the Boy in Green to the Man on the Green, working as director of golf at the Craig Ranch, located in McKinney, not far north of Dallas. He seamlessly transitioned from footballer to golf pro upon retirement. He hadn't envisioned life would have taken him to Dallas, nor keep him there. 'When I came over here I wasn't looking to stay long term. I was just looking to come over for a couple of months and get fit and go back to Europe. I came over and I enjoyed the feel, I enjoyed the lifestyle. I played golf a couple of times when we were looking around. I just really enjoyed it,' he told the *Irish Independent* in 2021, ahead of the Craig Ranch hosting the PGA Tour's Byron Nelson Championship.

1) John 'Jack' Kirwan carved out a fine career as a player in England before he took his first steps into management with AFC Ajax in 1910. He later managed in Italy, with Livorno.

2) Having led Real Betis to their first – and to date only – La Liga title in 1935, Patrick O'Connell (third from left, middle row) celebrated with his squad shortly before taking over at FC Barcelona.

3) Frank Stapleton joined Johan Cruyff's Ajax after thirteen years at Arsenal and Manchester United, but his time in the Netherlands was marred by injury.

4) Liam Brady and France captain Michel Platini exchange pennants at Lansdowne Road in October 1981. Months later, Platini's arrival would force his departure from Juventus.

5) Anne O'Brien (second from left) left home to join Stade de Reims aged just seventeen, where she starred for the French side under the tutelage of Pierre Geoffroy (left). Her career in Italy would later take her to unprecedented heights for an Irish player, male or female.

6) Claire Scanlan's long search to find professional football ended when she signed for Japanese side OKI FC Winds in 1996. She spent a year in Honjō where she played alongside some of the game's leading lights.

7) Roy O'Donovan takes to the field at Newcastle Jets' McDonald Jones Stadium, with son Alfie as mascot. Following his time in Asia, the Cork-born striker enjoyed the most prolific period of his career Down Under.

8) Claiming the 2019 C-League title in Cambodia was the result of a major turnaround at Svay Rieng FC, masterminded by their Head Coach, Limerick man Conor Nestor – in his first managerial role.

9) Brian Kerr is one of a select few Irish coaches who have taken charge of a foreign senior national team. He spent two years as manager of the Faroe Islands between 2009 and 2011.

10) Moving from Ireland to France provided Stephanie Roche with her first taste of professional club football, but her time at ASPTT Albi didn't turn out as she would have hoped.

11) Ronnie O'Brien's move to Juventus in the spring of 1999 prompted lots of attention, with the media flocking to Bray to meet Ireland's latest Serie A export.

12) Diane Caldwell spent six seasons in the Frauen-Bundesliga with FC Köln and then SC Sand (pictured) where she played against many of women football's leading players.

13) Limerick's Claire O'Riordan played regularly in the Frauen-Bundesliga for three years between 2018 and 2021, missing just three of sixty-six league games for MSV Duisburg.

14) Sean McDermott has carved out a reputation as one of Norwegian football's best goalkeepers but has struggled to garner senior international recognition.

15) Kevin Walker, son of ex-Ireland Under-21 international Pat, lined out for Sweden Under-16s against the Republic of Ireland in a friendly in Dublin. He is pictured with cousins Craig Kearns and Luke Keogh.

16) Few could have envisaged quite how successful Robbie Keane's time in Los Angeles would be when he signed for LA Galaxy in August 2011. He is regarded as among MLS's most significant foreign imports.

From Teesside to Turin, the DDSL to Dallas, O'Brien has enjoyed a career like few others. He's had the time of his life. Though his path took a different turn, he remains the only Irish player other than Brady to tog out for the Italian club. A year after his move to Juventus, though, another promising young Irish talent – who had also featured in Ireland's Under-18 European Championship-winning team – would make his way to Italy.

Almost twenty years on from Liam Brady signing for the Old Lady, Robbie Keane would follow in his footsteps by blazing a trail to Serie A. This time, rivals Inter Milan were the team to put their money on the line in banking on Ireland's great young hope. Brady, at twenty-four, was four years Keane's senior, but while Juventus had paid a paltry £600,000 for Brady's services, Inter Milan splashed an eye-watering £13 million on the young striker. Transfer fees, of course, had inflated to multi-million sums in the decades between. However, even in 1980, it was widely thought that Juve had masterminded a bargain deal for one of the continent's leading players.

Keane was not in that bracket of player yet, but was young and his career trajectory was pointing only upwards. In the space of twelve months, he had moved from Wolverhampton Wanderers in England's First Division to the Premiership with Coventry (as British football's most expensive teenager, no less), where he hit twelve goals for Gordon Strachan's team. Four of his five international goals up to his move to Italy had come across a six-month spell during that season too, marking the then teenager out as a likely record Irish goalscorer. There seemed no challenge too mountainous for the Dubliner to climb. Even at a young age, he did not lack the self-belief to back himself, whether it be to take on a defender, to score or to succeed in more general terms.

There remained a novelty about seeing an Irish player moving abroad to play for one of Europe's leading sides. Not since Brady had an Irishman played in Serie A, while in the decade preceding Keane's spell in Milan, only Tony Cascarino at Marseille and David Connolly at Feyenoord had spells in the top flights of leagues in Italy, Germany, Spain, France or the Netherlands.

With few Irishmen having forged this particular path, Keane turned to Republic of Ireland manager Mick McCarthy (who spent a season at Lyon in 1989/90) for advice, as well as former Sampdoria midfielder David Platt. Platt told the youngster that whatever happened in Milan, Keane would emerge a better player for the experience, and that nugget of advice underpinned Keane's natural inclination to take the challenge.

The move happened quickly in the end, from Strachan enquiring whether his young player would like to speak to Inter at training on Friday morning to Keane jumping on a Milan-bound flight hours later to talk terms. The clubs had already agreed on the fee, and Keane's eagerness to test himself against and alongside some of the world's best meant a departure was inevitable.

Ireland's young star signed a five-year deal with Inter Milan, just as O'Brien had a year earlier with Juve, but commensurate with Keane's achievements in a career still in its early stages, he would be earning a reported £30,000 per week in contrast to O'Brien's £3,000.

The youngster was mere weeks out of his teens when he put pen to paper on the deal that saw Inter splash out £13 million on the Tallaght native, more than doubling what Coventry City had paid Wolves a year earlier for his services. The Sky Blues chairman Bryan Richardson, and manager Gordon Strachan, were in no position to argue that Keane would be better served by staying put at Highfield Road. The similarities between Coventry and Milan were few, although both cities are known for being centres in their countries' respective automotive industries. On the pitch, they were incomparable.

Strachan had built a fine team at Coventry, one that included Keane, Gary McAllister, Darren Huckerby, Youssef Chippo, Mustapha Hadji and the England hopeful Steve Froggatt, who like Keane had moved from Wolves to Coventry. However, at Inter, Keane was walking into a San Siro dressing room that contained Christian Vieri, Ronaldo, Iván Zamorano,

Álvaro Recoba and new Turkish signing Hakan Şükür. Those were the players Keane was competing against for a place in Marcello Lippi's attack. French World Cup-winner Laurent Blanc, Clarence Seedorf, Colombian Iván Córdoba and a twenty-one-year-old Andrea Pirlo were also among the players at Lippi's disposal for other positions. The Inter squad were among the strongest not only in Italy, but in world football.

Lippi had been hired by Massimo Moratti after an eighth-place finish in 1999, and oversaw an improved showing the following season, as Inter finished fourth. But more was expected, in domestic and European competition. What wasn't expected was that much of the onus to catapult Inter back into trophy contention would fall on the twenty-year-old Irishman.

Not that it fazed Keane. Upon his arrival, he asked whether the number nine shirt was available to wear, fully aware that it was already worn by Ronaldo, the Brazilian striker whose latter years at Inter were ravaged by injury. 'It was worth a try,' Keane told the *Irish Daily Star* upon signing for the Italian giants. 'Some people may wonder if I can succeed at this level of the game, but there's no doubt in my mind that I will. I know that I will become a better player by playing for Inter Milan. I won't be fazed by this move. They have spent a lot of money on me and I'm confident in my own ability. I would not have signed for Inter unless I thought I would be playing regularly.'

The journalist Paul Lennon noted a definite strain of bewilderment in Keane's voice, perhaps betraying the fact that it was difficult not to be in some way overawed by the whole situation.

Now, just out of his teens, Keane was off for pastures new. McCarthy was adamant that the move would serve to benefit his young star and the national team, for whom Keane was becoming an increasingly important figure. 'It can only benefit him as a player and us as a country to have one of our brightest young talents learning his trade in the toughest league of them all. Even if Robbie only lasts a year in Italy, he will learn from the experience and his financial security will be sealed. There are no downsides to the move as far as I'm concerned. He cannot come back from Italy as a failure,' he told *The Star*.

Keane took to the task of immersing himself in Italian life well, and was studious when it came to his daily hour-long language lessons. He carried an English-Italian dictionary around too, which, pre-smartphone, was a necessity. He was accommodated in a plush apartment building a short distance from the San Siro. Ronaldo was a tenant too, but Keane and the striker never crossed paths, what with the Brazilian missing the entire season through injury and being back home working his way back to fitness.

Another helpful aspect in settling in was that John Ledwith, a friend from childhood, joined Keane in Italy and lived with him throughout his spell there. Ledwith had also lived with Keane at various times in his early days in England. He was no Ronaldo, but good company all the same.

Still, for all his eagerness to settle in, it soon became clear to Keane that he had joined a club in turmoil. In the previous five years, Moratti had overseen a transfer spend in the region of £150 million, and it was obvious to see, given the star names at Inter's disposal during that period, that the team were certainly underachieving.

Injuries to some of Inter's key forwards didn't help either. As it happened, when Keane arrived in the summer of 2000, Christian Vieri joined Ronaldo on the sidelines through injury. That meant the young Dubliner was thrust into Lippi's starting team and the limelight from the off, giving him no chance to adapt to a new country, league and style of play. The manager's future was dependent on him, even more so after an embarrassing 1–0 aggregate defeat to Swedish side Helsingborgs in the UEFA Champions League qualifiers.

Lippi spoke very highly of his bright young thing in the weeks following his arrival. 'Robbie has impressed us with his maturity,' he said. Keane had scored the winning goal in a pre-season friendly win over Real Mallorca, and was unlucky to see an impudent backheel hit the post in the defeat to Helsingborgs. Given Lippi's encouraging words – and the aforementioned injuries – it was no surprise that the Irishman was in the team for the most part in the early stages of that season, partnering Şükür, albeit in a more withdrawn role. He certainly showed promise, as when he scored his first goal for the club in the Supercoppa Italiana final against Lazio, finding the net after just two minutes at Rome's Stadio Olimpico. He beat seasoned pros Alessandro Nesta and Siniša Mihajlović to a forward ball and lobbed the onrushing Angelo Peruzzi before embarking on his already iconic cartwheel and tumble celebration. What began on the streets of Tallaght he had now taken to the biggest club game of his career. Inter lost the game 3–4.

Nine years Şükür's junior, Keane was still forced to shoulder as much of the goalscoring burden as his fellow new signing. He hit the net in a 3–0 win away to Polish side Ruch Chorzów in the UEFA Cup and sprung from the bench to create two more goals in a 4–1 win in the second leg. When Keane chipped the Lecce goalkeeper to net his third Inter goal in the second leg of a Coppa Italia tie, things seemed rosy in the garden. He had made a relatively impressive start to life at a new club in a new country, where expectations were heightened and allowances were few.

However, things took a turn when Inter Milan lost the first game of the league season to Reggina, on 1 October. Within twenty-four hours, Lippi was sacked. Keane was stunned. 'It's quite a shock, the Italians certainly don't mess about,' he told *The Star* in the immediate aftermath of the sacking. 'I would have preferred a more settled environment [but] I don't think it will affect me.'

In reality, it would affect Keane. Lippi, it seemed, had taken to Keane, and while it is impossible to speculate how Keane would have fared had Vieri and Ronaldo been fit for selection, the Irish frontman had seen regular early-season action – and was producing the output to suggest a longer-term future at the club. However, that was clearly not the feeling of the new Inter Milan boss, Marco Tardelli. Keane would start only three Serie A games for Tardelli, appearing as a sub in two more, without scoring.

It didn't help that a foot injury ruled him out of three games shortly after Tardelli's appointment, and by the time he returned to fitness, so too had

Vieri. It stands to reason that the new boss was keen to get the prolific and experienced Vieri back into the fold. The Italian international would go on to plunder eighteen goals that term, even as Inter ended in a disappointing fifth place. Vieri, who grew up in Australia, was one of the few players in the dressing room who spoke fluent English, and he and Keane had struck up a close friendship. There was no animosity between the pair. Vieri was the senior man, and although Keane was not the reverential type, he couldn't help but acknowledge his status in the game, even as he relished the idea of competing with him for a place in the team.

Though Keane may have been out of favour with Tardelli, the manager clearly still thought highly of the Dubliner. In Paul Lennon's biography, *Robbie: A Striker's Story*, Tardelli said at the time – clearly unaware that their paths would cross eight years later when he was part of Giovanni Trapattoni's Republic of Ireland coaching staff, with Keane their captain and goalscorer-in-chief – 'Robbie Keane is a player who really impresses me. With luck, he has many more years ahead of him in the game.'

Reggina attempted to sign Keane on loan as his game-time dried up in Milan, but the club quickly dismissed that offer. As his spell on the sideline lengthened, doubts began to form in Keane's mind about his Italian adventure. 'I didn't come here to go shopping. I came here to play football. I've nothing against Mr Tardelli. He is a great man and a great manager but unfortunately, I didn't feature in his plans,' Keane told *The Star*. So, only a few months into life in Milan, he began to consider looking elsewhere for first-team football.

Leeds United were competing in that season's Champions League group stages – they would ultimately reach the semi-finals under David O'Leary – and were in the city for a clash with AC Milan on 7 November. O'Leary's squad contained four of Keane's international teammates: Gary Kelly, Ian Harte, Stephen McPhail and Alan Maybury. The night before the match, Keane stopped by the San Siro to watch them train. As Gary Kelly recalled to Paul Lennon, the striker made a beeline for the Leeds manager.

'Tongue in cheek, he went to David O'Leary and said, "any chance of getting me to that club or what?" And within a matter of weeks, David, out of the blue said, "get on to Robbie and make sure he comes here".'

He duly rejected overtures from Chelsea to sign for Leeds on loan in December. The move was made permanent by the end of the season.

Despite the short and disappointing nature of his spell in Milan, Keane is not big on regrets, and doesn't view his time at Inter Milan in a negative context. He left to play football and would repeat the trick later in his career when out of favour at Tottenham Hotspur, setting off across the Atlantic to join Los Angeles Galaxy. Speaking of his time in Milan in 2014, he told the *Daily Mail*, 'Do I regret it? I honestly don't. It was an unbelievable experience. It was a good learning curve for me to understand the game when I came back. I wanted to come back. Every club, if I am not playing, I want to leave because I want to play football. I get paid to play football, not sit on the bench. I don't enjoy that.'

Remembering his arrival at one of European football's grand old clubs, the then twenty-year-old from Tallaght said, 'The first few weeks flew by and I was sort of speechless to be playing for one of the best teams in the world.' Anyone who knows Keane well would attest that takes some doing. He still made plenty of noise in a career that would eventually take in five countries and see him score sixty-eight international goals for Ireland.

As Brady was an inspiration for the likes of Keane, so was Anne O'Brien for the next generation of Irish women footballers. And after her misfortune at the Dash, modern-day star Stephanie Roche soon found her attention turning to Italy.

International football had been a major factor in Roche's decision to pursue a professional career, even though she didn't always think that it was right for her. She made her debut for the senior national team in 2008, while playing for Dundalk City Ladies. A prolific scorer at Raheny United and later at Peamount, Roche established herself as a regular in squads under Noel King and then Sue Ronan. 'I was scoring goals, playing really well and I'd go to play for Ireland and then be told that's not good enough if you want to play international football. To be honest, I was a little pissed off with that. But that was always the attitude – that you need to go abroad. I don't necessarily think it was the right thing. Players need to enjoy their football and establish themselves before they go over and play in England or wherever it may be. It was definitely an influence on my career because there was a pressure to go and play professionally, particularly going to France.'

Colin Bell, who replaced Ronan in 2017, was another advocate of his players playing at a professional level, meaning they trained every day and played against as high a calibre of opposition as possible.

Knowing what was required of her, Roche signed for WSL side Sunderland shortly after returning from America. This was her first time playing in the UK, where many of her international teammates were based. She spent three years there, but her time was curtailed by a leg break sustained when the Republic of Ireland played Northern Ireland in a World Cup qualifier in Lurgan in September 2017. When she returned to training in the autumn of the following year, by now out of contract at Sunderland, Bell again impressed on her the need to play full time. Sunderland had explored the option of re-signing the forward, but having decided against applying for a Women's Super League licence, they were to play in the part-time National League North Division.

Instead, she settled on a move to Tuscany, Italy. Roche joined Serie A's Florentia San Gimignano. 'My only option at the time was Italy. I had heard so many negative things about Italy. I was nervous about going but it was my only option. I was being told I had to go and play abroad [if she wanted to stay in the international picture].'

Roche does not recall her time at Florentia with any great sense of fondness. On the surface, they were an ambitious outfit with no affiliation to a men's club, like most of the other teams in the top flight of Italian women's football. Founded in 2015, three successive promotions had lifted them from the anonymity of the regional leagues to Serie A.

Forty years after Anne O'Brien had blazed a trail in Italian football, Roche was just the second Irishwoman to play in the country. However, her experience was to prove to be the polar opposite of O'Brien's.

Roche was conscious that her options were limited, but she still had valid concerns about the move. While at Sunderland, teammates Anke Preuß and Dominique Bruinenberg, who played together at AGSM Verona, told of instances when wages were left unpaid. Assurances were made that this would not be a problem for Roche, until it was. Having signed in November 2018, she wasn't paid until December, and then again in January, before a five-month wait until her next payment in June. It was irregular, and in Roche's own words, 'unorganised and flimsy'. For example, she recalls having to get a bus and two trains before embarking on a twenty-five-minute walk to get to training every day; it was all far from what she'd expected.

A stress fracture in her right ankle put paid to much of her first season in Italy, which she describes as 'not an enjoyable professional experience'. Despite the lack of enjoyment and irregular, late wage payments, Roche 'stupidly' signed on again for the 2019/20 campaign.

Her regret wasn't felt immediately. The summer of 2019 saw her have what she described as the best pre-season of her life, hitting nine goals in four games. The standard of opposition mattered little when regaining form; fitness and consistency was paramount.

Trouble was brewing. Roche butted heads with coach Michele Ardito regularly during her time at the club. Having started the season in the team, she was soon looking on from the sidelines again. Ironically, her international status was causing trouble. The sole international player in their squad, Roche's departing on international breaks created a further distance between her, the coach and the team in general.

She recalls being called up to play in Ireland's 1–1 draw away to Greece in Athens in November 2019, a match in which Roche was a late substitute. Anastasia Spyridonidou's ninety-third-minute equaliser broke Irish hearts, the girls in green having led for eighty minutes after FC Köln striker Amber Barrett's early lob. On her return to Tuscany, Ardito, Roche remembers, asked her for her Ireland shirt from the game. Roche obliged. Despite this kind gesture, her career at Florentia would amount to a further forty-seven minutes across three months. 'The first opportunity he had to take me out of the team, he did.' Though in a strange turn of events, later, 'He asked me if he went to another club, could he sign me,' she says. 'Was he serious?'

Her time at Florentia ended midway through her second season, and just weeks before the global breakout of the Covid-19 pandemic that would change the modern world. She returned, with a large amount of relief, to Peamount United.

In reality, Roche never harboured serious ambitions to leave Ireland in pursuit of a professional life, in football or not. As a teenager, she had turned down opportunities to embark on soccer scholarships in the United States – a well-worn path for many young Irish players, both female and male. 'I've always been a homebird. I like being at home. I love Ireland. I didn't think I'd ever go away. It probably wasn't until I got into the senior national team that I realised the opportunities that were there in women's football. The seasons were short [in America], it wasn't all about football. You were a student athlete. It just never really appealed to me. I wanted to stay in Ireland.'

Reflecting on her time in Europe and in America, she says it was anything but easy. The glitz and glamour of the Ballon d'Or awards in Zurich was the exception, a world away from the norm. 'I had issues that people didn't know about. I was put in the spotlight. I was doing interviews every day, doing that to promote women's football. But at the same time, I was going through so much shit that nobody knew about. I couldn't highlight it and then contradict myself. It was very difficult.'

It is becoming an ever more common complaint in modern football that observers struggle to look beyond what they see between the white lines, to acknowledge the human side of those they cheer for or root against. They have to perform, or else. Excuses don't tend to wash, for the most part. Roche's unprecedented fame was little consolation during these personal ups and downs, being dragged from pillar to post, from France to the US, England to Italy and home again.

As with Roche, Louise Quinn's route to playing in Italy was a meandering one, via Dublin, Sweden and London. During her first stint away from home, she found herself in Eskilstuna, a small Swedish city in Södermanland County in the south-east of the country. There, a team of girls in blue were well on their way to producing their own fairy tale of Leicester City proportions in Sweden's Damallsvenskan.

Having earned promotion from the second tier of women's football two years earlier, Eskilstuna United were going head to head with reigning champions Rosengård for a league title in 2015. Rosengård had won Sweden's top flight in four of the previous five seasons, and in their ranks were stars such as the Swiss forward Ramona Bachmann, the prolific German striker Anja Mittag, New Zealand star Ali Riley, experienced Swede Lina Nilsson and Marta, the Brazilian forward. With six Damallsvenskan titles under her belt already, as well as five FIFA World Player of the Year awards, Marta was undoubtedly the league's star. Rosengård were the best team, and when it came to discussions about who could stop them, few fixed their gaze on a team that had finished seventh in their first season in the top flight.

A Blessington native, Quinn had starred in Eskilstuna's two previous seasons, helping the Viktor Eriksson-managed team to an Elitettan title in 2013 and then that solid mid-table finish. A strong, aggressive centre back, Quinn had shone for Peamount United for years before moving to Sweden to pursue a professional career. Now she was a key player in their Leicester City-style run.

All that was lacking, ultimately, was the result. Eskilstuna needed results to go for them on that final day in October 2015. They beat Göteborg, but with nothing to play for, Linköpings were unable to stop Rosengård sauntering to a 5–0 victory. In the end, Quinn's team finished second, pipped to the post by Rosengård. There was a solitary point in it. Quinn still remembers the disappointment. 'That was a journey, so then when it got right to the end and we didn't win it, there was deflation. We gave everything. There was nothing left to give.'

Eskilstuna's rearguard, marshalled by Quinn and English defender Vaila Barsley, conceded just fifteen goals, a league best. The club's Cameroonian striker Gaëlle Enganamouit outscored Bachmann, Macedonian Nataša Andonova and the coming star Pernille Harder, as well as everyone else. She did so well, in fact, that she joined Rosengård for the next season. Quinn had played every minute of the campaign at centre back and contributed two goals – a breakthrough goal against Mallbackens in the second week of the season, and then a lead goal against Göteborg when Eskilstuna hit back after a Lieke Martens opener. Quinn's aerial ability in both boxes remains one of the defining characteristics of her game, and has for years been a potent weapon used by her clubs and national team.

On reflection, the players knew that they didn't need a trophy to validate their success in that very special year. And at least UEFA Women's Champions League qualification had been secured.

Quinn was where she wanted to be, living the dream life of a professional footballer in Europe.

Quinn had roomed with Fiona O'Sullivan on international duty, and it was from discussions with the American-born striker that the seed of pursuing a professional career on the continent was planted. Having finished her Sports and Exercise Management degree at UCD, the wheels were set in motion.

She was tentative, but available. Eskilstuna called. Quinn thought the second division would be a better fit. Self-esteem wasn't lacking, exactly, but self-doubt was in plentiful supply. It's a typical Irish trait. 'Is it for me? Am I good enough?' she wondered. Years later, she looks back and rues not starting her professional career earlier.

Her biggest driver to go abroad, as has been the case with several interviewees spoken to for this book, was international recognition or, more accurately, securing a starting position for the Republic. 'You want to give yourself the best possible chance of playing at a high level and being at your physical peak, so that when the Ireland call comes, you're ready to go.'

Barsley's near-simultaneous arrival at Eskilstuna in January 2013 – Quinn had known her from their time together at Peamount United – helped the settling in process no end. Similar in stature and with both possessing an ability to dominate aerial challenges, it was strange that the club wanted to sign them both to partner at centre back instead of looking for a more complementary pairing. Neither friend was about to complain.

What would have been a language barrier for some amounted to a language barricade for Quinn, who had taken the leap to move to Sweden – and later Italy – despite living with dyslexia. While at school in Wicklow, she had been exempt from taking a language at Leaving Cert level. One of her major struggles was, and remains, language.

Quinn and Barsley embarked on a government-run SFI (Swedish for Immigrants) programme. Around the time of her arrival in Eskilstuna, the country was processing a large number of asylum applications from countries such as Syria, Iraq, Somalia, Eritrea and Afghanistan. Already intimidated by languages in general, the course wasn't conducive to a positive learning environment for Quinn. 'It was a really intimidating place,' she remembers. 'You were coming into a classroom with people at all different levels, from all different cultures. Some didn't speak English.'

The move was a stab in the dark for Quinn, but she arrived with the knowledge that plenty of Irish internationals before her had chosen

Scandinavia as their new pasture. Galway's Méabh De Búrca arrived at the club at the same time as Quinn, following a year at Amazon Grimstad in Norway. Her friend, the California-born striker O'Sullivan, had spent two years in Sweden a few years previously, while another American-born player, Shannon Smyth, was also on the books at Amazon Grimstad.

Language barriers aside, Quinn felt accepted at Eskilstuna. From modest beginnings, the club was much more than a women's team struggling to find their place in the hearts and minds of the prospective supporters. For her debut against Älta, there were 324 people in the crowd. As Eskilstuna beat Göteborg 4–0 on the final day of the 2015 season, the Tunavallen was hosting 6,300 supporters.

Community spirit was integral to building their supporter base, and the foreigners found themselves immersed in such off-field duties. 'It was about us getting stuck into the community spirit. We visited schools quite a bit, just to play a bit of football. They found us really interesting. We were the really tall, crazy foreigners. The community took us under their wing. It was incredible. Anything that was going on in the city, they wanted Eskilstuna players there.' Quinn judged a Bake Off competition on one occasion. It was a decent standard, but nothing to call home about. Another time, she recalls standing outside a shopping centre in a thunderstorm handing out leaflets advertising the club's upcoming games.

By the time Eskilstuna had been promoted to the Damallsvenskan, overshadowing their men counterparts who were languishing in the second tier, attendance skyrocketed. The women's team were the hottest ticket in town.

Her success with the club proved that she had made the right choice in choosing Sweden. With the second-place finish came the coveted Champions League qualification. However, as a result of the Swedish calendar – the domestic league is played between April and October – the Swedish clubs had to wait twelve months between qualifying and actually playing in the tournament itself. Quinn described the wait as a minor irritant. Her

overwhelming feeling was one of joy, not simply to return to the elite competition for women's football in Europe, but to do so with such a modest outfit.

A 3–1 aggregate win over Glasgow City in the round of thirty-two
put Eskilstuna in dreamland before a meeting with German giants Werder
Bremen swiftly brought them back down to earth, as they put eight past
the Swedes over two legs.

Quinn, for all her success during her time in Sweden – she also
established herself as a first-choice player for Sue Ronan's Republic of
Ireland team during her time there – never let go of some of that insecurity
that had originally made her question the move. In four years at the club,
she only ever signed one-year extensions. A two-year deal frightened her.

Women's football, she had learned from experience and anecdotes, was
an unstable environment. That would become all too real for Quinn after
deciding to leave Eskilstuna at the end of the 2016 season. She joined
Women's Super League outfit Notts County, only for the club to fold
before the start of the new season. Mercifully, she signed with top-flight
side Arsenal weeks later, and would go on to win a league title and league
cup during her two-and-a-half years at the north London club.

Her move to England had been prompted by a need to be closer to
family, but also by a feeling that her time at Eskilstuna had reached a natural
conclusion. After their near miss in a thrilling title race, the following
season they dropped one place to third, but finished a seismic twenty-four
points behind champions Linköpings. Quinn had been made captain for
her final season at the club, an indicator of the standing she had among
the coach and her fellow players. 'I knew I got to a stage in Sweden where
I needed to be closer to home, without doubt. I just felt so distant from the
people I loved the most. I've always been a homebird.'

Quinn is as acquainted with the Champions League as any professional
Irish player today. She played in it first with Peamount United in 2011
when they secured a passage through to the last thirty-two, with Quinn
hitting a hat-trick against Slovenia's Krka en route. Further appearances

would come with Eskilstuna, Arsenal and Fiorentina, whom she joined in August 2020, mid-pandemic.

Having swapped Sweden for the UK to be closer to home, the Italian move seemed counterintuitive for a player who looks forward to being able to settle back in Ireland once her professional career ends. Such is the transient nature of the game, however; often choice isn't a luxury afforded to players.

Quinn had featured for Arsenal as they beat Fiorentina 6–0 over two games in the Champions League in the autumn of 2019, a match that brought the tall centre back to the attention of coach Antonio Cincotta. She had enjoyed the visit to Florence for that European second-leg. The Italian way of life had caught her eye, meaning overtures from France and Germany were dismissed.

She liked the team, was excited by the city and was encouraged by a conversation with Cincotta. She was still reluctant, though. 'I was scared shitless,' she admits. Was she going to regret moving away from home comforts again? Was learning another language going to push her over the edge? Was moving to Italy – which just months earlier had been the continental epicentre of the coronavirus pandemic – really a wise move? 'I had a really tough time making the decision. It's not like even some of the men's teams in the lower leagues. They're probably still making more than us. It's not like you can just pack up and bring your family or your partner with you and set them up in a big house. You have to go and do it on your own.'

She signed a one-year deal with an option to extend for another year at the end of her debut season.

'I was definitely going into the unknown. It's a constant battle. Sometimes, you have to dig deep, really deep. Vera [Pauw, Ireland WNT manager] said Italy would challenge me in every way. In a short space of time, I've learned a lot about myself. It's been a real roller-coaster. On the pitch, it's been really up and down.'

Ireland was never far from her mind while in Italy. 'I do feel that I'm trying to represent Ireland while I'm here and show we have a country full of talent. I'm showing just as much pride as the Italians are.'

Quinn was born on 17 June 1990. While Pat and Jacinta Quinn were awaiting the arrival into the world of their third daughter, the country was gripped in Italia '90 fever. In fact, baby Louise was delivered at 8.43 a.m., just hours before Ireland played Egypt at the Stadio La Favorita in Palermo. Every television in Mount Carmel Hospital in Churchtown was tuned to RTÉ's coverage of the game. With mum and newborn daughter doing well in hospital, her father did manage to make it to the pub for 3 p.m. to catch the game. He could hardly have missed it, regardless of the circumstances.

Little did the Quinns know, their little girl would become as absorbed in football as any man, woman or child had during those feverish, euphoric summer days. It isn't lost on Quinn that she is among just a handful of Irish who have played top-level football in Italy. She is aware that she has joined illustrious company.

It is only in recent years that the story of Anne O'Brien, a pioneer of Irish women's football and a bona fide legend in Italy, pierced the consciousness of the wider football community. Even Quinn, herself immersed in the game, had not known much of her predecessor. 'I feel like I've only got to learn about Anne more recently. She's been in a few more articles and she's come to more journalists' minds. A few years ago, I didn't know much about her. She was so popular and then did not get a look in with Ireland. Vera knew her and we had a small chat about her. She really was an absolute legend in Italy, which is class.'

Furthering her international prospects and cementing her national team place while Ireland vie to qualify for a major tournament for the first time remains the key motivator for Quinn to look beyond the myriad challenges that come with playing away so far from home.

As a teenager, the defender declined the opportunity to take up a soccer scholarship in the United States because she was so single-mindedly chasing a place in the Irish senior team. Back then, there was no guarantee that the FAI would fly fringe players back for national team duty. Quinn had seen some slip away and out of the reckoning once they swapped home for the US. That was only ten years ago, but much has changed in the interim. 'It has been amazing to be part of where the change is happening.'

And while Quinn's own time in Italy is now over – she departed Fiorentina in July 2021 – she is proud to have followed in the footsteps of an icon such as O'Brien, who has done so much to change what young Irish girls, just like Quinn, feel they can achieve in the game.

9

THE EURO STARS

In the last decade, a new wave of Irish talent has taken to continental Europe – and not just Italy – to further their careers and chase glory and opportunity they may otherwise have never been afforded. Naturally, Europe has been the location for the majority of the country's footballing emigrants given ever-improving transport links and historically long-established domestic football infrastructure across the continent.

It hasn't just been lower league journeymen or League of Ireland stalwarts that have sought a new start on European soil either. Full internationals, both men and women, continue to look to Europe. None have committed themselves to the notion of playing abroad quite like Cillian Sheridan.

It was September 2014. Martin O'Neill had been in the Republic of Ireland hotseat for ten months. The Derry man was sitting in the media room at the FAI headquarters in Abbotstown, North County Dublin, flanked by the association's then communications director, Peter Sherrard, as O'Neill announced a thirty-seven-man squad for the upcoming Euro 2016 qualifiers against Gibraltar and Germany. It was customary during O'Neill's tenure to name expanded squads, which would then be reduced as the matchdays approached. Speaking to the assembled media, he joked,

'The only player missing from the last thirty years is Paul McGrath. I've excluded a few fellas who've just died.'

The laughter in the room was far from riotous. As tends to be the case when members of the press are attempting to curry favour with a manager, it was more sycophantic in tone. Given what was considered to be a genuine paucity of players from which to choose, O'Neill's bloated squads were designed to be an indication of his willingness to cast his net far and wide. After all, Ireland were in no position to overlook any player who may add something to a squad that had over several years seen their representation in the English Premier League dwindle.

One interested observer of the squad reveal was in Cyprus, fostering his own hopes of making the provisional panel. Cillian Sheridan was following closely the news emanating from Abbotstown. However, the APOEL Nicosia striker turned out to not be among the eight strikers picked for O'Neill's squad. Having not received a call-up since 2010 under Giovanni Trapattoni, his exclusion was no surprise. Sheridan had hopes, but not expectations.

Nevertheless, the manager's joke rankled with him. If he wasn't to get a shot now, then when? Six days earlier, Sheridan had led the line for APOEL in their UEFA Champions League clash with Barcelona at the Nou Camp, in which Gerard Piqué's goal had secured a narrow win for the Catalans.

Since the Cypriot club had qualified for the group stage – making Sheridan Ireland's only representative in the competition that season – O'Neill had been regularly questioned on whether or not Sheridan would be called up. As England's top clubs no longer had Irish players in their squads, local interest in Europe's premier club competition had all but petered out.

Could Ireland really afford to ignore a player who was rubbing shoulders with Lionel Messi, Luis Suárez, Neymar, Zlatan Ibrahimović and Edinson Cavani? Fifteen members of O'Neill's squad were plying their trade in England's second tier, the Championship. LA Galaxy's Robbie Keane was, at thirty-four, two years away from his international retirement. Goals and where they were to come from now and in the future dominated the thoughts and minds of those invested in Irish football matters. Sheridan never considered it a certainty that he would do any better than the players at the manager's disposal, but he was convinced he was deserving of an opportunity to be amongst them.

'I was annoyed at that joke,' Sheridan says. 'I'd like to think he knew who I was, I don't know. I was never afraid to go abroad and think it was going to damage my chances.' Still, he felt that O'Neill's tactics made it difficult for him, or any other striker. 'Watching games, even if there were really good strikers playing, I don't think they would have been scoring. The way the team played, it would have been hard to play there as a striker.'

O'Neill indicated to the media that day, and on several other occasions, that he did in fact know Sheridan. After all, the Bailieborough man had begun his career at Celtic, where O'Neill had enjoyed five trophy-laden years. However, on that day in Dublin he did admit to journalists that he hadn't watched the Champions League group game from the week before.

The well-travelled striker says he was embarrassed by much of the coverage he received that season. The Irish media were very keen to talk about 'the only Irishman in the Champions League'. Between 2000 and 2010, nineteen Irish players had taken part in the competition proper. In the decade to follow, that number fell to just six. Three of those – Anthony Stokes, Eoghan O'Connell and Jonny Hayes – played for Celtic. Therefore Sheridan, playing on the continent and in a group containing the might of Barcelona, the petrodollar-fuelled Paris Saint-Germain and European greats Ajax, was someone to really latch onto. Still, Sheridan was certainly showing strong form at the time. And he believed he was now finally getting the sort of opportunities that validated his decision to play outside of the UK, a choice that had led him down a winding path.

At just twenty-one, he had left Celtic and signed a three-year deal with Bulgarian side CSKA Sofia. Historically, CSKA were the country's most successful club, with thirty-one league titles to their name. Having weeks earlier broken into the Republic of Ireland senior set-up, it was considered a bold move. Wasn't Sheridan concerned of being out of sight, out of mind? Not particularly, as he believed he was moving to a level superior to what he had experienced during loan spells at Motherwell, St Johnstone and Plymouth Argyle. After all, by the time he arrived, CSKA were a qualifying tie away from a group stage appearance in the UEFA Europa League. The contract dwarfed the terms he was on at Celtic too, which went some way to assuaging any doubts about swapping Parkhead for the Parva Liga.

Those doubts likely resurfaced, though, when, within days of Sheridan signing for the club in August 2010, manager Pavel Dochev was sacked, having lost his first two games of the league season. Two months later, his replacement, Macedonian Gjore Jovanovski, was removed. It was to prove a turbulent season, although Sheridan's third manager in two months, Milen Radukanov, did lead the club to a third-place league finish and a Bulgarian Cup win. According to Sheridan, however, he favoured homegrown players. 'At the time there was a split in the dressing room between the foreign guys and the Bulgarians. He played a lot of Bulgarian players. I felt the dressing room was more hostile than others I've been in.'

The dressing room dynamics and managerial upheaval didn't take the Cavan man by surprise, but those issues were mere indicators of the instability that undermined the club. Sheridan's long-time agent, John Inglis, who is based in Bulgaria, at least knew the lay of the land. Inglis was forced at one point to advise his client to fake a departure so that he could force through an overdue wage payment, as, at the end of Sheridan's third month at the club, he had yet to be paid.

Advised that a failure to pay Sheridan as he approached ninety days since his signing would enable him to terminate his contract, the striker called the club's bluff. He put on a show of saying goodbye to teammates and staff. He didn't attend the following day's training session. Instead he stayed home but told the club he was at the airport. His outstanding wages appeared in his account hours later.

'It was a game,' he says. 'It happened quite a lot. I've never been at a club that had so much instability. The panic can start to set in. So many things happened in Bulgaria that after that things were pretty calm. That was almost the best thing to happen to me. For it to go as bad as it went helped me with all the other places I've been abroad.'

Things weren't all bad for the 6'5" targetman in Sofia. He scored seven goals in twenty-six appearances in his first season, but serial changes in the dugout and boardroom ultimately led to him being frozen out. As he was a high earner amongst a constantly evolving playing squad, CSKA were keen to offload.

Opportunities to move to the United States passed by. After a season back in the SPL with St Johnstone, in which Sheridan came to the realisation that he had personally failed to meet professional standards in Bulgaria, he decided to return to CSKA. He did so in a buoyant mood. 'I wanted to go and prove myself, show them a different player than was there in my first year. I went back with a totally different attitude towards everything.'

Unfortunately, while his mindset had undergone a transformation, the continued unpredictability at the club proved too big an obstacle. In the first leg of a UEFA Europa League tie against Slovenian minnows Mura 05, Sheridan was dismissed by English referee Lee Probert for an elbow on an opposition defender. Despite no language barrier, Sheridan's resigned protests fell on deaf ears. The game finished scoreless. He missed the second leg, a 1–1 home draw, and CSKA were out.

Fans' reaction to the ignominy of their European exit led to a huge turnover of players. Some of the sixteen players who had arrived during the summer were told to leave weeks into multi-year contracts. Sheridan was not one of them, but he was conscious that he was unlikely to be first choice moving forward. Therefore, after playing in just three league games at the start of the season, Sheridan departed for Scotland, joining

Kilmarnock. Soon, though, he would again be heading for the continent –
this time, Cyprus.

APOEL Nicosia's new manager, Paulo Sérgio, had earmarked Sheridan as
one to watch two years earlier. While manager of Hearts, Sheridan had fired St
Johnstone to a 2–0 victory and the next season, with Sérgio no longer in situ
but surely watching on, Sheridan hit a hat-trick against the same opposition.

As it was a club that had reached the quarter-finals of the Champions
League in the spring of 2012, a little over a year earlier, Sheridan never
believed he would be in line for a move to a club of its premier pedigree.
In a bizarre turn of events, within months of his arrival, he faced a battle to
be even the most popular Irishman among the fervent APOEL supporters.

The club had been knocked out of both Champions League and Europa
League qualifiers, and faced a season focused only on matters domestic.
That was until the intervention of an unlikely Irish saviour. After Turkish
side Fenerbahçe had been banned from European competition as a result
of a match-fixing scandal probe, their replacement was to be selected at
random from the teams that had lost at the playoff round.

Attending the draw for the UEFA competitions in Monaco, *The Irish
Times* journalist Emmet Malone – as a media representative from a country
without a club in the draw – was invited onto the stage at the Méridien
Beach Plaza hotel to randomly select the name. APOEL were the team
handed a reprieve.

To say Malone instantly garnered cult status at the club would be an
understatement. The journalist was invited to Cyprus as a guest of the
club's president, while there were suggestions that fans would produce a
banner bearing his name. Amid countless offers of free beer, one fan had
his name printed on a club shirt, while some reports claimed an overzealous
supporter named his newborn child after the correspondent.

Sheridan tweeted his reaction: 'Shit way to qualify but don't care.'
Malone has since recalled how surprised he was by the reaction to his
chance intervention.

Sheridan too was taken aback at the time, but by the size of the club he had joined. 'It probably took me by surprise at how big the club was, and the pressure the fans put on the clubs there.' He added, 'People will say, "it's a big team but it's in a small, little league, small country". Pressure is still pressure.'

Still, he quickly sought to replace Malone as the fan's favourite Irishman, leading the club to a league and cup double that year, with APOEL earning another league title in Sheridan's second and final season. His previously mentioned Champions League duels with Europe's leading lights were as much a highlight of his time with APOEL as the five winners medals (including two Cypriot Super Cups) he picked up along the way. One of several standout moments was scoring the second goal in a 2–0 Cypriot Cup final win over Ermis Aradippou on 21 May 2014.

Somewhat controversially, he joined cross-city rivals Omonia Nicosia that summer, where the goals flowed with more regularity, even though the trophies did not. After eighteen months at Omonia Nicosia, in February 2017 he left Cyprus behind to seek a new challenge in Poland. In the goalscoring form of his life, he sought to strike while the iron was hot.

He still had the Irish set-up at the forefront of his mind. 'I wanted to go because I thought it would give me a better chance to get into the Ireland squad. I thought they would have deemed the Polish league a better league than Cyprus.' And he was able to continue his fine form in Poland. 'When I moved to Poland, playing with Jagiellonia, I was playing really good, scoring. If I was Polish, for that period, I probably would've been called up to the Polish national team. They're quite good at that – when players are doing well in the [domestic] league they call them into the national team.'

Sheridan's arrival in Białystok, in the north-east of the country, came in the middle of their best-ever Ekstraklasa season. Sheridan hit eight goals in fourteen appearances for the club between March and June of that year, as they finished runners-up. He was scoring as regularly as any Irish striker receiving call-ups at that time. But his phone never rang. There was no new-message 'ping'.

His first coach at the club, Michał Probierz, offered a helping hand. 'I remember at international breaks, he'd say to me, "Do you want me to phone someone? Do you want me to phone Martin O'Neill?".' Sheridan, with his laid-back demeanour, which perhaps betrayed his genuine desire to achieve further international recognition, declined the assistance. 'Nah, it's okay. I don't want to look too desperate.'

Jagiellonia followed up a second-place finish by again ending the season as runners-up in 2018. European qualification was secured in both instances. In the years since, Sheridan has laid his hat at Wellington Phoenix in the A-League, Israel's Ironi Kiryat Shmona and back in Poland, with Wisła Płock. His start at Płock had begun in auspicious circumstances. Making his debut in early February 2020, he entered the fray as a seventy-fourth minute substitute with his new club 2–0 up on Pogoń Szczecin. By the end, they had lost 2–3. A matter of weeks later, Poland, and the world, much like the Płock defence that day, shut down.

Arguably Ireland's most well-travelled footballer, it is a blessing that Sheridan had the nomadic tendencies that opened his eyes to opportunities all around the world. He believed it would have been difficult to return to any level of prominence in the UK at any time in the last decade after he first made the move east. 'It's very hard to get back into the UK once you've left. It doesn't help when every move you make is being described as "obscure". When I went abroad, I probably felt I was playing the best I ever had compared to when I was younger. I feel like I was a better player, playing with more technical players.' But the stigma of playing away from the UK still exists, Sheridan feels. 'It's seen as not good. It's deemed a bad move. You're not good enough to play in the Premier League or the Championship, so you go abroad.'

As a result, Sheridan believes there is still a reluctance among Irish players to look overseas for career opportunities. And Sheridan admits that he thought likewise, for a time. 'Before I went to Cyprus I probably underestimated the quality that was there of players and teams. It's hard to blame people for being ignorant towards it if they don't know anything about it. I'm not going to expect people to have a great knowledge of the Cypriot league or the Polish league. I've always been lucky that I have Celtic appearances. It gives me a springboard in my career that I've played at Celtic. A lot of clubs would start off and say, "he played at Celtic, we'll give him a chance".'

However, despite the stigma, it can lead to incredible opportunities. 'There's much better players than me that have never got the chance to play in the Champions League or even Europa League because they've been in England. They've probably made a lot, lot more money, but in terms of getting the chance to play in Europe it's definitely a better, a more accessible way to do it.'

Sheridan took those opportunities. His varied career is unparalleled, at least by another male Irish footballer – though the same could be said for one Irish stalwart who has enjoyed a decade-long spell in the very best leagues in women's football.

Diane Caldwell was just a Girl on the Train. As a teenager, she attended Mount Temple Comprehensive School in Clontarf. Every morning, she would leave her home in Balbriggan and get the train to the city centre's Connolly Station before hopping on a bus for the final leg of her journey.

One morning, a twelve-year-old Caldwell was reading a football magazine en route to Connolly when she caught the attention of a man sitting opposite. He asked for a look at the magazine. Deviating from the 'Don't talk to strangers' edict she had been taught ad nauseam at home and school, she obliged.

The magazine had a photo of the Republic of Ireland's women's national team on the back cover. The man, Dermot Kilmurry, told her that one of the players photographed was Claire Scanlan, his best friend's daughter. He knew one of the Irish international players. Caldwell processed the information. This was big. In her eyes, this man was someone to know.

Such is the way with morning commutes, they would continue to see each other on occasion, Caldwell heading for Clontarf and Mr Kilmurry leaving the train at Connolly to make his way to the city centre, where he worked for CIÉ. They talked on an intermittent basis whenever their paths crossed. Football dominated the discussion. After one such discussion on a return trip home, he passed on the young girl's details to Scanlan, who was playing at Leeds United at the time.

Caldwell was playing for local team Balbriggan United, not one of the benchmarks in women's junior football. No one had heard of them, and the prospect of playing for Ireland seemed remote, a pipe dream. The kind of thing football-mad kids read about in magazines. However, against all the odds, a debut for the Republic of Ireland Under-17s – at the age of just fourteen, no less – soon followed. Almost twenty years later, Caldwell still cannot be sure that it was Scanlan who had a word with the national team's underage coaches to give her a shot. She'd just call it an educated guess on her part.

Mr Kilmurry went on to become a family friend, and would regularly attend her international games at underage and senior level with her father, Kenneth. He and the Caldwells stay in touch to this day.

As for Scanlan, having returned from America and her one season playing professionally in Japan, she had re-joined the Irish national team and proved her worth immediately, being named the 1999 FAI Women's Senior International Player of the Year. During this period, she would send her young fan memorabilia and autographs, including from fellow professionals such as Arsenal and Ireland stalwarts Emma Byrne and Ciara Grant. Soon Scanlan and Caldwell would be teammates. In fact, Caldwell would go on to play alongside Scanlan, Grant and Byrne in that Irish team. She made her debut for the senior side at seventeen, playing alongside a thirty-four-year-old Scanlan, who still had three more years of service to the Girls in Green left to give.

'It was surreal,' Caldwell remembers of her international debut on 16 March 2006. It was against Denmark in that year's edition of the Algarve Cup, an annual invitational cup for women's national teams. 'Claire was someone I certainly wanted to emulate. I was lucky I had her to look up to. You hear a lot of female players who didn't have any role models. Claire was a massive inspiration for me.'

Both players entered as substitutes that day, in a 4–0 loss. Nine days later, Caldwell's competitive bow came as a replacement for Scanlan in a World Cup qualifier against Switzerland at the Gurzelen Stadion in Biel/Bienne.

Scanlan, seventeen years Caldwell's senior, herself grew up completely unaware of the scale, scope and opportunity of women's football. That said, her time playing in Japan alongside some luminaries of the women's game marked her out as someone unique – a trendsetter, a globetrotter too. And now Caldwell looked to follow her example.

Following a spell in the United States at Hofstra University, Caldwell's first taste of the professional game came in Iceland, during a short stint at Þór/KA. She soon moved onto Norway, where she spent four seasons in which she was exposed to virtually everything the game could throw at her.

Avaldsnes were a club with no history to speak of but bountiful supplies of ambition, owned by Arne Utvik, an über-wealthy businessman who operates as one of the largest property developers in the private market in the Haugaland region in western Norway. Utvik has been a long-time investor and board member at the club, and is believed to have injected over twenty million Norwegian kroner into the club over the previous decade. Since arriving at the club in 2008, his financial backing has helped them gain promotion to the Toppserien, win the NM Cupen Women in 2017 and get into the Champions League. That has been via capital investment in facilities and bankrolling their rise with a number of high-profile acquisitions from Europe and beyond. He was a man convinced that success was for sale, and he certainly had the financial wherewithal to buy it.

They became the first fully professional club team in Norway, with Caldwell just one of a host of foreign international players brought into the fold. The Irishwoman played alongside Brazilian stars Rosana and Debinha (whom she has since been reunited with at North Carolina Courage), and prolific Norwegian striker Cecilie Pedersen.

In four seasons at the club, she played under four managers: Tor Martin Hegrenes, Roar Wold, Arne Møller and Tom Nordlie. The latter left the club before the end of the 2015 season, with a cup final imminent and with his team on the cusp of Champions League qualification. (It emerged in 2018 that he had been removed following allegations of sexual harassment made against him by a player, the Icelandic international Hólmfríður Magnúsdóttir.)

Caldwell, all steely-eyed determination and with a burning desire to compete at the very top of elite women's competition, felt at home at Avaldsnes despite the on- and off-field drama that often threatened to overshadow efforts on the pitch. 'The project was so motivating. We were gunning to be the best. I loved that.' There was also a level of competition for places that she hadn't experienced before. 'You're challenged. You don't know who's going to come in the next window. They signed two centre backs in one window so there were five centre backs competing for two places. I was thinking, "Okay, let's do this". I've never had that much competition before and I relished it. For the first time, I thought this was what professional football really was. We were quickly becoming the best team in Norway. But it was turbulent, every season there was turbulent.'

The ambition was to turn Avaldsnes into a seat of power in women's football, but they only partially succeeded in doing so. For all their star power, they wanted more and sometimes failed in their attempts to bring players in. US superstar Abby Wambach came close to signing but ultimately did not. Utvik, who was a constant presence in the dugout and during team meetings, failed to hide his displeasure when not getting what he wanted. Looking back,

Caldwell can see that something was missing. 'There was always something in the club that wasn't right. It wasn't cohesive. There was something that divided the team in many different areas. You need team camaraderie; you need everyone working together. For me, that was the difference. Every year, there was some drama. We changed coaches every year.'

While there, she appeared in two cup finals but ended up on the losing side in both. (Avaldsnes would eventually win the cup in 2017, two years after Caldwell departed for Germany.) The versatile player at least only had memories of one cup final defeat. She suffered a potentially serious – but mercifully not – head injury in the 2013 showpiece final defeat to Stabæk, just eleven minutes into the match. It prematurely ended the biggest game in her career to that point.

'I remember being so excited and so confident that we would win and I had that collision early on. Five or ten minutes later my vision was blurry and it was the first time it had properly happened to me. I had a few concussions in America, but nothing as bad as that. I couldn't really focus on the ball after that, and I was thinking that obviously you don't want to be the cause of a goal because of a mistake and you can't see. I kept thinking I should go off, but obviously it's a cup final and you don't want to go off, so I thought I'd keep going and just brush it off. And I stayed on and we got to half-time and I just remember sitting there and I didn't tell anyone. The coach looked at me and asked if I was alright. I think my eyes were glazed over. I said yeah and I wanted to play on but everyone was looking at me. At the time there were no concussion protocols and I just wanted to play on.'

Caldwell went back on for the start of the second half, before finally accepting that she could no longer play. 'I was all over the place. I signalled to the bench that I had to go off. The next thing I remember was, I was in the locker room on one of those emergency beds surrounded by ambulance staff in the brace where they don't let you move your neck and spine, and I remember saying my arm was numb and that was a symptom of the concussion and they rushed me to hospital and did a CT scan on my brain.

And then I was released from hospital in the early hours of the morning and we had to travel back to Avaldsnes by plane, so that was my cup final.'

Soon Caldwell decided to move on to Cologne in Germany. But this was to prove a difficult and short-lived period in her career. Upon arrival in February 2016, FC Köln were bottom of the Frauen-Bundesliga and staring relegation to the second tier in the face. The team had promised Caldwell she would be one of several new signings to help catapult Köln to safety, from a position of apparent and seemingly inevitable doom. A promise made was not a promise kept, however, and the Irish international ended up being the only new arrival in the mid-season window. The manager who signed her, Willi Breuer, was then moved into a technical director role. His replacement, Marcus Kühn, was a strange coach, according to Caldwell, who believed his constant chopping and changing of formation and personnel contributed to the team's downfall. Ironically, his failure to generate any kind of consistency in selection, performance and results was one of his few consistent traits. Kühn could not prevent Köln from being relegated, bottom of the twelve-team division. They had managed just three wins in twenty-two league games, shipping sixty goals in that time.

Caldwell realised early on in her time there that this wasn't the right club for her. 'Cologne just didn't fit. It is a big city and I'm not a city girl. The team wasn't good. I got the feeling at Köln we were "the women's team". No one really cared. It didn't mean anything to them. It's a nice club. There's a lot of history, but they had to have a women's team and we never felt supported.'

Caldwell completed ninety minutes just once in six appearances for Köln. New to such a high-class league, it was natural she took time to adapt to the standard. 'It was tough,' she says. Still, as one of only a handful of international players in the squad, her total of 315 minutes across nine games was meagre. After relegation, she knew it was time to move on.

Caldwell's first taste of Germany lasted just four months. It says something about her single-minded, goal-orientated determination that she was undeterred by her unhappy experience at the club, and it did not taint her dream of playing in the country, in a league she had long considered to be the best in Europe.

Determined to stay in Germany, she just had to find a new club. Mercifully, she had caught the eye of SC Sand when they travelled to Cologne that March. In just her third outing for the club, she played in midfield and impressed sufficiently to garner interest and ultimately a contract – even though Köln lost that game 1–5.

Located in the south west corner of Germany, Sand is just over seven miles from Strasbourg across the French border and an hour away from the nearest German city, Freiburg. It offered Caldwell a small-town lifestyle and, more importantly, women's football was the headline act at SC Sand.

The deal to bring the twenty-seven-year-old to the club was nearing completion when she attended the 2016 DFB-Pokal final, where Sand were narrowly beaten 2–1 by a Wolfsburg team containing Lena Goeßling, Alex Popp and Swedish legend Nilla Fischer. This was the level to which she was ascending.

Her time at Sand mirrored that of Avaldsnes in that Caldwell formed part of a group that punched above their weight, going toe to toe with more established teams and regularly bloodying their noses. Her first season there culminated in Sand earning an eighth-place league finish and a DFB-Pokal final appearance. They went down narrowly again to Wolfsburg, losing 2–1. Cup success continued to elude her.

Colin Bell, the manager, left in February of that season to take over as Republic of Ireland manager. It was a bittersweet moment for the player, who was losing a respected coach on a day-to-day basis. However, she was confident her Ireland team would benefit greatly from their new man at the helm.

The Irishwoman would spend four seasons at Sand, ultimately being named club captain in her final campaign. With her short time at Köln included, she has spent more time in Germany than anywhere in her career. But it wasn't perfect. Widely considered – including by Caldwell herself – as the world's best league when she first arrived in 2016, it doesn't hold that exalted status today. 'The DFB [the German Football Association] are living in the Stone Age. They are predominantly males who are making decisions at the highest level, and the majority of clubs aren't interested in the women's game. They probably think they are one of the best, but I think they are stagnating and not forward thinking to stay ahead of everyone else, or even get back ahead. The standards are going down. The level has diluted a lot.'

Eager to continue to test herself against the best, in early 2021 Caldwell left Europe behind, signing for North Carolina Courage, one of the leading teams in the National Women's Soccer League in America. Ironically, her arrival at the Courage, co-owned by tennis superstar Naomi Osaka, marks the first time since she left Raheny United in 2006 that Caldwell has shared a club dressing room with an international teammate. In fact, Denise O'Sullivan played a significant role in Caldwell's U-turn decision to swap Europe for the US. 'Denise is a lot like me. She's very goal-orientated and she's very determined. What she values is what I value. It was a no-brainer with the stature of the club and the players that are there. It is the biggest move of my career in terms of who they are and what they've done.'

It's not as though the States is an unfamiliar place to Caldwell. 'I was in America for a long time, five years, through university and doing my master's. I loved my time there, but I had never foreseen myself going back. I was enjoying playing in Europe and being close to Ireland. The leagues are developing in Europe. I thought I'd stay there.'

As for her life after the game, Caldwell will likely return to Germany and set up home there once her time has come. It has been the perfect fit for her. 'I wouldn't call myself a homebird. Two weeks at home and I'm ready to go back. I know I don't have what I have in the US, and in Germany, available to me in Ireland.'

But for now she's enjoying the experience of travelling, seeing the world through playing football. 'The experience of moving and challenging yourself to fit into a new environment doesn't seem as daunting as when I was younger. I was never nervous about making moves. I was never homesick, luckily. I took to travelling quite well because I was so focused on my football and so goal orientated.'

For certain Irish players, like Sheridan and Caldwell, looking to the continent has turned the aspirational, almost fanciful, to the attainable. The same is true for Claire O'Riordan.

'Yesterday is history, tomorrow is a mystery but today is a gift. That's why it's called the present.' It is one of those popular, oft-quoted, sometimes misremembered internet inspirations. No one is quite sure who originally said it. Some say Eleanor Roosevelt, others not. Claire O'Riordan, a Republic of Ireland international who plays for German Bundesliga side MSV Duisburg, remembers the quote from the animated movie *Kung Fu Panda 2*. After three years in the industrial, inland port city, she is certainly open to whatever comes next in her burgeoning, if belated, professional career.

O'Riordan takes things day by day, week by week. She has never had a grand plan for her life, sporting or otherwise. Football easily could not have been part of it. Even at nineteen, in her second year of study at Carlow IT, she was, by her own admission, utterly naive to the infrastructure and opportunities available to her to play the game at a high level, having only played soccer with her friends – mainly boys – on the roads of Newcastle West in Limerick.

In the same year, 2013, O'Riordan discovered that Ireland had underage and senior women's national football teams. The former had passed her by completely. At least the senior national team was something to aspire to, she thought – little realising that five years later, she would sign a first professional contract with a top-flight team in what many considered the best league in Europe, the Frauen-Bundesliga.

She arranged a trial with then Wexford Youths boss John Flood, who reminded her of the obligations required. A college student juggling club and county commitments in hurling and Gaelic football, as well as representing Carlow IT in third-level competition, O'Riordan was already committed to sport. However, she knew that these other sports would have to suffer if she wanted to succeed at football. Ultimately forced into a choice of where to centre her focus, she chose football. And her commitment was total. 'My weekends would be dedicated to Wexford. I wouldn't be able to see my family. It was good that I was in my second year when I went to Youths, because in first year, I couldn't wait to get home to see my family. I was so homesick.'

Here was a player who possessed a steely determination, often masked by an easy-going, personable exterior. Weekends often involved nine-hour bus journeys – three buses there and three back – to attend games. 'John still talks about that to this day. He wanted a player like that. Looking back, I probably couldn't kick snow off a rope. I had to learn to come up to the level of the Women's National League. I had never been coached before. I'm ashamed to say it but I barely knew the positions on the pitch.'

After joining Wexford Youths, O'Riordan would go on to win three league titles in five seasons at Ferrycarrig Park. A latecomer to the game in a structured sense, O'Riordan's exploits at Wexford – where she scored in excess of seventy goals in her five seasons – garnered her international recognition by the age of twenty-one. Her rise has been rapid, not that she sees it that way. The Limerick woman believes her late start means she is still playing catch-up. 'How much you put into it is what you'll get out of it. I wish I was as talented as Katie McCabe [Irish international and Arsenal midfielder] but that's just not me. I have to work on other areas to get up to the standard. It's been a long journey. I came to the realisation that I am about three years behind in terms of my development.'

After making her Ireland debut under Sue Ronan in the 2016 Cyprus Cup, it was her replacement Colin Bell who impressed on O'Riordan – as he did with many of his home-based players – that she should pursue a professional career. While the majority of non-Ireland-based players at his disposal were based in England in the growing Women's Super League, Bell's history in Germany, where he had coached for the majority of his thirty-year career, led to an opportunity for the versatile forward. He recommended her to MSV Duisburg coach Thomas Gerstner. A trial followed in the summer of 2018.

Flying to Düsseldorf for her trial was the first time O'Riordan had ever flown alone. Even aged twenty-three, she found the experience a daunting one. She does remember, though, how a chance run-in with Bell at Dublin Airport allowed him the opportunity to pass on some words of encouragement. 'Colin knew he had a player who was committed to doing whatever it took to become a professional player. I was willing to do whatever it took. I didn't have an agent. I wasn't the face of anyone. I was a Limerick girl who came to Wexford. I did the best I could. I was committed and raw. Very raw.'

She obviously impressed at the trial, getting her first professional contract. One year in length, but it was still a contract.

Arriving in Duisburg in the summer of 2018, where home games are played at the unassuming PCC-Stadion in Homberg, O'Riordan says she found the experience 'mindblowing', much as she had upon stepping onto the Ferrycarrig Park pitch for the first time five years earlier. In Germany, she says, there are Under-15 girls teams who have more weekly training hours than teams playing in Ireland's senior national league. 'The speed and quality blew me away,' she says. The departures of players the ilk of Pernille Harder and Melanie Leupolz for England and elsewhere have made the task for the likes of O'Riordan easier, but only slightly.

Duisburg itself is historically known as one of Germany's major industrial and trade centres. After the Second World War, in which large swathes of the city were destroyed by Allied bombs, the city had to be entirely rebuilt. What followed in the decades to follow was the decline of the mining and steel industry that had supported the city's growth to that point. While, O'Riordan says, it offers relatively little in terms of aesthetic or cultural pleasures, nearby Düsseldorf and Cologne make up for the shortcomings in that area.

Her first game as a professional is memorable for all the wrong reasons. Duisburg were turned over 0–4 at home by SGS Essen. A week later, a trip to Bavarian giants Bayern Munich ended in the same scoreline. The visitors were no match for a team featuring stars of the women's game like Jill Roord, Lina Magull and Sara Däbritz.

It was not the easiest of starts for O'Riordan. 'I turned around after the first game and said I don't know if I can do this.'

Perhaps in those early moments she might have considered how it would have been easier for her to move to England rather than Germany, where language and other cultural differences can prove obstacles in the way of succeeding on the pitch. 'It's typical of anyone to look at England. I would like to experience it, but I decided to play professionally and explore the world.' And she wanted to stick with her desire to experience the world beyond the British Isles. 'Through football, I'm getting to see the world.' She envies the likes of Denise O'Sullivan, who in-between seasons with North Carolina Courage in the NWSL, has turned out for W-League's Western Sydney Wanderers and Brighton & Hove Albion in the WSL.

Still, it's true that acclimatising to Germany was a hurdle she struggled to jump at first. She resented being in Germany, away from her family, friends and the livestock on her family farm. Still, she persevered, and soon began to prosper. Having signed a one-year deal on arrival, she subsequently penned a two-year extension twelve months later – a clear indication of her importance in the eyes of Gerstner. That usefulness has manifested itself in her utility to her team. The Limerick woman has lined out at centre back, full back, right wing, attacking midfield and as a central striker. The initial change from striker to defender when she arrived in 2018 has been replicated at international level, and what is to come in the future will be with that in mind. She is resolute and proud of the progress she has made. 'It is difficult, but I know I'm here for the right reasons. I'm family-orientated and I miss them. I had to refocus on my task, being a professional footballer. Knowing what I have overcome and achieved over the last few years, since I was seventeen, I never would have thought this is where I would be.'

All of these sacrifices have allowed her to play professionally among Europe's elite, and become a better footballer. 'Moving here, my ultimate goal was to become a better player. It was ultimately to help the women's national team. If that meant leaving home and leaving my family and friends, then it was something I wanted to do. It was an amazing opportunity. It's been difficult, but it's the best thing for me.'

Such has been O'Riordan's assimilation into German life that when she returns to Dublin to take part in international camps now, some of her on-field instructions are barked out in German. That is something her teammates, including Louise Quinn, can attest to. 'It's scary,' the defender says. Despite her command on in-game instruction, she admits the language is 'mind-boggling'. It wasn't a subject she took in secondary school, when she studied at Scoil Mhuire agus Íde. It wasn't something she ever felt she would need. That was, of course, until football – the global game – came along.

Another marker of her success in Germany came in March 2021. An Irishwoman abroad, St Patrick's Day holds an obvious significance for a player who wears her Irishness as a green badge of honour. That was the day the Irish striker-turned-defender scored her first professional goal. After shipping an eighty-ninth-minute goal to SC Sand, it looked as if Duisburg were set to fall to an eleventh defeat of a difficult season. That was until, moments later, O'Riordan capitalised on an error by Sand goalkeeper Jasmin Pal to poke into the net. It was a reward for all her hard work.

For this late bloomer, the hard work will continue for as long as she continues to play the game – in Germany or elsewhere. It is a work ethic forged in her formative years, which were spent not on the pitch but in the paddock with her father. 'I'm a mini-John O'Riordan,' she says of her father. 'It's something we've always done together. It's such hard work. It's real manual labour. You could go out to the farm at 5 a.m. and not come in until eight or nine that evening. There is nothing I'd rather be doing at that moment.'

Except maybe playing ball, that is.

While O'Riordan endured some rudimentary difficulties in acclimatising to life in Germany, some others ventured to far more volatile parts of the continent to earn their living, and in doing so found they learned much more about themselves than they could have ever imagined.

At twenty-six years of age, a late-night trip to a Donetsk branch of McDonald's became a chastening experience for Darren O'Dea. Something so straightforward, so everyday in its simplicity, became a depth so low, he can recall it in vivid detail years later.

Five weeks earlier, the Republic of Ireland international had swapped Canada – where the defender had spent a year starring for the MLS franchise in Toronto – for Ukraine. He was now a Metalurh Donetsk player. Living, temporarily, at the club's state-of-the-art training complex located south of the city, O'Dea was in the process of securing an apartment so that his wife Melissa and two-year-old daughter Lucia could travel from Glasgow to join him.

One night, alone and somewhat stifled in the small bedroom provided for players to lodge at the facility, the Dubliner decided to make a dash for some fast food. He hadn't left the training ground alone before, despite getting a car a few weeks previously. Unsure of himself in his surroundings, and with no handle whatsoever on an alien language, the short trip generated no shortage of anxiety. 'I was miserable, I wasn't sleeping. From being driven around, I had seen a McDonald's down the road from the training ground. I had it mapped out in my head how to get there.'

Or he thought he had.

'It was pitch black,' he recalls. 'There are no streetlights on the roads in Donetsk. The signs aren't only a different language but a different alphabet. I got lost. And eventually parked up.' To make matters worse, his car had no sat-nav, while his foreign phone was rendered useless when not connected to Wi-Fi.

As a result, O'Dea found himself alone on a desolate stretch of an obscure side road. 'I thought I was going to have to sleep there until the light came up. I sat there for around twenty minutes.'

He eventually called Melissa, 2,000 miles away in Glasgow. He was in a total panic. Her words at least had a calming effect. He had left the training ground at 9 p.m. and eventually found his way back, returning five hours later, at 2 a.m. An attempt at a routine trip had shaken him, reduced him. He didn't have as much as a chicken nugget to show for his efforts. 'I woke up the next day and didn't have anyone to confide in, to tell them what had happened or to ask for help. I had so much anxiety.'

He is reluctant to use the term 'depression', but his early weeks in Donetsk mentally tested him to a degree he had never felt before. He was failing, in his own eyes. His face was a tell. When Melissa eventually arrived in Donetsk weeks later, she could immediately see her husband's stress. He looked gaunt. He'd aged three years in six weeks, she thought.

The experience of Donetsk had already hit him like a tonne of bricks. He wanted to shy away from anyone and everything. He wasn't sleeping, and panic became his default setting. The anxiety of getting his hair cut or ordering a taxi were too much. The latter forced him into shaving his head, a close cut he hadn't opted for before or since.

O'Dea had moved to Ukraine at the second time of asking. Upon leaving Celtic in the summer of 2012, and prior to his move to MLS, there had been interest from another Ukrainian Premier League outfit, Arsenal Kiev. They had offered a huge financial package, dwarfing anything O'Dea had received at Celtic, where he had performed in the

UEFA Champions League to high praise. Despite an initial 'no' from the player, a more in-depth analysis at the figures prompted further investigation. He was close to signing, but ultimately the talks led nowhere. The club went bankrupt the following year, before reforming in a new guise in 2014.

O'Dea joined Metalurh following his exit from Toronto FC, and in doing so followed in the footsteps of some high-calibre players who had represented the club, including Yaya Touré, Henrikh Mkhitaryan and Jordi Cruyff. Arriving in July 2013, he soon had to get his head around a managerial change. Two weeks on from his debut, Yuriy Maksymov was replaced by the Russian Sergei Tashuyev.

A journeyman manager for which Metalurh was his fifteenth posting in a twenty-year career, Tashuyev couldn't speak a word of English, nor had O'Dea any Russian to begin with. He would pick up some phrases along the way. The manager would refer to his Irish defender as 'Fucking Shit', not because he was, but due to that being O'Dea's most common refrain on the training pitch. 'That's all he heard. That's all he could hear. He'd just hear me say it. He didn't know what it meant. I was always moaning about something.' O'Dea had grown up in an institution at Celtic, a title-winning behemoth with European Cup pedigree too. He was single-minded about how he acted, behaved and trained. He was right, and the rest was 'Fucking Shit'.

The level of player he shared a dressing room with shocked the Irishman, who in his own words believed he was walking into a 'bang average Ukrainian team'. Still, what he came to understand in Ukraine was that there were different ways to do things. It proved an eye-opening experience for the centre back. At first, 'I was banging my head against the wall. It's like screaming at the top of your lungs but nobody can hear you. Eventually, I shut up and opened my eyes. I accept there are a million ways to live, to coach, to behave. I accept everything and everyone now. Ukraine broke me down in that respect.'

O'Dea was substituted at half-time in his debut game for Metalurh, a 1–1 draw at home to Karpaty Lviv. Seven days later, away at Vorskla,

O'Dea scored what turned out to be the winning goal in a 2–1 victory. It was a reasonable start to life in the old Eastern Bloc.

He planned to cruise through his time in Ukraine, earn his money and be off on his way. He had signed a lucrative three-year contract. O'Dea believed, as an international player who had played in the Champions League and won titles in Scotland, that he would arrive at Donetsk's second club (Shakhtar are the city's major footballing force) as their big signing. It turned out that he was far from their best-paid player, but as if to prove that he was a key addition to the squad, he stepped up into a rich vein of form. 'I was physically and technically at my peak in Ukraine because of the training. My life was as miserable and boring as you can get, so I lived in the gym 24/7. I was at my peak. I was actually getting better. I was playing some of my best football there.'

Not that everyone noticed, particularly his new international manager. When joining the club, O'Dea had been included in every Republic of Ireland squad picked by Giovanni Trapattoni since 2009. He hadn't always played – amassing only twenty caps – but with the Italian known to be loyal to players, O'Dea was always selected. His involvement continued when he had left Britain behind to join Toronto, and he expected it would continue during his time at Metalurh. A change of manager in the autumn of 2013, however, would change things. Trapattoni was out and Martin O'Neill, via interim boss Noel King, was appointed.

O'Dea was not selected by King for the World Cup-qualifying double-header against Germany and Kazakhstan in October, and he didn't receive a call from King, or the FAI, to break the news. It was a gripe for the defender, who felt disrespected. A member of the FAI's administrative staff phoned to tell O'Dea he was on standby. She said King would call, but it didn't come.

That signalled the end for O'Dea, who acknowledged as much soon after. He never expected a call from O'Neill. 'I was out of sight, out of mind. I probably would have agreed with the fact that I wasn't playing at a level that was perceived to be good enough to play for Ireland.'

Not that he necessarily agreed with the perception. 'I could argue against that. I was better than I was before, but no one knew it.' The former Celtic player was playing in a team competing towards the top of their domestic league. They had beaten Dynamo Kiev 2–1 and Metalist Kharkiv 3–0, while they drew 2–2 with Shakhtar at home.

Were prejudices at play? Once a player leaves behind the English (and to a lesser extent Scottish) leagues, were they cast aside, left on the scrapheap of 'proper' football consciousness? At both international and club level, O'Dea believed so. 'I was never really bothered about the Ireland thing, because I understood their thinking. But, looking back, it probably isn't the right way. They should know every player. Ireland doesn't have a big-enough pool of players to dismiss anyone.'

Meanwhile, football people in Britain – managers, coaches, scouts, chairmen – were quicker to dismiss him once he left the British Isles behind for Eastern Europe. For example, when his time in Ukraine was up, he struggled to be taken seriously in England. 'This is not my opinion, it's a fact. I'd left two years previously as an international player and had half a dozen offers from clubs that wanted to sign me for thousands of pounds a week. Two years later, I was physically and mentally in a better position and had more experience. But no one would go near you. You have no interest. England was a closed market. If you go abroad, you have to accept you're not coming back. If you do come back, it's at a much lower level. It probably is ignorance, but not purposely. I had that ignorance too. When I was growing up, in terms of football, I was ignorant to everywhere else.'

By his own admission, the move to Ukraine was rooted in pragmatism, the driving force being financial. He was there to maximise his earnings for a year, maybe two or even three, should he complete his full contract. Unlike in Toronto before, setting up roots was never on his mind. 'I was going in absolutely blind to it. I wasn't going to move there, buy a house, try to set up roots there. I wasn't going to have real stability. I knew it wasn't going to be home. In the Ukraine it was "How much am I getting paid?"

I had no emotion in it. There was no emotion for the club. I couldn't care less. I wanted to win, I wanted to compete. I wanted to be the best, but with the club it was, "You pay me". The rest of the clubs I gave my heart and soul to. I integrated myself into it. With Ukraine, it was about earning money and playing football at a good level.'

It transpired that O'Dea would never have been able to make Donetsk a home, anyway, even had he been inclined. A wave of demonstrations and civil unrest in the country, primarily in Kiev, against the President Viktor Yanukovych, began in late 2013 and escalated in the new year. It led to the removal of Yanukovych, an overthrown government, and then to Vladimir Putin's annexation of Crimea, which resulted in significant pro-Russian unrest in the east of the country.

At its very outset, the anti-government protests in Kiev were viewed from afar by O'Dea. He had been home in Glasgow for Christmas and was aware of the protest movement. It hadn't spread to the east of the country by the time he was to return, and with football seemingly continuing as normal, he saw no reason not to go back.

At the end of a six-week mid-season training camp in Antalya in Turkey, Metalurh returned to the city in March. However, by that time, the protests had spread. Putin's forces had moved into Crimea by this point, while pro-Russian protesters had taken control of some government buildings in Donetsk, which was the very epicentre of the unrest in Donbas, the city now gripped by a civil war.

Things had gotten very real – but football, as ever, ploughed on regardless.

O'Dea's life was affected only slightly at first. Text messages from club staff or teammates would advise players not to leave their accommodation if there were protests nearby. He was aware of the trouble without ever really grasping the seriousness of his strange circumstances. Danger lurked a stone's throw away. He did at least make some concessions to the precarious nature of his situation. 'That's when I started to carry my passport with me at all times in case I had to get out.'

Having left the training ground residence, O'Dea was now holed up in a hotel. It was, he decided, the easiest way to live there, as he needed help with everyday living. He missed Melissa back in Glasgow, on whom he relied heavily. At home, coverage on the ongoing and escalating violence in Ukraine was inescapable, which only made Melissa and his family worry more over his well-being. This was becoming a major international story.

There was even the extraordinary incident aboard the team bus when, with air space closed, the Irishman and his teammates were accosted by machine-gun-toting Russian militants at a fake border established on the edge of Crimea. During a four-hour stand-off, he himself had a weapon thrust in his face during an innocent attempt to go to the toilet. It is the story O'Dea most often regales to those who ask about that time in Ukraine. 'It was mad,' he says simply.

In eleven games played amidst the backdrop of the ongoing civil war, the death count rising daily, Metalurh enjoyed six wins and two draws. It was by some distance their best patch of form of the season. Their Irish defender played in seven of these games, featuring in all six victories and helping his team to four clean sheets in that run. He also scored the club's forty-fifth and final goal of the season, a consolation in a 1–3 loss to Dnipro on the final day. It would prove to be his last act for the club.

An ankle break during the off-season delayed O'Dea's return to Ukraine – much to a twisted sort of delight for Melissa, friends and family. Then it was revealed that fighting was having an effect on the club. They were forced to leave Donetsk and their small 5,000-seater stadium to play their home games in first Lviv and then more semi-permanently in Kiev. An inevitable decline began.

While recovering from his ankle break, O'Dea received word that the club were making drastic attempts to remove high-earners from their employ. He was told either to accept a fifty per cent wage cut or to leave the club as a free agent. With two years to run on a fruitful contract, he politely declined and finally returned to Ukraine, but not Donetsk, to complete his rehabilitation. 'It was a stand-off. I was waiting to get paid up. They were hoping I walked,' he remembers.

A compromise was ultimately reached and a year into his Eastern European adventure, it was all over. By that time, the club was based out of an unused holiday resort in Irpin, on the outskirts of Kiev. The club would ultimately declare bankruptcy in the summer of 2015.

Donbas, and the solitary shell of a life O'Dea had lived there became distant in theory but not in memory. If anything, it is only in hindsight that O'Dea can see how unhappy he was during that period. 'I probably never realised how unhappy I was until I broke my ankle and realised I was delighted I was getting to stay at home. Yet, with the injury, my career was in tatters.'

Looking back at his initial weeks in Donetsk – the loneliness, disorientation, self-doubt and all – led O'Dea to question the motivation for his move to Ukraine. It quickly dawned on him that money was not the be-all-and-end-all. What use was money when he had to live without his young family and friends? What the fuck had he been doing? Sure he adapted, and there had been brief periods of time – moments – where pleasure and satisfaction were gained, but they had not been worth the unhappiness.

Still, now he can say that his twelve months in an ostensibly modern European city (it has hosted games during Euro 2012) turned war zone has moulded him more so than any other experience in his life.

10

THE SECOND GENERATION

The majority of players focused on in the book so far have been Irish-born, with some exceptions, such as English-born Caleb Folan. He is far from alone in the list of British-born Republic of Ireland stars who qualified for the country by virtue of Irish mothers or fathers, grandparents too. But while those players represent a large swathe of those Irishmen who take to continental Europe and beyond for their next career step – see Tony Cascarino (France), John Aldridge (Spain), Mick McCarthy (France), David Connolly (Netherlands) and Aiden McGeady (Russia), for example – there are others with roots elsewhere. They include Patrick Kohlmann, the German-born defender who represented Republic of Ireland's Under-21s while on the fringes of Borussia Dortmund in the early 2000s, and Barry Maguire, the Dutch-Irish midfielder who once helped FC Utrecht vanquish Celtic from the UEFA Cup. They, however, are just the tip of the iceberg.

There is also the Norwegian-born Sean McDermott, whose early years involved a brief stint living in his father's home county of Donegal. For Robert, Sean and Kevin McDermott, adapting to life in the small village of Mountcharles was far from easy. Having grown up in Kristiansand in Norway, the brothers had moved to Ireland's north-west with their father Terence and mother Arna. There, they lived near their beloved grandparents, Patsy and Ann.

Upon arrival in the summer of 2002, the opportunity for the sports-mad brothers to try their hand at Gaelic football with local club St Nauls was one the older siblings welcomed with both arms. That summer was an adventure but soon turned to an ordeal, when the three boys were enrolled in a nearby national school. It turned out the transition from Norwegian schooling to that in rural Ireland was a tricky one for the McDermotts.

At break times, Sean remembers being segregated from his brothers. The classes were not permitted to mix, and neither were boys and girls allowed to play together – even if they shared a classroom. Sean wasn't allowed to go to the front of the school to check in on Kevin, who was just five years old at the time.

The boys had come from a school in Kristiansand where there were no uniforms and children could move freely around the playground during break. They also found the teachers much stricter than their Scandinavian counterparts.

Sean remembers his first day at the school vividly. He recalls his teacher saying, 'Sean, I was expecting a lot more from you today.' The nine-year-old was speaking English, but it hadn't been his first language up to that stage in his young life. 'The school was terrible,' Sean says. 'I did not like it at all. It was completely different to Norway. Maybe it was different up in Donegal, a small town compared to places like Dublin.'

Everything in Donegal had been great to that point, especially for the young boys who adored their grandparents and treasured the chance to be close to them at their home in Glencoagh. However, their summer in the Irish sun was over, and even before the cold snap, the reality had begun to bite. 'As soon as school started, everything changed. It was downhill from there. Of course you need time to adapt. School plays a huge part in that because you are there most of the day, most of the week. The school was a terrible experience, but other than that I was happy there.'

Fortunately for the McDermott children, their stay at the school was a short one, as was the family's time in Mountcharles. Six months later, having failed to settle in Ireland, they travelled back to Norway to resume their life there.

Bar his six months living in Donegal as a boy, and three years in London while playing in Arsenal's academy, Sean McDermott has virtually spent his entire life in Norway. Since 2017, the goalkeeper has played in the country's top flight, the Eliteserien, with Kristiansund – not to be confused with Kristiansand, his hometown. One letter and 344 miles separate the towns, located at opposite ends of the country.

Released by Arsenal in 2012, McDermott has carved out a reputation as one of the finest goalkeepers in Norway. He debuted in the top division there at nineteen, an embryonic stage for a goalkeeper, when playing for Sandnes Ulf, and quickly established himself in a team battling relegation, a fight he helped to win.

McDermott himself was already an Irish underage international by this stage, and had been part of Paul Doolin's Under-19 squad that reached the semi-finals of the European Championships in Tallinn in 2011. Regardless of his growing up immersed in Norwegian life – and his few months of miserable schooling in Donegal – the youngster only had eyes for Ireland.

He had always dreamt of playing for the country where his father was born. He credits his dad for teaching him everything about the game. 'Ireland has always been the team I watched since I was a child. I wanted to play for them, but I love both countries.'

A fixture in Irish youth teams through to Under-21 level, Norway did not prioritise approaching McDermott to switch allegiances, but that moment arrived in 2013, when the Norwegians offered the stopper a chance to compete for a place in their squad for the upcoming European Championships in Israel. There is something of the pragmatist in McDermott. He considered the offer, but ultimately declined. Norway boss Tor Ole Skullerud had offered him a place in the provisional squad, but no guarantee of selection in the final panel. Had there been, Ireland may have lost him.

For a time, McDermott was unsure whether he'd made the right decision. In the years between winning his final Under-21 cap for Ireland against Montenegro in March 2014 and first establishing himself as Kristiansund's number one, McDermott believed he had become a lost soul, especially in the context of international football. He felt he had been consigned to history, forgotten about.

There had been much water under his personal and professional bridge since then. Having fallen down the pecking order at Sandnes Ulf to Iceland international goalkeeper Hannes Þór Halldórsson, he returned to his hometown with IK Start, where again he warmed the substitutes bench. A loan move to second-tier Ullensaker/Kisa in 2016 offered him the chance to reacquaint himself with match minutes before he joined Kristiansund, where he hasn't looked back since.

McDermott, broad shouldered and standing at 6'1", is physically imposing, and he possesses an inner determination and confidence in his ability. Finding himself playing regularly in an upwardly mobile team, his apparent severance from the national team picture disturbed him. 'I remember when I was with the Under-21s, I was playing in the top division in Norway – for Sandnes Ulf – and doing really well. When I was too old for the Under-21s, I should have automatically been considered for the seniors. Of course, I'm young and Ireland had a lot of good goalkeepers. Maybe I wasn't going to be involved anyway. But my name should have been in there. They should be watching you and keeping in contact with you. I needed to at least be in the discussion. That's how football is. When you're not on the biggest stage, you're not that important.' He concedes, however, 'That's how the game is. It's very cynical.'

The goalkeeper, now in his mid-twenties, had fallen through the cracks. Squad announcements would come and go, and though his hope of a call-up never wavered, the outcome was always the same. 'I was never in it. It didn't make sense.'

At the time, Martin O'Neill was selecting goalkeepers such as Aaron McCarey, who had spent much of the season as a substitute at the Scottish

Premiership's Ross County, and Kieran O'Hara, a twenty-two-year-old Manchester United youth player whose first team experience at that point totalled six games on loan at Stockport County and Morecambe in the National League and League Two respectively. In contrast, McDermott was the first-choice goalkeeper at a team looking towards the summit of Norway's top flight.

He surmised that the Irish managerial team didn't know who, or where, he was. He took the initiative to contact the association, first by email and via contacts back in Ireland. Having gotten nowhere, his next punt was contacting the FAI's official Instagram account. Sliding into their DMs is a very millennial way to chase down a senior international call-up. Unconventional in the extreme, it was to pay dividends.

The media team member with responsibility for Instagram took McDermott's message – which simply outlined that he felt he was deserving of a chance – and passed it on to Seamus McDonagh, the former goalkeeper who was serving as O'Neill's goalkeeping coach. Seven days after Ireland beat the United States 2–1 in a friendly at the Aviva Stadium in June 2018, McDonagh flew to Norway. He was in the stands at Kristiansund's modest stadium to see the goalkeeper keep a clean sheet as Kristiansund beat Molde, managed by Ole Gunnar Solskjær, 1–0. It was a landmark result for the club, and was all the more notable as Solskjær is the town's most famous son.

Having taken the lead through a goal from Stian Aasmundsen, the team needed McDermott to preserve the lead late on, and he rushed off his line to superbly block an effort from Molde's much trumpeted young striker. His name? Erling Braut Haaland. Suitably impressed, McDonagh would recommend McDermott be included in Ireland's next two camps in September and October that year. He was back.

'Seamus did a fantastic job of taking the opportunity to come out to Norway and watch us playing Molde. I appreciated that. He took the approach to come out, I didn't ask him. I just wanted them to recognise that I'm playing. There's something wrong when they lose track of players.'

While a debut cap eluded him, he was selected again under Mick McCarthy the following year, when he was at least given the number one shirt (due to first-choice keeper Darren Randolph's desire to wear number 23) if not the in-game chance to stake a claim for it on a regular basis.

That is as close as McDermott has come – so far, anyway. McDonagh departed the FAI when O'Neill stepped down in November 2018. Alan Kelly has since come and gone as goalkeeping coach, replaced by Dean Kiely. McDermott has not received a call-up under Stephen Kenny, and with emerging talents such as Caoimhin Kelleher and Gavin Bazunu staking claims under Ireland's latest manager, McDermott may feel he will again have to remind those making the decisions of his worth.

In part to further his international aspirations, McDermott took a gamble in January 2019, ending his five-season spell at Kristiansund to join Dinamo București. The goalkeeper's time at the eighteen-time Romanian champions was to last a mere seven weeks, however, and a total of three games.

Dinamo were a fallen giant of Romanian and European football. Once perennial qualifiers for European competition, they hadn't made a tournament proper since appearing in the group stage of the Europa League ten years earlier. McDermott was convinced that their dual ambitions were aligned: theirs to re-establish themselves as Romanian's premier team and his to become Ireland's number one goalkeeper.

Anecdotal research was coming back less than positive, and after a trip to the city to scope out the club, his first answer was no. However, after further consideration – and no other offers – the Irishman decided to consider Romania a stepping stone to continental Europe. 'I didn't really get the right vibe at first. But nothing happened with the other teams. I decided to get out of my comfort zone. I'm not afraid to take a risk.'

Joining a struggling team who had won just five of the previous twenty-two league games, McDermott enjoyed a dream start. He kept clean sheets in two victories. It marked the first time in the entire season that Dinamo had secured back-to-back wins. That run would end abruptly a week later when they were defeated 1–2 at home to FC Botoşani.

Two days later, local media reports suggested the club were to bring in a new goalkeeper. The new signing – the Congolese international goalkeeper Parfait Mandanda – duly arrived, and, days later, McDermott asked to leave. Speaking at a press conference, the manager Mircea Rednic said, 'I asked for a goalkeeper, not a libero. He didn't have to be upset,' he added, responding to a question over the decision to drop a new goalkeeper from first to third choice in the space of a week, having taken to life on the field well. 'That's life,' responded an unmoved Rednic. 'I'm very demanding.'

McDermott was shocked by the speed at which things turned sour. 'I got no explanation. I started to speak to people and they were saying that this was normal in Romania – they change the coach and the players every half season if they're not happy. This wasn't a good place for my career.'

Upon his arrival at the club, the number one shirt was already being worn by Romanian Vlad Muţiu. McDermott chose to wear 55, his parents' age at the time. In reality, in the space of seven days, he was as far from the number one position as he could have imagined.

When, within weeks of his arrival, McDermott, via his agent, asked to leave, the club happily agreed, citing his status as their number three goalkeeper. The club, to their credit, released him from his contract and allowed a smooth return to Kristiansund. He was welcomed back home with open arms. 'Life feels so much more stable in Norway.'

However, that experience has not discouraged the goalkeeper from seeking more opportunities to further his career beyond Norway. He is goal-oriented off the pitch, though his main concern on it is more preventative. He is keen to try his luck elsewhere soon, with international ambitions remaining high on his agenda.

In recent years, the goalkeeper has become much closer to God, and it has offered him a fresh outlook on life, but in particular his career. 'I put all my trust in God. I feel like when you look to God, instead of the world, all things are possible.'

He remains optimistic about his future in the game. 'My best years are ahead of me. A move doesn't have to happen right away, it can happen in two years or five. It is out of my control. I feel if I am going to go to the very top it doesn't matter the football system, it doesn't matter who the coach is, what way things are going, no one is going to stop it. I have my focus on God and feel I'm going to get to the top anyway. I'm focusing on developing myself. Everything is in God's timing, not mine.'

While some second-generational Irish footballers choose the nation of their parentage, others decide to play for the country that they see as home. Not that this choice guarantees success either.

In March 2009, Kevin Walker's fledgling career was on an upward curve. Nineteen and having already broken into the senior team at Stockholm's AIK a year earlier, the midfielder looked for all the world like he was set for a far more central role in the team going forward. With another pre-season under his belt – they play a summer season in Sweden, as they do in Ireland – Walker received a first call-up to the Swedish Under-21 national team.

His call-up was a source of pride for the youngster, who was born and bred in Sweden, and especially for his mother Annette, who hailed from the country – even if his father Pat, a Carlow man, had harboured hopes of his son becoming a Boy in Green. Still, he had likely already given up that particular fight, as eldest son Robert had already represented Sweden at various underage levels.

Walker flew to Belgium with the expectation that he would make his Under-21 bow in one of a double-header of friendlies against their Belgian counterparts, a team that included Toby Alderweireld and Radja Nainggolan. He watched his first game from the bench, as the Red Devils churned out a 2–1 victory, but before the second fixture four days later, his world would be turned upside down.

A high fever and sharp pain floored him. He sat out training and the second game, which ended with a Swedish victory by the same score, as doctors monitored his condition. He was put on a flight back to Stockholm, a journey which only heightened his pain. It was only once he had touched back down in Stockholm that the teenager was diagnosed as having blood poisoning.

Walker's football career was stalled but, more starkly, his life was in danger. He was put on a heavy course of antibiotics, taking twelve tablets a day for six months. Having seemingly rid himself of the illness, Walker returned to training, but still he felt pain. When the fever returned, he was hospitalised for a week. It was touch and go. The unpredictable nature of the sepsis meant that neither the young footballer, nor his parents, brother or anyone close to him, could take anything for granted. While the spectre of an on-field injury lurks at every turn as a professional footballer, serious illness is beyond an occupational hazard.

In total, it was thirteen months between appearances on the field. 'I missed the whole season. I had to build myself back up. I had to take a U-turn in my career.'

Walker's period on the sidelines also coincided with a shock title victory in 2009. One of Sweden's most illustrious clubs, they had not claimed a championship since 1998. The year earlier, in Walker's breakthrough season, they had finished a disappointing fifth. A Svenska Cupen triumph completed a double success and accentuated the pain for the youngster.

By the time he was fit to return to play, Walker had fallen down the AIK pecking order, and he had to drop down to the second tier for three separate loan spells. A shot at further international honours passed him by, having represented the Swedes at Under-16, 17 and 19 level.

It is with no small degree of irony that Walker's international debut for Sweden, at Under-16 level, came in Dublin. On 25 April 2005, aged fifteen, Walker turned out for Sweden against the Republic of Ireland.

There was plenty of interest in the Swedish player of Irish heritage, so much so that Sportsfile photographer Brian Lawless singled the young man out to pose for individual shots while leaning casually against a goalpost.

Despite not representing Ireland, a big contingent of family arrived from County Carlow to cheer him on. He posed for photos with his younger cousins Craig and Luke, who were somewhat torn as to exactly who they were supporting on the day.

Terry Dixon and future senior international Harry Arter were the stars for the home side on the day, as senior boss Brian Kerr watched from the sidelines. Relatives weren't shy in making a beeline to Kerr to inform him of Walker's parentage. He knew all about it. Anyone who knows him will attest to that. There are few players, young or old, at any serious level of the game Kerr isn't aware of.

'The status of playing in Sweden is not good enough for the standards that they allegedly have,' Walker says, sixteen years on from that day. He has not represented either country at any level since the last of his Under-19 caps in 2008.

'Realistically, I knew there was a very slight chance of getting into the Ireland squad unless I was in England. In that stage of my career, I was in the Under-19s and I was called up for the Under-21s and I got blood poisoning,' he says of how his career trajectory was set back by that illness. 'That put a dent in my progress. Fulham and Celtic were going to watch me but I sat beside the scouts in the stand instead of playing in that game in Belgium. I had to rebuild myself.'

As for the possibility of playing for Ireland, he explains, 'We had the citizenship papers but I don't think we ever got them through. I've lived my whole life here in Sweden. It had been on the cards at one stage to move to England. There had been other interest from all over the world but it was too far from interest to make me get on the plane and move. Who knows what would have happened?' He adds, 'I never felt any contact or approach from the FAI. They were probably looking at their own fields and in England.'

His father, Pat, had to accept that Ireland wouldn't come calling. There is another reason why his father was so keen on him representing Ireland – Kevin would have actually been following in his father's footsteps.

Pat, who was a former professional player and later a successful manager in both Sweden and Norway, set up home in Sweden in the 1980s with his wife Annette, who came from near Gothenburg. An ex-Republic of Ireland Under-21 player, Pat Walker played in the same youth team as Steve Bruce at Gillingham before returning to Ireland, where he won an FAI Cup with Bohemians – though he did spend most of his professional career in Sweden, before moving into management with, among others, GIF Sundsvall, Örebro and Sandefjord. In fact, Pat's stature in the game in Sweden is such that he has been considered for other important positions. For example, he has been asked at various junctures about his openness to working with the Swedish Football Association, mostly with their younger age groups. He doesn't take such an invite lightly, as neither the senior men's nor women's team have ever had a foreign coach. He was also in the running for the role of the FAI's high performance director in the mid-2000s, and came close to taking the Galway United job in 2008, before ultimately deciding to stay in Sweden.

Still, as Kevin struggled to recover from his illness, Pat no doubt gave little further thought to what country his son would represent; he just wanted him to be fit and healthy again.

Kevin's year out from football, convalescing, also allowed him to rediscover his love of music. As a teenager, Walker had developed a keen interest in music. He describes a weekly ritual of watching broadcasts of the early seasons of *American Idol*, including its first incarnation, which was won by Kelly Clarkson. He would retreat to his bedroom at the family home in Örebro and start belting out his own spin on the tracks performed on the shows. 'I was probably killing the neighbours!' he jokes.

As he recovered, he started playing guitar and keyboard, a development that would ultimately lead to a life-changing series of events four years later.

Then a midfielder with Superettan side GIF Sundsvall, a teammate was due to perform at an open mic night in the city. When he couldn't make it, he asked Walker to stand in. The then twenty-three-year-old performed four songs, and the recording found its way to producers of the Swedish version of *Idol*. Approached about auditioning for the 2013 edition, he went for it, with little expectation of making any serious dent in the competition.

Little did he know, the idea of a professional-footballer-turned-pop-star would capture the imagination of the Swedish public, but also football fans around the globe. His endeavours on the show made front-page news in Sweden and waves in Ireland, the UK and further afield. During the course of the show, he balanced his playing commitments for Sundsvall with practising and performing weekly from Stockholm's Globe Arena, where the Friday night live event was filmed.

The midfielder described his life at the time as being like 'Bruce Wayne', but his time on the show was not without controversy. TV4, the broadcaster who showed *Idol Sverige* also owned the rights to Superettan games, and they moved a game scheduled for a Friday night to a Sunday to facilitate Walker's participation in both. Then head of sport at TV4, Emir Osmanbegovic, was asked at the time whether it was realistically possible to combine starring on a TV talent show with life as a professional footballer. He said it was, 'as long as the company owns the broadcast rights for both events'. Other players and managers felt GIF Sundsvall were being given special treatment. Additionally, some commercial flights from Sundsvall to Stockholm were delayed to allow Walker to go from training to the airport and make the 360km journey to the capital.

Over the course of the eleven-week-long finals, Walker didn't miss a minute of football. He played the full ninety minutes in all seven of Sundsvall's remaining fixtures, as they ultimately missed out on promotion to the top flight when they lost a promotion playoff to Östersunds, then managed by Graham Potter.

Looking back, he sees how crazy that period of time was for him. 'It was overwhelming in a lot of aspects. I was trying to enjoy it of course, but I was doing the day job and living the dream. It gave me something beautiful outside of football to make me grow as a person. I truly felt on the edge of my comfort zone.'

His football became something of a refuge, if anything, during that period. 'When I stepped back onto the football field, I was so much calmer. There wasn't the same nervous feeling you would get when you were younger. It was the experience from standing there on a live show. I managed to put it together and learn on the spot and what my limits were at the time.' And his newfound confidence did seem to translate to the field. Walker scored four goals for his club that season, and three of them came during that seven-game spell when football and music overlapped.

If promotion to the top flight eluded him, a recording contract with Universal Music was a fine consolation. The highlight of his run on the show – outside of winning the show outright, of course, which he ultimately did – came in the finale, when he and fellow finalist Elin Bergman joined special guest Robbie Williams on stage to duet on his song 'Shine My Shoes'.

Having to combine his dual interests of football and music in that time was a tricky task, and Walker considered himself an outsider in more ways than one during his time on *Idol*. Splitting his time between Sundsvall and Stockholm, he never truly felt part of what had developed into a tight-knit friendship group over the weeks between the other contestants. Winning the competition outright had been fanciful thinking, but at no point during the run did he have to take part in the dreaded bottom two sing-off. Subsequently, his debut album *Belong* went platinum in Sweden, where it reached number two in the charts. His single, of the same name, went one better and topped the charts.

Still, amid this success, he realised that football was his primary passion. He ultimately decided to put his football before a music career, for the most part, and cut ties with Universal Music so that he could control his output on his terms while also pursuing success on the field.

That has arrived in plentiful supply in the years that followed, as Walker and GIF Sundsvall went one step further in 2014, earning promotion to the Allsvenskan with a runners-up finish. (They lost out on the championship on goal difference only.) The midfielder, having been vice-captain a year earlier, was promoted to captain at the start of the season by co-managers Joel Cedergren and Roger Franzén.

A permanent move to Stockholm followed with Djurgårdens IF. In 2016, in his second season at the club, Walker was named captain by manager Pelle Olsson. He was keeping illustrious company, as in the next two seasons he was followed in the role by Kim Kallstrom and Jonas Olsson, a duo with over 150 international caps between them.

Walker ultimately helped the club to a cup win in 2018, followed by a league victory a year later – exactly a decade since he had been laid out by the bout of blood poisoning that ended his hopes of a first league medal and threatened his life and career.

In 2021, Walker rejoined his hometown club Örebro, themselves a top-flight team with ambitions of reaching Europe. Approaching his thirty-second birthday, it felt like he had come full circle.

A move to the continent had been on the cards, with interest in Scandinavia and further afield, but he elected to stay in Sweden. It also meant being close again to his father Pat, who lends an ear and words of encouragement when needed. Rather than Dad offering unsolicited advice, it is Walker who seeks it out. 'It's often me coming looking for advice because he is a top, internationally qualified coach. It's an asset not every player has. I can use the footage of the training sessions and we sit at the kitchen table and go through it. We live and breathe football. It's been a massive part of our lives.'

Kevin, partner My and kids Kaylie and Aiden all moved back into the Walker family home when they made the decision to return to Örebro, as more permanent solutions were sought. The house was again alive with activity, energy and song.

Things had come full circle for the neighbours too.

From Örebro to Stockholm and back, via near death, chart-topping success and a title-winning season with Djurgårdens, Walker has crammed so much into his three decades to date, all the while retaining a strong link with his Carlow clan.

Senior international recognition with either the country of his birth or his heritage proved elusive in the end – as it has so far for Sean McDermott – but Walker's journey is the envy of many. For those two, it all started when their fathers made their respective homes away from home in Scandinavia.

11
COMING TO AMERICA

Between Paul Keegan and Ian Hennessy's debut season in Major League Soccer back in 1996 and 2010, Irish interest in America's great football enterprise was virtually non-existent. College soccer afforded some Irish the opportunity to balance academia and athletic achievement, but these cases often went under the radar. Apart from Ronnie O'Brien's partial career rebirth in Dallas, Toronto and San Jose, plus ex-Shelbourne winger Richie Baker's stint at New England Revolution, Irish eyes really had little reason to cast a curious glance over the Atlantic.

Robbie Keane's arrival at LA Galaxy in the summer of 2011 certainly changed that.

In the eyes of LA Galaxy supporters and impartial observers of Major League Soccer, what stood Keane apart from all others was that he bought into the league in a way that most of his high-profile, designated player predecessors – and those who have followed him in the decade since – never did. It was a distinction that marked Keane out even from his teammate David Beckham, a man largely responsible for bringing the Irishman to Los Angeles in the first place.

Admittedly Beckham was a bona fide trailblazer, in that he had arrived at Galaxy four years before Keane and long before it became a more accepted norm for high-calibre players to swap chasing glory in Europe's epicentre of elite football for life Stateside. The former Manchester United superstar joined LA Galaxy in 2007 with a provision in his contract offering him the option to buy an MLS expansion franchise when he eventually departed from the league. (That team would become Inter Miami, who debuted in MLS in 2020.) As a result, he was, in a more literal sense, buying into the development of this emerging, ever-expanding league in the greatest untapped market in the globe. Many supporters consequently felt as if Beckham's time at Galaxy was merely a stepping stone to a life after retirement, a 'brand Beckham' expansion into the lucrative US sporting and cultural space. His behaviour, at times, backed up this view. For example, in 2009, the ex-England captain missed the first half of the league season with Galaxy while on loan at Serie A giants AC Milan. It led to comments from teammate Landon Donovan, who explicitly questioned Beckham's commitment to the LA cause. Upon his return from Milan, where a two-month loan was ultimately extended to five months, he was the subject of ire from supporters who supported Donovan's sentiments.

The same criticism could never be levelled at Keane, who has become as synonymous with LA Galaxy as he is with any of his seven clubs in England. One of three designated players at the club when he signed in the summer of 2011, alongside Beckham and US star Donovan, Keane's five-and-a-half years in California offered the Dubliner a new lease of life after fourteen years in Britain.

At first, it seemed like an odd move for a player who had established himself firmly among the pantheon of great Premier League goalscorers. For Beckham and Keane, read Gerrard, Lampard, Ashley Cole, Henry, Drogba, Kaká, Nesta and Zlatan Ibrahimović – that is, the list of global football A-listers who have arrived in MLS in the late stages of celebrated careers. However, Keane, having just turned thirty-one when he arrived in Los Angeles, was younger than them all. The 'retirement home' cynicism that was peddled in the summer of 2011 when he swapped Spurs for Galaxy didn't stick in this instance. His performances on the field didn't allow them too, as he quickly established himself as their main goalscorer and, within months, played a key role in Galaxy winning the 2011 MLS Cup. And fans had still only seen the beginning of what Keane had to offer.

The standard of defending in the league often left a lot to be desired – Keane hadn't been scoring goals in that volume or mould for a few years by that point – but it was still easy to conclude that Hollywood suited him. Keane has exuded an air of confidence since childhood, and with justification, but in LA, his added layers of humility and strong work ethic provided an antidote to fans' attitudes towards the very best designated players that rightly or wrongly prevailed.

With Keane in tow, the Galaxy's attack was the most consistently fearsome in the country. His sense of timing and movement was exquisite, meaning should a pass arrive into the vicinity of the penalty area, he was always ready to receive. At that point, it was almost always a matter of time before the net bulged. So often, he made solid professionals – goalkeepers and defenders alike – look foolish. Facing him was the stuff of nightmares.

Keane seemed fuelled by the chance to seize glory for himself in the land of opportunity. He had short shrift for anyone who questioned whether he was wasting his last years in the obscurity (in a football sense, at least) of LA, all palm trees and blue skies. Keane yearned to beat all comers. Whether there was a goal, game or trophy on the line, it was always sweet for him, seemingly more so in a city with which his affinity remains strong. His intelligent movement and unerring finishing ability made fools of defenders and memories of a lifetime for supporters. Keane seems a shoo-in to one day manage LA Galaxy. It is simply a matter of when.

Keane also possessed a near-maniacal competitive streak. His career up to that point had amounted to one League Cup win in 2008 with Tottenham. It wasn't enough for a man who believed that winning was everything. In Galaxy, he saw an opportunity to make up for his lack of silverware. 'I could have played in the Premier League again for a few more years, no problem,' Keane remarked in a conversation with broadcaster Kevin Egan on his *Kickin' Off* podcast in July 2020. 'Was I going to win anything in the Premier League? Possibly not.'

This competitiveness – and his reliable goalscoring – led Keane and Galaxy into an era of unprecedented success. It even got him invited to the White House, as is custom for all the winning teams in the MLS Cup. 'I love playing the game. It's simple. And when you're playing, you're enjoying yourself, but you play to win games. You play to be champions,' Keane told *Sports Illustrated*. 'They're the feelings that don't happen to many players and you don't get that very often. I've had it for a few years now and I want that buzz again. I want to come back again to the White House. I want to see the President again.'

And he did. In fact, Keane spearheaded LA to one of the most dominant stretches in MLS's twenty-five-year history, scoring and creating freely as the team won the 2011, 2012 and 2014 MLS Cups, as well as the 2011 Supporters' Shield.

Galaxy's success, and Keane's stature, became such that soon he was talking about legacy. 'I want to make the Galaxy one of the biggest names there is. That's about winning. People forget about the people who lose. You go without a championship for two or three years and other teams start taking over. But for me, it's about winning. Leave a legacy here? I think I probably already have with what I've achieved since I've been here. But for me, that's not good enough. I want to keep going and make a bigger legacy.'

Proof of Keane's impact on Galaxy came on the day that Keane played his last-ever game for Ireland against Oman at the Aviva Stadium at the end of August 2016. The Galaxy took out an advertisement on the front page of *The Irish Times*, paying tribute to an international career that remained always at the forefront of Keane's mind. From the outset of his time in LA, Keane refused to let the distance interfere with his international career. For example, he appeared in as many international friendlies for his country during his time in the US as he had in the previous five years while based in the UK. He would travel 5,000 miles and more to play for his country. He was no pretender in that regard. He even managed to add seventeen goals to his international tally during his time in the US, bringing the total to sixty-eight.

Few could have imagined the impact that Ireland's record goalscorer would have in America, where he became a statesman-like figure within the club and the city. It ended a far cry from his early days in the city, where he was once infamously described as an 'unidentified fan' in a caption of a Reuters agency photograph in which he posed with Beckham and the actor and comedian Russell Brand at an LA Lakers game at Staples Center.

Galaxy boss Bruce Arena described his striker as a 'tough bastard' and hailed his skill, competitive nature and influence in a dressing room that, DPs aside, consisted mostly of young and unheralded domestic players. His years in the US were defined by a focus and ruthlessness that earned the Galaxy its three championships. He sensed an opportunity to do something unique there, and his seemingly unquenchable thirst for the game drove the team to achieve its own goals.

In five-and-half years, Keane scored ninety-one regular season and playoff goals, and he created a further fifty-one goals in those 146 games. Named to the MLS Best XI in 2012, 2013, 2014 and 2015, he won the league's Most Valuable Player award in 2014. More goals arrived in cup and continental competition too.

His 104 goals in all competitions for LA Galaxy are a collection of strikes as varied as any high-calibre striker could hope to call their own. From tap-ins to impudent lobs, six-yard box headers to long-range drives, Keane scored them all, and with unfailing regularity. Goals were Keane's currency and, in a long career, he never wrote cheques his many clubs weren't able to cash to their great benefit.

Keane's five years in Los Angeles coincided with – and in no short measure contributed to – a rise in MLS's profile and standing in the eyes of the watching world. The Irishman helped make the US a viable option for high-calibre players to seek a new challenge that wasn't merely one last payday. His time in LA unquestionably surpassed all expectations. Arena described his Irish star as the club's 'greatest advocate'. What Keane did for his own career, LA Galaxy and the perception of what a fulfilling lifetime in elite football could be is without comparison in the modern game. Keane will forever be associated with the Galaxy. He was its star that shone the brightest.

He also created an avenue for some international teammates to follow suit with moves across the pond. While Caleb Folan had beaten Keane to it by four months, more integral members of Giovanni Trapattoni's squad soon followed, like Darren O'Dea, Kevin Doyle and Sean St Ledger (the latter two at Colorado Rapids and Orlando City). And other non-international Irish footballers also looked to follow his example.

In nine years in the United States, James O'Connor has tried his hand at everything. A stalwart of England's Football League, where he played just short of 500 career games, he spent his career in towns and cities that hardly scream glamour: Stoke, West Bromwich, Burnley and Sheffield. It should have come as no surprise then, that at thirty-two years of age, he decided to leave England behind and move to Florida.

There, he would play for Orlando City, a USL Pro team (a level below the MLS), under Adrian Heath. A well-travelled former player, Heath had turned out for Stoke City and Burnley during a lengthy career, just as O'Connor had done. He was probably best known for representing Everton in the 1980s, where he won two league titles, an FA Cup and UEFA Cup Winners' Cup under Howard Kendall.

O'Connor and Heath were ultimately brought together by a mutual friend, the one-time Stoke City director Phil Rawlins. The self-made millionaire had set up a team in Austin, Texas in 2008 – the Austin Aztex – that would ultimately relocate to Orlando when he purchased the city's USL rights. Heath was the first manager there before following Rawlins to Orlando.

It so happened that even before the move, O'Connor was a regular in Florida, as he owned a holiday home in Orlando. The Bray native would bring his family out annually for sunshine and golf. He had envisaged making it a more permanent residence by the time he reached his mid-thirties, but after eighteen months of slogging it out in League One with Sheffield Wednesday, the urge was too strong to delay further. Only thirty-two, O'Connor was ahead of schedule, but ready to see what America could offer.

'It was probably a bit earlier than I'd originally planned, but I felt as if it was a great next step,' he says. 'I could see how the game was growing here. It was very clear to see there was a serious appetite for the game. In the nine years since I've been here, the growth has been incredible.'

It was a case of the stars aligning for O'Connor, when he joined the club owned by a contact, managed by an acquaintance and in a city he loved and in which he owned a house. His children were also young enough that a transatlantic move would not have disrupted their lives too much: Ollie nearly three and Maisie just one.

Having already finished his Pro Licence course in the UK, O'Connor was conscious that his choice of destination should be somewhere with plentiful opportunities to employ his learnings and advance his coaching career. America fit the bill. 'At that point, I'd played over 500 games in England. I'd experienced quite a bit. What was the next step? You can get to thirty-two and continue playing. Some – like Graham Alexander [the Scottish international and O'Connor's former Burnley teammate] – go on and on. He played until he was forty. For me, having gone through the coaching licences, I was pretty clued into what were the next steps for me.'

He signed on with Orlando City in January 2012 – months after Robbie Keane's high-profile arrival – and a year later was combining his playing role with assisting Heath on day-to-day coaching matters. Orlando City were going places. In his second season at the club, they lifted the

USL Pro Championship. At thirty-three, that was O'Connor's first major trophy as a player – notwithstanding the Football League Trophy he won with Stoke in the year 2000.

By 2015, O'Connor had decided to leave Orlando to take on a managerial role – though it was, in a sense, with the same team. Louisville City, a brand-new franchise, had purchased the rights to Orlando City's USL franchise. After Orlando had joined MLS, their USL franchise moved 850 miles away to establish a new club in Kentucky. That's American sport for you.

As O'Connor was preparing to make his dugout debut, Orlando set about attracting some major star power for their first foray into Major League Soccer. Brazilian superstar Kaká joined from Real Madrid, the 2007 Ballon d'Or winner ostensibly O'Connor's midfield replacement. The Irishman was moving in very different circles than he ever had before. 'When you first come over, certainly as a player – I wanted to get an understanding of the players' mentality. I wanted to understand what the culture was, the differences. It allowed me, while I was still playing, to get an understanding of expectations, both from a player's perspective and, obviously, from a coach's perspective. It was a nice phase where I was able to continue playing and understand the environment and the expectations.'

His time in charge of Louisville, from 2015 to 2018, was widely successful given the club were newly in existence. The opportunity had intrigued him and he grasped it firmly. He guided his team to the Eastern Conference Finals in his first two years, before Louisville won it in 2017. They needed penalties to beat New York Red Bulls in the final, before then beating Swope Park Rangers in the Championship decider.

This success brought about the opportunity to return to Orlando, this time to manage their MLS team. His tenure in charge of Orlando City, where he replaced Jason Kreis, was less successful. He won just thirteen of fifty-six league games in his term, ending both seasons second-bottom of the Eastern Conference. Kaká had long since departed by that stage, though he did at least have Portuguese winner Nani at his disposal. But O'Connor left his post as manager at the end of that second disappointing season.

A meticulous man by all accounts, O'Connor's current hiatus from the dugout hasn't left him shorn of a platform on which to demonstrate his skills. He likes to plan, to prepare, and now working as executive vice president of development back at Louisville, he has no immediate wish to return to management. America offers up all kinds of opportunities, after all. 'This is a club very close to my heart. This is an interesting challenge for me and when I looked at it, it was something that definitely appealed to me. Having had the experience of coaching and understanding what a coach is more than likely going to want and need, that's probably been a big benefit to me. There are a lot of aspects to this role and I'm really starting to enjoy it.'

Since starting in the role in January 2020, O'Connor has been responsible for overseeing the delivery of a $15 million new training ground, as well as launching an academy and new women's team. For all his planning and preparing, his coaching licences won't have prepared him for this. 'It's been a whirlwind,' he says.

However, it hasn't just been the MLS and USL that have attracted Irish footballers to the States; increasingly in recent years, Ireland's women footballers have taken to North America to pit themselves against the world's best.

When making career decisions, it is wise to keep good counsel. Sometimes, others can see things that you cannot. They can bring a fresh perspective that you haven't considered. For Denise O'Sullivan, her options are plentiful. A popular member of the Republic of Ireland squad, Denise can call on a host of teammates and coaches past and present to talk about what's next and what's best. That is before her attention turns to home, where the midfielder has her mother Nuala and nine siblings in whom to confide and seek advice. The extended O'Sullivan family from Knocknaheeny in Cork – brothers, sisters, in-laws, nieces, nephews and cousins – have all taken a keen interest in how O'Sullivan's career has taken shape over the last decade.

More recently, she has established herself as one of the world's best midfield players, starring for North Carolina Courage in the NWSL. O'Sullivan is a key component in the Courage machine that won back-to-back Championships in 2018 and 2019. Their end-of-season playoff wins were underpinned on both occasions by being the team with the best regular season record.

Her time in the States began in more mixed circumstances, however, with an eighteen-month spell at Houston. The decision to up sticks from Glasgow – where she played for Glasgow City – and move to Texas in 2016 was difficult for the family-orientated then twenty-two-year-old. Personal considerations were at the forefront of her mind, particularly given the huge distance between Texas and Cork when compared to Glasgow. 'Leaving my family, that was huge. I really had to think about that. I was going through a tough situation with my family at the time. My dad passed away right before actually going to Houston, just days before. That was another consideration. I had to take into account going away while actually going through that process of losing my dad.' She had at least been able to seek guidance from her father, John, shortly before his passing from cancer. 'He knew about the opportunity that came about to go to Houston. He told me I needed to take this opportunity.'

The rest of her family were equally supportive. 'My family was behind me the whole way. They wanted me to get over there and pursue it. America was the dream for me, and was where I wanted to go, so for it to come about right after was very special and was a proud moment for me and my family to get that contract.'

She had been discovered by the Dash in January 2016, when the Corkonian was part of a Republic of Ireland squad that travelled to

California for a friendly encounter with World Cup holders USA. In front of a crowd of over 23,000 people, the Irish fell to a 5–0 defeat, with Carli Lloyd's twenty-two-minute hat-trick putting the result beyond doubt inside the opening half hour. But the game had at least acted as a shop window for O'Sullivan, who drew the attention of the Dash. Though she didn't know it yet, soon O'Sullivan would be calling Lloyd, arguably the world's best player, who had six months earlier scored a hat-trick in the World Cup final, a teammate.

It had always been a dream of O'Sullivan's to play in the States at some point in her career. She hadn't embarked on a scholarship across the pond as a teenager, and with two seasons as a professional at Glasgow under her belt – where she had been happy enough, to be fair, with Champions League participation an annual affair – she now, unexpectedly, found herself in an opportune moment. She felt that she needed to step up from the Scottish Women's Premier League. America would require climbing several rungs.

Houston Dash might have brought her or any Irish football fan out in a rash given another Ireland player's first, last and ever-so-brief dalliance with the club a year earlier. Stephanie Roche had joined the club exactly eleven months earlier, and her short-lived time in Houston was the stuff of nightmares. Randy Waldrum, the coach who signed Roche and then was powerless to see her waived as an injury crisis took hold elsewhere in his squad, was still the man in charge. Ironically, it was while he scouted for a striker that he was moved to pursue O'Sullivan instead.

The playmaker took to the NWSL like a duck to water, quickly garnering the respect of her teammates and opposition players. She played in eighteen of the Dash's twenty league games in her debut season, scoring twice. Having started life on the bench, she was soon starting games. Learning happened on the job. 'It was very tough for the first few matches. As soon as you get on the ball, you take two touches and then you have to pass again. The calibre of players they have in that league – every USA player at the time were involved. It was very athletic, with very fit and physical players, so I think I had to adapt to that. It took me a while to do that. The biggest thing was getting used to playing in that league and getting up to the speed of the game. It took me a while but I eventually got used to it. It was very competitive but it got me where I am today.'

Despite her integrating well, the yearning for home never left her during this period. However, her ability to cope has evolved. 'I don't think it ever goes away. You miss your family. That's natural, you're going to miss them. You just learn to deal with it.'

Despite her solid start to life at the Dash, a change of circumstance forced her hand to leave Texas less than eighteen months into her time in the Bible Belt.

Seven weeks into the 2017 campaign, Waldrum was out of the club, having lost five of the opening seven games of the season. His replacement, Omar Morales, dropped O'Sullivan. She made just two starts in the next three months. To the manager's credit, results did at least pick up. 'He preferred different players. I wasn't on top of his list of his preferred players and I was coming on in the last two minutes of games. I lost my confidence. It was just awful. So frustrating.'

The Dash agreed to release O'Sullivan but with a caveat. They wanted her to go overseas, not to a rival NWSL club. It was not a contractual clause, more of a gentleman's agreement. She was going to return to Europe, to Germany, before Paul Riley's intervention. Riley, the North Carolina Courage coach, made contact and the rest was history.

How did Morales take the reneging of the agreement? O'Sullivan never waited to find out. 'He probably wasn't happy but he was willing to let me go so easily, I don't know if he was really worried to be quite honest. I had to think about myself, not the Dash or the coach. I had to make that move.'

The Courage were at a level above the Dash, so the approach – and subsequent offer – was something of a surprise for O'Sullivan. 'It was a bit of a shock that the Courage came in for me, within twenty-four hours of being put on the waiver list. It wasn't about proving anyone else wrong, it was about proving I can be better. I knew I could be better and push past my limits. That was my mindset at that moment.'

And O'Sullivan has certainly broken past those limits, to the point where she is today at the vanguard of Irish football. A two-time NWSL Championship winner with North Carolina Courage – and a three-time Shield winner to boot (the Shield goes to the team who finish top of the regular league standings, before the championship knockouts begin) – the Cork midfielder was also named in the NWSL Players' Team of the Year in 2019. Voted for by her peers, that award holds particular significance for those selected. Furthermore, her teammates voted her as their own MVP for both Championship-winning seasons, underlining her worth in the Courage locker room. 'It was huge to get MVP. To be picked by your own teammates, it's always special.' Those accolades are in addition to the eight major honours secured while at Glasgow City.

Now, though, playing in what many consider to be the strongest women's league in the world, O'Sullivan has made the transition from possessing promise to commanding total respect from all in the game.

O'Sullivan says that she has learned so much from her time in the US, like how despite their successes – they also did reach the Championship decider in her first half-season in North Carolina, with the Irishwoman scoring an eighty-ninth-minute winner in the semi-final – Riley keeps them grounded. 'The environment and the culture of the club, I had never been in an environment like that before, everyone from the top down. Paul would be in his office from 6 a.m. to 3 p.m. watching videos. Throughout the whole year, Championship isn't mentioned. We're not allowed to mention it. It is all about everyday growth.'

She has come a long way from her early days back in Knocknaheeny, where the young O'Sullivan would spend hour upon hour playing with her friends and neighbours on the greens and the fields surrounding her estate. She was her own person from a very young age, never shy to mix in with the boys in combative and aggressive fashion, facets of her game she continues to employ today. Her mother Nuala never had to waste too much energy worrying about where her youngest was whiling away the hours after school. Football – first in Scotland and then in America – gave her the chance to spread her wings and fly. She continues to soar, searching out new adventures when given the opportunity.

In-between the lengthy winter-long off-seasons in the States, O'Sullivan has spent time on loan at Brighton & Hove Albion and in Australia, with first Canberra United and then Western Sydney Wanderers. Her desire to play all year round speaks to an enduring love of the game and a wanderlust, a need to travel and to experience. 'I was always surrounded by a big family. But I just wanted to be independent, away doing my own thing. Growing up with that support system was huge for me. My family are the biggest part of my life. Every single one of them calls me, every day of the week. I have them all there to fall back on when I need support. Growing up my mam and dad didn't have much money but they still managed to give me everything that I needed to fulfil my goals, my dreams of being a professional football player.'

She has, undoubtedly, made the most of the opportunity that her father urged her to take.

Soccer in the United States continues to grow exponentially, with grassroots participation involving both boys and girls skyrocketing in the past decade, while Major League Soccer has expanded from eighteen teams in Keane's first season in 2011 to twenty-seven a decade later, with more expansion teams on the way. Its rise, and that of the USL below it, has afforded more and more opportunities to players from Ireland and elsewhere to try their hand at life Stateside.

Additionally, the National Women's Soccer League has been going strong for a decade now – and like the MLS is rapidly expanding too. With the majority of US international players based domestically, the likes of O'Sullivan and teammate Diane Caldwell are assured of facing opponents of the highest quality on a weekly basis.

What American clubs – or franchises, if you prefer – have in their favour are sizeable untapped supporter bases and the infrastructure required to attract serious competitors from most other places in the world, bar, perhaps, some of Europe's biggest leagues. What is certain, however, is that the Irish-American connection in MLS, NWSL or USL will continue for a long time yet.

EPILOGUE

The merits of pursuing a football career away from home and beyond the familiar landscape of Irish and British football are plentiful. Nothing broadens the mind quite like a foreign excursion. The well of opportunity is seemingly bottomless too, but beware the pitfalls. There are many. After all, there is never a guarantee of a more prosperous life, or in football terms, success. Leaving home behind for foreign pastures throws many more variables into the mix.

This book has covered just some of the stories – both good and bad – covering periods of careers that range from wildly successful to distinctly underwhelming and everything in-between. Some foreign adventures lasted a lifetime in football career terms, while others were cut short for one reason or another.

Roy O'Donovan, for example, put his Indonesian nightmare behind him to start afresh in Australia's A-League, where he has become one of the country's most feared goalscorers. Since the league's inaugural season in 2005, only three foreign players have scored more than O'Donovan's fifty-six goals. One of those is Ireland's own Andy Keogh. The Dubliner has scored all fifty-nine of his A-League goals for Perth Glory, in spells interrupted only by short stints in Thailand with Ratchaburi and then in the Indian Super League with NorthEast United. Down Under has been kind to both players, offering a home and a sense of belonging to two Irishmen who had amassed a collection of fourteen English and Scottish clubs between them before upping sticks for their new lives half the world away.

Australia has long been a haven for the Irish, over 114,000 emigrating there between 2008 and 2019. Footballers are no different. Both strikers have in recent times become Australian citizens. The country has also been temporary home to Denise O'Sullivan, Julie Ann Russell and Simon Cox (all Western Sydney Wanderers), Damien Duff (Melbourne City), Cillian Sheridan (New Zealand's Central Coast Mariners), Jay O'Shea (Brisbane Roar), Wes Hoolahan (Newcastle Jets) and the late Liam Miller, who spent three years there representing Glory, the Roar and Melbourne City.

Major League Soccer in America continues to retain a certain attraction. Derrick Williams, a German-born Republic of Ireland international in possession of a US passport, became the second Irishman to represent LA Galaxy in 2021, when he swapped Lancashire for Los Angeles. It is, for obvious reasons, understandable. A veteran of over 250 Football League games with Bristol City and Blackburn Rovers, Williams won't make the kind of mark left at the Galaxy by Robbie Keane, but few – Irish or otherwise – can even consider making a similar impact. As his country's all-time record goalscorer, the same rules didn't apply to Tallaght's tyro. Keane was, and remains, an outlier.

These players' experiences, like those of the Irish in England, Scotland, Europe or across the continents, were a mixed bag. For every Keane, Liam Brady or Anne O'Brien, there are others for whom the experience of playing abroad is a chastening one that leaves them yearning for home. Whether they are successful or not, however, these are experiences that mould a person. For example, as nightmarish as his twelve months in war-addled Ukraine were, Darren O'Dea, in an interview for this book eight years after the fact, believes that experience has changed him more so than any other in his life. He emerged, mettle well and truly tested – if mentally exhausted.

Moving forward, it feels as if Irish players with aspirations of taking their game to a higher level – and earning senior international recognition in the process – may be becoming more amenable to the prospect of a move beyond the Irish and British football pyramids.

Essex-born Josh Cullen, a lieutenant of Stephen Kenny during their time together in the Irish Under-21s, left West Ham United in search of first-team football in the autumn of 2020, but instead of looking to the lower leagues (where he had already spent time on loan at three clubs) he followed Vincent Kompany to Anderlecht, Belgium's most successful team. There he has excelled.

Jack Byrne, having endured a number of trying moves following his departure from Manchester City in 2017, decided to leave Shamrock Rovers for APOEL Nicosia, forgoing the chance for now to write his own redemption arc in England. As APOEL are perennial top dogs in Cyprus and regular European contenders too, Byrne opted to decline a return to England for a different challenge. Sheridan, a veteran of two Cypriot league titles and that high-profile Champions League campaign with APOEL, said in an interview for this book that criticism of Byrne's decision to swap Tallaght for Nicosia was 'ridiculous and annoying'.

In July 2021, another star of Kenny's Under-21 team, Zack Elbouzedi, swapped Lincoln City of League One for Swedish side AIK. Given that, in his early days as Ireland manager, Kenny has selected players from England's third tier, as well as the League of Ireland, the winger arrivesd in Sweden knowing that his location may be less of an obstacle to being selected for international duty than under previous managers.

Another major change, moving forward, comes as a consequence of Brexit. In a departure from the norm, UK clubs are now prohibited from signing Irish players until they turn eighteen. (For example, between the summers of 2017 and 2020, a total of ninety-one Irish-based players of all ages – but mostly teens – were snapped up by British clubs.) This change will allow Irish clubs to keep hold of their young talents for longer, potentially leading to improvements in both the standard and coffers of the League of Ireland.

It also means that clubs within the European Union will likely look to avail of opportunities previously hoovered up predominately by English clubs. Recent moves for home-based Irish teenagers Kevin Zefi and Glory Nzingo by Inter Milan and Reims, with a host of other trial opportunities being secured by other youngsters, suggest clubs in the continent are already beginning to use the shifting of the goalposts within the market to steal a march on their British counterparts. However, as Mainland Europe is considered by many to be a far superior environment for a young player to hone their technical ability and understanding of the game itself, this could well turn out to hugely benefit the next generation of Irish players.

In a further indication that things may be changing, in May 2021, Republic of Ireland Under-21 boss Jim Crawford named five European-based players in a squad for three friendly internationals in Marbella: Ryan Johansson (Sevilla), John Joe Patrick Finn Benoa (Getafe), Conor Noß (Borussia Mönchengladbach), Anselmo Garcia McNulty (Wolfsburg) and Dan Rose, an English-born goalkeeper who plays for Schalke 04 in Germany. This all points to a potentially more cosmopolitan future for Irish football.

In the women's game, Europe and the USA still represent a significant step up for players competing in the developing Women's National League. What may slow more players' movement to established European leagues, however, is the rise of the Women's Super League across the Irish Sea. Opportunity abounds there, although US college scholarships remain popular with young players. Diane Caldwell and Claire Scanlan can speak to the benefits of taking that route.

The world, the game and the story of Irish emigration have evolved over many decades and, as seen with recent developments, continue to do so. Some intrepid members of Ireland's football fraternity have followed a centuries-old path in an ever-changing world. However, the changing face of football hasn't necessarily left the Irish behind – many have journeyed to meet it, in all corners of the earth. As globalisation has made the planet smaller, the Emerald Exiles' global footprint has made its mark, and they will continue to do so moving forward.

BIBLIOGRAPHY

Books

Brady, Liam. (1980), *So Far So Good*, London: Hutchinson

Byrne, Peter. (2012), *Green is the Colour: The Story of Irish Football*, London: Andre Deutsch

Conroy, Terry. (2015), *You Don't Remember Me, Do You? The Autobiography of Terry Conroy*, Worthing: Pitch Publishing

Cruyff, Johan. (2017), *My Turn: The Autobiography*, London: Macmillan

Curran, Dr Conor. (2017), *Irish Soccer Migrants: A Social and Cultural History*, Cork: Cork University Press

Fanning, Bryan. (2018), *Migration and the Making of Ireland*, Dublin: University College Dublin

Foot, John. (2007), *Calcio: The History of Italian Football*, London: Harper Perennial

Kimmage, Paul. (2005), *Full Time: The Secret Life of Tony Cascarino*, London: Scribner

Lennon, Paul. (2012), *Robbie: A Striker's Story*, Dublin: Paperweight Publications

Lynch, Declan. (2010), *John Giles: A Football Man*, Dublin: Hachette Books Ireland

Lynch, Declan. (2010), *Days of Heaven: Italia '90 and the Charlton Years*, Dublin: Gill and Macmillan

O'Callaghan, Eoin. (2019), *Behind the Lines: Great Irish Sports Stories from The42.ie*, Dublin: Journal Media Ltd

O'Connell, Sue. (2016), *The Man Who Saved FC Barcelona: The Remarkable Life of Patrick O'Connell*, London: Amberley

Rowan, Paul. (1994), *The Team That Jack Built*, Edinburgh: Mainstream

Stapleton, Frank. (1991), *Frankly Speaking*, Dublin: Blackwater Press

Vermeer, Evert, van Hoof, Marcelle. (1999) *Ajax 100 Jaar: Jubileumboek 1900-2000*, Amsterdam: Luitingh-Sijthoff

Walker, Michael. (2017), *Green Shoots: Irish Football Histories*, Liverpool: deCoubertin Books

Wilson, Jonathan. (2013), *Inverting the Pyramid*, London: Nation Books

Digital Media

Away with the Faroes (RTÉ)

Balls.ie

Billboard.com

FAI.ie

Kickin' Off with Kevin Egan (Podcast)

Off the Ball (Newstalk)

RSSSF.com

RTE.ie

Soccerway.com

Sport Stories (Virgin Media)

The42.ie

Transfermarkt.com

UEFA.com

Wikipedia

WorldFootball.net

Newspapers

Aftenposten (Norway)

The Boston Globe (USA)

Daily Mail

Fingal Independent

Het Nieuws van den Dag (Netherlands)

Il Calcio Illustrato (Italy)
Irish Daily Mirror
Irish Daily Star
Irish Examiner
Irish Independent
The Irish Sun
The Irish Times
The Guardian
The Independent

Interviews
Cahill, Ollie, Phone Interview, 5 March 2021
Caldwell, Diane, Phone Interview, 1 March 2021
Folan, Caleb, Phone Interview, 13 March 2021
Keegan, Paul, Phone Interview, 9 February 2021
McDermott, Sean, Phone Interview, 6 February 2021
Nestor, Conor, Phone Interview, 5 February 2021
O'Connor, James, Phone Interview, 8 February 2021
O'Dea, Darren, Phone Interview, 3 February 2021
O'Donovan, Roy, Phone Interview, 2 February 2021
O'Riordan, Claire, Phone Interview, 18 March 2021
O'Sullivan, Denise, Phone Interview, 10 April 2021
Quinn, Louise, Phone Interview, 5 February, 18 February and 16 April 2021
Roche, Stephanie, Phone Interview, 17 March 2021
Ryan, Richie, Phone Interview, 11 March and 26 April 2021
Scanlan, Claire, Phone Interview, 3 February 2021
Sheridan, Cillian, Phone Interview, 4 February 2021
Stapleton, Frank, Phone Interview, 31 March 2021
Walker, Kevin, Phone Interview, 4 February 2021
Walker, Patrick, Phone Interview, 4 February 2021

IMAGE CREDITS

ACKNOWLEDGEMENTS

The idea of writing a book exploring the stories and celebrating the legacies of Irish footballers, coaches and managers all around the world is one that I had floating around in my head for a number of years. However, in all honesty, by 2020 it had been long forgotten. That was until I received an unsolicited email from Caoimhe Fox at New Island Books, who enquired as to my willingness to take on this project.

The opportunity came as a surprise, but the enthusiasm afforded to both myself as a first-time author and the project itself gave me the confidence that this could work. Thank you to Caoimhe, Aoife Walsh and especially Stephen Reid at New Island for their guidance, support and patience throughout the entire process. They backed me when many would not have. I am eternally grateful to the whole team at New Island for the chance to write this book. Credit should also go to Caoimhe's partner John Carroll, who was aware of our online presence and first planted the idea that Emerald Exiles could be the basis for a book. Huge thanks should also go to Noel O'Regan, who knocked my work into something cogent and publishable.

Writing a book for the very first time was a daunting experience for me and, in the midst of a global pandemic when travel and in-person meetings and interviews were impossible to conduct, it was more trying than I could have possibly imagined.

In undertaking this project, I spoke to many current and former professionals, as well as agents, union representatives, historians, authors and journalists for on-the-record interviews and background. I want to thank everyone who kindly gave up their time to speak to me about their experiences. I'm humbled by how available people have made themselves to me and how open they were in answering my questions. It was a pleasure to speak to them all at length about the game. It was obvious to me that, if we had one thing in common, it was our love of talking about football. Friends of mine will surely testify that this is when I am at my most content. Perhaps worldwide lockdowns and the lack of other distractions helped me when trying to tie down some interview subjects who were at home, with little else to entertain themselves but to talk to an author about their lives in football. Either way, I am grateful for their company, and I hope to see them all again soon – this time in person.

Some of the interview subjects were harder to locate and contact than others, and I want to thank all of the various journalists, club press officers, representatives and friends of friends who helped me get in touch with the interviewees. While it may not seem like much, without their help I would not have been able to speak to many of the players and coaches whose stories live on these pages. Their assistance was invaluable.

I'm also very grateful to everyone who helped source photography for the book, a process that proved more testing than I had anticipated. To the photographers who graciously allowed us to reproduce their work, thank you.

Thanks also to Andrew Deering, who helped with transcribing the many hours and hours of audio from interviews conducted for the book. Cheers to P.J. Murray, who also assisted with some transcribing. It is greatly appreciated. The staff at the Louth County Libraries were also very obliging in assisting in sourcing research material.

The idea for the book first originated from a final-year university project I produced back in 2013. My old university tutor Ross Hawkes was the first person I ever pitched the idea of *Emerald Exiles* to, and he backed it all the way. To this day, he still does. Thanks Ross. That project involved a website and social media presence that, for years now, I have put upon my great friend Kelvin Farrell to help me run. He has always obliged, and I'm so thankful for that, and his friendship.

During the early days, when I was seriously doubting my ability to write this book, my friend Angel Feliciano gave me words of encouragement that I held on to for the duration of the writing. Thanks, Angel.

Finally, and most importantly, a very special word of thanks should go to my mum Carmel, brother Alan and sister Hannah for their continued support – before the book and during the writing process. Hannah especially brings such joy to my life and makes every day special. I'm so very grateful to have you.

INDEX

Aasmundsen, Stian 170
AC Milan 36–7, 44, 124, 182
Accrington Stanley 9
ADO Den Haag 113
AFC Cup 81
Aganovic, Armin 110
Agence France-Presse (AFP) 99
agents 36, 64, 104, 109, 117, 140, 172
Agnelli, Gianni 39
AGSM Verona 127
AIK (Stockholm) 173–5, 198
Aim Sovannarath 80
Ajax 4, 6–9, 27–32
    De Toekomst academy 30
Alberto, Carlos 49, 105
Alderweireld, Toby 173
Aldridge, John 166
A-League (Australia) 112, 144, 196
Alexander, Graham 187
Ålgard 111

Algarve Cup 147
Allsvenskan 179
Al-Muhtadee Billah, Crown Prince of Brunei 72–3
Ålta 132
Aluminium Hormozgan 113
Alviž, Robert 72
amateur teams 6, 70, 84
Amazon Grimstad 132
American Idol 176
Amond, Pádraig 3, 112–13
Amsterdam 28
Amsterdamsche FC 12
Ancelotti, Carlo 117
Anderlecht 198
Andonova, Nataša 130
Anschluss 12
APOEL Nicosia 26, 138, 142–3, 198
Ardito, Michele 127–8
Arena, Bruce 185

Arizona, FC 112

Army United, Thailand 66

Arsenal 21, 27, 34–6, 133–4

Arsenal Kiev 159–60

Arter, Harry 175

AS Ambrosiana-Inter 11 see also
Inter Milan

Åsane 111

Ascoli 40

Asia 55–73

Asian Football Confederation
(AFC) 67 see also AFC Cup

ASPTT Albi 97–100

Aston Villa 12

Atatürk, Mustafa Kemal 10

ATK (India) 55

Atkinson, Ron 27

Augustesen, Susanne 43

Austin Aztex 186–7

Australia 77, 110, 196–7
National Premier Leagues 112
national team 89

Austria, national team 11–12

Avaldsnes 147–50

Azerbaijan 112–13

Babb, Phil 26

Bachmann, Ramona 129–30

Baker, Colin 56

Balbriggan United 146

Ballon d'Or 35, 97, 128, 188

Banks, Gordon 47

Barbance, Solène 99

Barcelona see FC Barcelona

Baresi, Giuseppe 40

Barrett, Amber 128

Barrett, Paddy 81–2, 113

Barrett, Tommy 77

Barsley, Vaila 130–1

Bastrup, Lars 25

Bayern Munich 156

Bazunu, Gavin 171

Beattie, Stephen 113

Beckenbauer, Franz 25, 49, 105

Beckham, David 181–2, 185

Belfast Celtic 18

Bell, Colin 126, 151, 155

Belluno 44

Benjaminsen, Fróði 86

Bergkamp, Dennis 30

Bergman, Elin 178

Birmingham City 24, 64

Blackburn Rovers 9, 71, 197

Blanc, Lauren 121

Blau-Weiß 23

Blind, Danny 30–1

Boateng, George 63

Boeung Ket, Cambodia 81

Bohemians 8, 54, 90, 109, 176

Boniek, Zbigniew 39

Boniperti, Giampiero 39

Borneo 69–70

Bornes, Chloé 99

Borussia Dortmund 166

Borussia Mönchengladbach 199

Bosman ruling 27

Boston Breakers 101

Boston College Eagles 49–52

Boston Globe 92, 94

Boston Rovers (Beacons) 47–8

Botoşani, FC 172

Bourges, FC 113

Bradford City 65

Brady, Liam 2, 4, 26, 27–8, 34–40,
    45, 93, 114, 119

Brady, Sarah 36

Brand, Russell 185

Bredania 't Zesde 7

Brentford FC 9

Brescia 37

Breuer, Willi 150

Brexit 198

Brighton & Hove Albion 156, 194

Brisbane Roar 197

Bristol City 197

British Home Championship 13, 18

Bruce, Steve 176

Bruinenberg, Dominique 127

Brunei 68, 71–3

Brunei DPMM 68, 71–3

Brush, Ellie 101

Buckley, Liam 113

Bukovi, Márton 10

Bulgaria 139–41

Bulgarian Cup 140

Bulova 57–8

Burnley 186

Burns, Liam 109

Burns, Mike 93

Butler, Peter 63, 65

Byrne, Emma 146

Byrne, Jack 3, 198

Byrne, John 32

Byrne, Mick 113

Byrne, Stuart 109

Cagliari 37

Cahill, Ollie 110, 112

Caldwell, Diane 145–53, 199

Cambodia 74–82

Football Federation 75–6

Cambuur 3, 113

Cameron, John 6

Campbell, Anne 22

Campbell, Noel 20–3, 32–3, 108

Campionat de Catalunya 16

Canada 104–6

Canberra United 194

Cascarino, Tony 120, 166

Casey, Dan 113

Castagner, Ilario 40

Castellazzi, Armando 11

Catanzaro 39

CBS 46

Cedergren, Joel 179

Celtic 139, 145, 159, 166

Central Coast Mariners 197

Central FC, Trinidad 68

Chambers, James 110

Champions League see UEFA
    Champions League

Charles, John 36

Charlton, Jack 32, 49, 76

Chelsea FC 47

Chim, Mr 58

Ching, Brian 101

Cincinnati, FC 108

Cincotta, Antonio 134

Clarke, Alan 23

Clarkson, Kelly 176

C-League (Cambodia) 74, 79

Cleveland Stokers 47

Colchester United 110

Colorado Rapids 64, 92, 186

Connolly, David 120, 166

Conroy, Sue 56

Conroy, Terry 56–9, 63

Conte, Antonio 117–18

Conway, Jimmy 41

Cook, Paul 103

Cooke, Mick 62

Cooper, Scott 69

Copa del Generalísimo 15

Copa del Rey 15

Coppa Italia 37, 43, 123

Córdoba, Iván 121

Cork City 71–2

Coupe de France 97

Coventry City 27, 119–20

Covid-19 81, 128

Cox, Arthur 32

Cox, Simon 197

Coyle, Owen 55

Crawford, Jim 199

Crimea 162

Crotone 118

Cruyff, Johan 27–9, 31–2, 35

Cruyff, Jordi 160

CSKA Sofia 139–41

Cullen, Josh 198

Curran, Conor 23

Cypriot Cup 143

Cypriot Super Cup 143

Cyprus 138, 142–3, 145, 198

Cyprus Cup 155

Cyprus First Division 26

Däbritz, Sara 156

Daily Mail 125

Dallas, FC 104

Dallas Burn 118, 181

Damallsvenskan 129, 132

Danielsen, Atli 86

Davids, Edgar 117–18

Davies, Hunter 40

Davoren, Iarfhlaith 113

de Boer, Frank 30
De Búrca, Méabh 132
Debinha 148
Del Piero, Alessandro 116
Denmark, national team 147
Derby County 32
Derry City 110
Devine, John 35
DFB (Deutscher Fußball-Bund) 152
DFB-Pokal 151
Dinamo Bucureşti 171–2
Diouf, El Hadji 72
Dixon, Terry 175
Djurgårdens IF 179–80
Dnipro 164
Dochev, Pavel 140
Domenech, Raymond 86–7
Donnelly, James (Jim) 9–13, 18
Donovan, Landon 182
Doolin, Paul 168
Dordrecht, FC 7
Doyle, Kevin 186
Drogheda United 112
Drumcondra AFC 89
DSK Shivajians 112
Duff, Damien 197
Dublin City FC 113
Dundalk City Ladies 126
Dundalk FC 30–1, 81–2, 89, 109, 113
Dundee United 104, 118
Dunne, Richard 116
Dunne, Tommy 110
Dutch football league 6
Dy Vichea 78
Dynamo Kiev 162

EA Sports Cup 104
Eastern Conference (USA) 92, 94–5, 188
Egan, Kevin 184
El Clásico 15
Elbouzedi, Zack 198
Eliteserian 168
Elitettan 129
Elliott, Jimmy 10
emigration 2
Enganamouit, Gaëlle 130
English football league 1–3
   Premier League 1
   Championship 138
Eredivisie 3, 113
   playing style 28–30
Eriksson, Viktor 129
Ermis Aradippou 143
Eskilstuna United 129–34
Estonia, national team 87–8
Ekstraklasa 143
Europa League see UEFA Europa League
European Championships
   1972 (Belgium) 21

1988 (West Germany) 32
2012 (Poland–Ukraine): 165;
  qualifiers 83, 87–8
2016 (France) qualifiers 137
Youth 86, 116–17, 168
European Cup 21
European Super League 107
Everton 5, 186
Evra, Patrice 86

FA Cup 6, 34–5, 186
Facchinetti, Gilbert 25–6
FAI Cup 54, 103–4, 112
Fall Championship (NASL) 106
Falvey, Colin 106, 113
Faroe Islands, national team 83–8
FC Arizona 112
FC Barcelona 4, 13, 15–16, 18, 138
FC Botoșani 172
FC Bourges 113
FC Cincinnati 108
FC Dallas 104
FC Haka 112
FC Köln 150
FC Porto 26
FC Utrecht 166
Fenerbahçe 10, 142
Ferguson, Alex 27
Feyenoord 120
FIFPro tournament 109–12

Finland 112
Finnan, Steve 3
Finn Benoa, John Joe Patrick 199
Fiorentina 38, 134
First World War 8
Fischer, Nilla 151
Fitzpatrick, Glen 109
FK Haugesund 111
Flood, John 154
Florentia San Gimignano 126–7
Folan, Caleb 55, 63–8, 166, 186
Foley, Dominic 108
Foley, Peter 56
Football Association 9
Football Association of Ireland
  (FAI) 77, 170
Football Star Academy, Australia 77
Foran, Derek 113
Fortgens, Ge 8
Fortuna Köln 20–3
Foynes AFC 77
France 97–100
  national team 86–7
Franco, Francisco 15
Franzén, Roger 179
Frauen-Bundesliga 150, 154
French league, women's 97

Galatasaray 10
Galderisi, Giuseppe 92–3, 95
Galway United 110

Gamble, Joe 55, 70–2
Gartland, Brian 109
Garvey, Keith 77
Geoffroy, Pierre 41
Germany/West Germany 20–23,
    150–2, 154–8
Gerstner, Thomas 155–6
Getafe 199
GIF Sundsvall 176–9
Gignac, André-Pierre 87
Giles, John 41, 49
Gillingham 176
Givens, Don 24–7, 32–3
Glasgow City 133, 190–1
globalisation 2–3
Goeßling, Lena 151
Gorman, Dessie 113
Göteborg 130, 132
Gotor, Jorge 69
Gradanski Zagreb 9–10
Grant, Christopher 76–7
Grant, Ciara 146
Gray, Steven 112
Greaves, Jimmy 36
Gresik United 70
Gress, Gilbert 25–6
Guardian 117
Güneş SK 10

Haaland, Erling Braut 170
Haka, FC 112

Hamburg SV 35
Hand, Eoin 56
Hannigan, Ben 20
Hannigan, Mary 84–5
Happel, Ernst 25
Harder, Pernille 130, 155
Harrington, Christopher 113
Harrington, Kellie 113
Harte, Ian 3, 83, 124
Haslam, Harry 24
Hearts (Heart of Midlothian) 142
Heath, Adrian 186–7
Hegrenes, Tor Martin 148
Helsingborgs 122
Hennessy, Ian 51, 90, 181
Henry, Thierry 86
Herald 117
Het Nieuws van den Dag 6–7
Hitchcock, Fran 113
Hogan, Jimmy 7, 11–12
Holst, Chris 6
Honda, Keisuke 78
Hong Kong 56–9
Hong Kong FC 56
Hong Kong Premier League 56
Hong Kong Rangers 56
Hoolahan, Wes 197
Houston Dash 100–2, 190–2
Hughton, Chris 64
Hull City 63, 67
Hun Sen Cup 78, 80

Hunter, Billy 9
HVV Den Haag 6
Hyland, Paul 117

Ibrahimović, Zlatan 98
Iceland 147
Idol Sverige 177–8
IK Start 169
Il Calcio Illustrato 11
I-League (India) 112
Independent 40
India 55
Indian Super League 55, 196
Indonesia 68–71
Indonesian FA 70
Indonesian Super League 70
Inglis, John 140
Inter Miami 182
Inter Milan 11, 37, 39–40, 119–24, 199
Intertoto Cup 117
Inzaghi, Filippo 116
Iran 110
    national team 89
Ireland, Republic of, national team 13, 23, 32, 47, 56, 64, 83, 88, 124, 145–6, 161, 184–5, 198
    Charlton era 32, 49, 76
    Under-16s 86
    Under-18s 86, 116
    Under-19s 168

Under-21s 166, 169, 198–9
    women's: 41, 43, 62, 97, 101, 125–6, 128, 131, 133, 146–7, 155; Under-18s 59
Irish Daily Star 121–4
Irish Examiner 21, 48
Irish Football Association (IFA) 8, 18
Irish Independent 38, 102, 111, 118
Irish National Insurance Company 47–8
Irish Sun 89
Irish Times 84, 142, 184
Ironi Kiryat Shmona 144
Issy FF 99
Italian Football Federation 45
Italian football league 4, 34–45
Italy 8, 11, 34–45, 114–36
    national team 87–8

Jacksonville Armada 106
Jagiellonia 143–4
Jamshedpur 55
Japan 60–2
Jennings, Pat 35
J-League 55
Johansson, Ryan 199
Jovenovski, Gjore 140
Julian Vards women's team 41
Juventus 35–40, 45, 93, 115–17

Kaká 188

Kakkonen 112

Kakos, Anastasios 87

Kallstrom, Kim 179

Kampong Cham, Cambodia 80

Kanbawza FC (Shan United),
    Myanmar 66

Karpaty Lviv 160

Kean, Steve 71–3

Keane, Robbie 2, 4, 55, 104, 116,
    119–25, 138, 181–6, 197

Keegan, Kevin 35, 38

Keegan, Mary 52

Keegan, Paul 49–54, 90, 92, 181

Keegan, Peter 51–4

Keegan, Wayne 52–3

Kelleher, Caoimhin 171

Kelly, Alan 106, 171

Kelly, Dermot 103

Kelly, Ed 50–1

Kelly, Gary 124–5

Kelly, Tommy 48

Kendall, Howard 186

Kendrick, Joe 112

Kenny, Enda 102

Kenny, Stephen 109, 171, 198

Keogh, Andy 55, 196

Kerala Blasters 55

Kerr, Brian 52, 82–8, 116, 175

Kiely, Dean 171

Kilbane, Kevin 83

Kilmarnock 142

Kilmurray, Dermot 145–6

King, Noel 113, 126, 161

Kirwan, Jack 2, 4, 5–9, 18

Kitchee 56

Knudsen, Jens Martin 85–6

Kohlmann, Patrick 166

Kohn, Spitz 32

Köln, FC 150

Kompany, Vincent 198

Kotkan Työväen Palloilijat 112

Kraft, Jonathan 90–1, 95

Kraft, Robert 90, 95

Kreis, Jason 188

Krikorian, Mark 60

Kristiansund 168–9, 172

Krka 133

KSV Waregem 113

Kühn, Marcus 150

Kutner, Steve 117

LA Galaxy 91, 95, 104, 125, 138,
    181–6, 197

LA Lakers 185

La Liga 3, 4, 14–15

Lalas, Alexi 50, 93–4

Larsen, Henrik 84

Late Late Show 98

Law, Denis 36

Lawless, Brian 175

Lazio 41, 43–5, 123

Le Havre 32

League Cup (England) 56, 183
League of Ireland 96, 103, 198 see also Women's National League, Ireland
Lecce 118, 123
Ledwith, John 122
Leeds United 2, 67, 124, 146
Lennon, John 39
Lennon, Paul 121, 124–5
Leupolz, Melanie 155
Levante 3
Limerick FC 56, 72, 77, 89
Lincoln City 198
Linköpings 130, 133
Lippi, Marcello 121–3
Lithuania, national team 87
Liverpool FC 1, 35
Livorno 8
Lloyd, Carli 101, 191
Longford Town 54
Löring, Jean 22
Los Angeles Wolves 47
Louisville City 188–9
Lugano 117–18
Luppen, Martin 22
Luton Town 24
Lyon 120

Magnúsdóttir, Hólmfríður 148
Maguire, Barry 166
Magull, Lina 156

Major League Soccer (MLS) 49, 54, 66, 90–5, 104, 118, 181–3, 194–5, 197
College Draft 49–50
MLS Cup 183–4
Maksymov, Yuriy 160
Malaysia 63–5
Malaysian Super League 63, 72
Maldini, Paolo 106
Mallbackens 130
Malone, Emmet 142–3
Malta 113
Manchester City 59, 198
Manchester United 1, 13, 24, 27, 170
Mancini, Roberto 39
Mandanda, Parfait 172
Maradona, Diego 24
Marta 129
Martin, Tommy 84, 88
Martens, Lieke 130
Martins Pereira, Camila 101
Master 7, Laos 81
Maybury, Alan 124
Mbarga, Befolo 80
McCabe, Katie 154
McCaffrey, Sean 56
McCarey, Aaron 169–70
McCarthy, Mick 64, 120–2, 171
McCaughren, Tom 42
McDermott, Sean 166–73, 180

McDonagh, Jacko 113

McDonagh, Seamus 170–1

McDonnell, Johnny 86

McFaul, Shane 55, 112

McGeady, Aiden 166

McGrath, Joe 89–90

McGrath, Paul 91

McGuinness, Stephen 112

McHugh, Carl 55

McNulty, Anselmo Garcia 199

McPhail, Stephen 124

Mediterranean League 16

Meenan, Darren 109

Mehmet, Billy 55

Meijer, Hennie 30

Meisl, Hugo 11–12

Melbourne City 197

Melbourne Heart 112

Mercyhurst College 60

Merson, Paul 117

Messi, Lionel 98

Metalist Kharkiv 162

Metalurh Donetsk 158–65

Metidieri, Carlos 47

Metidieri, Gilson 47

MetroStars see New York/New Jersey
    MetroStars

Miami FC 106–8

Middlesbrough 115

Mihajlović, Siniša 123

Miller, Liam 197

Mitra Kukar, Tenggarong 69–70,
    73

Mittag, Anja 129

Mkhitaryan, Henrikh 160

MLS Cup 183–4

Modena 44

Molde 170

Møller, Arne 148

Molnár, György 9

Morace, Carolina 44–5

Morales, Omar 192

Moran, Kevin 59

Moratti, Massimo 121–2

Morecambe 170

Motherwell 140

MSV Duisburg 155–7

Mühren, Arnold 27, 30

Mulligan, Paddy 47–8

Mussolini, Benito 11

Mustoe, Robbie 116

Muțiu, Vlad 172

Myanmar 66–8

Nadeshiko League 60

NagaWorld, Cambodia 79, 81

Nahrawi, Imam 70

Nainggolan, Radja 173

Nani 189

Napoli 44

National Defense (Cambodian army
    team) 75, 79

National Women's Soccer League
(NWSL), USA 100, 156, 193,
194–5
Neftchi Baku 113
Neill, Terry 35
Nesta, Alessandro 106–7, 123
Nestor, Conor 74–82
Nestor, Larry 82
Nestor, Teresa 80
Netherlands 6–8, 27–32
football league 6
Neuchâtel Xamax 24–6
New England Patriots 50, 90
New England Revolution 49–51, 53,
90–5, 181
New York Cosmos 25, 105
New York/New Jersey MetroStars 51,
91, 94
New York Red Bulls 188
New Zealand, national team 89
Newcastle Jets (Australia) 197
Neymar 98
Nicol, Steve 53
Nikko Securities Dream Ladies 61
Nilsson, Lina 129
Nîmes 113
NM Cupen Women 147
Nob Tola 75
Nordlie, Tom 148
North American Soccer League
(NASL) 48–9

North American Soccer League
(NASL) (MLS), 104, 107, 113
North Carolina Courage 148, 152,
190, 192–3
North Mayo Heritage Centre 11
NorthEast United 196
Northern Ireland, national team
87–8
Norway 109–11, 147–50, 168–71
international team, Under-21s 168
Norwegian Cup 111
Noß, Conor 199
Notts County 133
Nzingo, Glory 199

Obama, Barack and Michelle 102
O'Brien, Anne 4, 40–5, 60, 62,
114, 125, 127, 135
O'Brien, Declan 113
O'Brien, Ronnie 4, 115–19, 181
O'Brien, Tony 44–5
O'Callaghan, Ellen (Ellie) 16–18
O'Callaghan, George 72–3, 113
Ochs, Stephanie 101
O'Connell, Dan 17
O'Connell, Ellen 14–15, 17
O'Connell, Larry 14, 17–18
O'Connell, Patrick 4, 13–19
O'Connell, Sue 16
O'Connor, James 186–9
O'Connor, Turlough 30

O'Dea, Darren 55, 158–65, 186, 197
O'Dea, Melissa 158–9, 164
Odisha FC 55
O'Donovan, Brian 92–3
O'Donovan, Ellen 68, 70
O'Donovan, Roy 4, 55, 68–73, 108, 196
Ogawa, Yudai 76
O'Hara, Kieran 170
OKI Electric 60
OKI FC Winds (Lady Thunders) 60–2
O'Leary, David 35, 124–5
Olsson, Jonas 179
Olsson, Pelle 179
Olympic Games Berlin (1936) 10, 12
Omonia Nicosia 143
O'Neill, Alan 31
O'Neill, Martin 137–9, 161, 169–70
Örebro 176, 179–80
O'Riordan, Claire 153–8
O'Riordan, Jim 158
O'Riordan, Neil 89
Orlando City 186–8
Osaka, Naomi 152
O'Shea, Jay 197
O'Shea, Tim 56
Osmanbegovic, Emir 177
Östersunds 177
O'Sullivan, Denise 152, 156, 189–95, 197
O'Sullivan, Fiona 130, 132
O'Sullivan, John 190
O'Sullivan, Nuala 190, 194
O'Toole, Olivia 100
Ottawa Fury 104–6
Oxford United 56

Paços de Ferreira 3, 112
Pagnam, Frank 9
Pal, Jasmin 157
Parva Liga 140
Pauw, Vera 43, 134–5
Peamount United 96, 99–100, 126, 128, 129, 131, 133
Pearman, Tammy 61
Pedersen, Cecilie 148
Pelé 49, 105
Pereira, Carlos 35
Peronace, Gigi 36
Persepolis 113
Perth Glory 196
Peruzzi, Angelo 123
Peyton, Gerry 55
Phelan, Terry 55
Phnom Penh Crown 81
Pilkington, Anthony 55
Piqué, Gerard 138
Pirlo, Andrea 121
Platini, Michel 39
Platt, David 120

Plymouth Argyle 140
Pogón Szczecin 144
Poland 143–4
Popp, Alex 151
Portilla, Cristian 69
Porto, FC 26
Potter, Graham 177
Powell, Colin 109–12
Pozzani, Ferdinando 11
Prato 44
Preah Khan Reach Svay Rieng see
    Svay Rieng, Cambodiaa
Preuß, Anke 127
Primeira Liga (Portugal) 3, 26
Pritchett, Keith 89
Probierz, Michał 144
Professional Footballers' Association
    of Ireland (PFAI) 109–12
Prohasca, Herbert 37
Pugh, Davy 48
Puskás Award 96–9
Putin, Vladimir 162

Queens Park Rangers 24
Queiroz, Carlos 51
Quinn, Louise 4, 129–36, 157
Quinn, Niall 30

Racing Santander 14, 16
Radukanov, Milen 140
Raheny United 126

Randolph, Darren 171
Raspudić, Boris 72
Ratchaburi 196
Raúl 105
Rawlins, Phil 186–7
Real Betis 4, 14, 16, 18
Real Madrid 14–15, 26, 188
Real Mallorca 122
Real Oviedo 14
Recoba, Álvaro 121
Rednic, Mircea 172
Reggiana 44, 124
Regionalliga West 21–2
Regis, Cyrille 27
Reims 199
Reynolds, Jack 8
Richardson, Bryan 120
Riise, Hege 61
Rijkaard, Frank 30–1
Riley, Ali 129
Riley, Paul 192–3
Robinson, Shane 112
Robson, Bryan 116–17
Roche, Stephanie 4, 96–102, 125–9,
    191
Rodríguez, James 98
Rogers, Dave 112
Romania 171–2
Ronaldo 120–3
Ronaldo, Cristiano 98
Ronan, Sue 126, 133, 155

Rooney, Fran 43
Roord, Jill 156
Rosana 148
Rose, Dan 199
Rosengård 129–30
Ross County 170
Rossiter, Mark 109
Rostov 117
Roy, Brian 30
Ruch Chorzów 123
Rummenigge, Karl-Heinz 39–40
Rush Athletic 59
Russell, Julie Ann 197
Ryan, Bobby 109
Ryan, Richie 4, 103–8
Ryan, Sean 38

St Johnstone 140–2
St Ledger, Sean 186
St Patrick's Athletic 20, 52, 82, 84, 112
Sabah FC 72–3, 113
Sampdoria 39, 120
Samsuri Mokhtar, Ahmed 63
Samuelsen, Símun 86
Samurai Blue 78
San Jose, California 60
San Jose Earthquakes 118, 181
Sandefjord 176
Sandnes Ulf 168–9
Santander 14
SC Cambuur 3, 113

SC Sand 151, 157
Scanlan, Claire 59–62, 146–7, 199
Schalke 04 199
Scheidel, Oskar 20
Schön, Helmut 21
Scottish football league 1
Scottish Women's Premier League 191
scouts 11, 24, 79, 109, 112, 162, 175
Second World War 155–6
    lead-up to 7, 12–13
Seiko 57
Senna, Marcos 105
Serbia, national team 86, 88–9
Sérgio, Paulo 142
Seria A 44
Seton Hall 51
Sevilla 16, 199
Seville 14
SGS Essen 156
Shakhtar Donetsk 161–2
Shamrock Rovers 47, 104, 113, 198
Shan United (Kanbawza FC),
    Myanmar 66
Sheffield United 24
Sheffield Wednesday 186–7
Shelbourne FC 62, 113
Shelley, Brian 109
Sheridan, Cillian 26, 137–45, 197–8
Sheringham, Teddy 55
Sherrard, Peter 137

Silva, Riccardo 106

Simonsen, Allan 84

Sindelar, Matthias 12

Singapore League 71–2

Singapore League Cup 68, 71

Skullerud, Tor Ole 168

Sligo Rovers 103–4

Sloan, Paddy 37

Slovenia, national team 87

Smyth, Shannon 132

Soccer Bowl (NASL) 106

Solskjær, Ole Gunnar 170

Song Chi-Hun 75–6

South China 56

Southend United 9

Spain 13–19

Spanish Civil War 15–16

Sparta Rotterdam 6

Sporting Fingal 103, 112

Sporting Lisbon 26

Sports Illustrated 184

Spyridonidou, Anastasia 128

Stabæk 149

Stack, Graham 55

Stade de Reims 41–3

Stamp, Phil 116

Stapleton, Christine 28

Stapleton, Frank 2, 27–33, 35,
    49–50, 53, 59, 90–5

Stein, Uli 25

Stielike, Uri 26

Stirling Lions 112

Stockport County 170

Stoke City 56, 186

Stokes, Anthony 55

Strachan, Gordon 119–20

Şükür, Hakan 121, 123

Sunderland AFC 47, 126

Sundhage, Pia 43

Sunyol, Josep 15

Supercoppa Italiana 123

Superettan 177

Supporters' Shield (USA) 184

Svay Rieng, Cambodia 74–82

Svenska Cupen 174

Sweden 129–33, 173–80
    national team: Under-21s 173–4;
    Under-16s 174–5

Switzerland 24–6, 117–18
    national team 147

Swope Park Rangers 188

Swords Celtic 59

Tampa Bay Mutiny 50, 91, 95

Tardelli, Marco 123–4

Tashuyev, Sergei 160

Terengganu FC 63

Thailand 66

Þór Halldórssen, Hannes 169

Þór/KA 147

Time magazine Person of the
    Century 114–15

Toppserein, 147

Torino 36–7

Toronto FC 113, 118, 158, 161, 181

Tosi, Rodrigo 72

Tottenham Hotspur 5–6, 125, 183

Touré, Yaya 160

Trani 43

Trapattoni, Giovanni 37, 39, 64, 65–6, 88, 124, 161, 186

Triads 58

Trinidad and Tobago 68

Tse, Sean 56

Tsimakuridze, Georgi 66–7

T-Team, Terengganu 63–5

Tubridy, Ryan 98

Tuohy, Liam 47

Turkey 9–11
    national team 9–10

TV4 (Sweden) 177

UEFA Champions League 122, 124, 138–9, 160
    Women's 130, 132–4, 191

UEFA Cup 21, 24–5, 123, 166

UEFA Cup Winners' Cup 30–1, 35–6, 47, 186

UEFA Europa League 82, 141

UK Elite 77

Ukraine 158–65

Ullensaker/Kisa 169

UMF Tindastóll 113

United Soccer Association (USA) 46–7

United Soccer League (USL) (USA) 113, 186–8, 195

Universal Music 178–9

US Saint-Romanaise 97

USA 46–54, 90–5, 100–2, 106–8, 152, 181–95, 197
    national team 93; women's 191

Utrecht, FC 166

Utvik, Arne 147–9

Valencia 35

Valenciennes 113

Valletta 113

van Basten, Marco 27

van Persie, Robin 98

van 't Schip, John 30

Vancouver Royals 47

Vard Haugesund 109, 111

Veikkausliiga 112

Venables, Terry 89

Ventre, Danny 103

Vieri, Christian 120, 122–4

Visakha, Cambodia 80

Vorskla 160

Waitakere United 112

Waldrum, Randy 100–2, 191–2

Walker, Annette 173, 176

Walker, Kevin 173–80

Walker, Michael 22, 37–8, 117
Walker, Pat 173, 176, 179
Walker, Robert 173
Walsh, Mickey 26
Wambach, Abby 148
Webber, Saskia 61
Welferinger, David 99
Wellington Phoenix 144
Werder Bremen 133
West Bromwich Albion 186 West
    Germany see also Germany/West
    Germany national team 21
West Ham United 35, 40, 63, 198
Western Sydney Wanderers 156, 194,
    197
Wexford Youth 154
Widodo, Joko 70
Williams, Derrick 197
Williams, Robbie 178
Williamson, Enith 7–8
Wilson, Jonathan 7
Winter, Aron 30–1, 113
Wisła Płock 144
Witschge, Rob 30
W-League (Australia) 156
Wold, Roar 148
Wolfsburg 151
Wolverhampton Wanderers 64, 119
women's football, generally 41–2, 62

Women's Football Association of
    Ireland 43
Women's National League, Ireland
    96, 100, 199 see also League of
    Ireland Women's Super League
    (WSL) 126, 133, 155, 156, 199
World Cup
    1938 (France) 12
    1990 (Italy) 76, 135
    1994 (USA) 76
    1998 (France) qualifiers 89
    2006 (Germany) qualifiers 83, 86
    2010 (South Africa) qualifiers 83–4
    2014 (Brazil) qualifiers 161
    Women's World Cup: 2011
    (Germany) 61; qualifiers 126, 147
    youth 86

Xamax see Neuchâtel Xamax

Yanukovych, Viktor 162

Zambra, Dean 99
Zamorano, Iván 120
Zayed, Éamon 55, 72, 110, 113
Zefi, Kevin 199
Zenga, Walter 40, 53
Zidane, Zinedine 116–17